God & Menzies

The Faith that Shaped a Prime Minister and His Nation

David Furse-Roberts

Connor Court Publishing Pty Ltd

Published in 2021 by Connor Court Publishing Pty Ltd under the Jeparit Press Imprint.

Jeparit Press is an imprint of Connor Court Publishing in conjunction with the Menzies Research Centre.

Connor Court Publishing Pty Ltd.

PO Box 7257

Redland Bay QLD 4165

sales@connorcourt.com

www.connorcourt.com

ISBN: 9781922449771

Cover Design by Vanessa Schimizzi (Branded Graphics)
Cover image: *Alamy*

Printed in Australia.

Contents

Preface

Separation of church and state in Australia is a tribute to the wisdom of the nation's founders. Freedom of belief is akin to freedom of conscience. Freedom to deny the existence of God is no less important than freedom to worship a deity.

Of the 30 prime ministers since Federation, only one entered office as a confessed non-believer. This suggests that the Australian public is comfortable with leaders who profess Christian values and, indeed, may even prefer them. The Menzies Research Centre commissioned *God & Menzies* in part to explain why that might be so, and the light it sheds upon the character of the nation and its citizens.

The candidness with which Sir Robert Menzies spoke about religion must be seen in the context of the times. In the 1966 census, the year Menzies retired as prime minister, 88 per cent of Australians identified themselves as Christian and fewer than 1 per cent were bold enough to state they had no religion. Menzies spoke about religion more than most prime ministers and articulated Christian values with rare clarity. These values were highly influential in developing the political philosophy of the Liberal Party, which has held office in 50 of the past 72 years. Indeed, to understand modern Liberalism it is essential to take these religious and spiritual influences into account.

In a practical community sense, Menzies' approach to religion has unusual, even unique significance. He was born into a highly sectarian society, with the conscription controversies of the First World War aggravating and deepening the sectarian divide.

During his entire public life, Menzies shunned sectarianism, it permeated not only society but even his own family and the people with whom he mixed. Challenging sectarianism in his conduct as parliamentarian and minister, and transcending it as party leader and prime minister, he played a leading role in diminishing a scourge in the political, professional and business life of Australia.

David Furse-Roberts investigates the foundations of Menzies' thinking and discovers it has deep roots in biblical tradition. Individual freedom and personal responsibility begin with the book of Genesis. The principle that every human being is of equal worth underlies the Liberal Party's commitment to egalitarianism; it derives from biblical teaching that every soul is equally precious in the sight of the Lord. The bonds of mutual respect that establish civic order are inherent in Christ's injunction that we treat our neighbours as we ourselves wish to be treated.

God & Menzies will have a particular appeal to those of religious conviction and may deepen their understanding of faith. Menzies was a Presbyterian, strongly influenced by the Methodism of his mother's family. For Menzies, the precepts of ethical conduct superseded formal distinctions between Christian denominations, and between Christianity and other religions. His career is marked not only by close relationships with the various Christian denominations, Roman Catholic as well as Protestant, but equally with the Jewish community.

Primarily, however, this work is intended as a secular contribution to an understanding of Australian history and society. It is especially valuable in illuminating our peculiar post-enlightenment colonial inheritance, and the motivation of 18th century reformers for whom Australia was not the fatal shore but a land of redemption.

Today we face concerted attempts to push religion to the margins of Australian life and draw boundaries around conscientious liberty. In Victoria, for instance, the exercise of some forms of prayer has been made a criminal offence under the pretext of outlawing discrimination. At the very least, this illustrates a careless approach, if not outright antagonism, to hard fought freedoms that sustain our liberal democracy.

This work will have served a valuable purpose if it leads to a more profound recognition of Australia's fortunate legacy and the importance of religion in sustaining individual liberty.

I congratulate David on this outstanding work. It is a noteworthy addition to the distinguished library which furnishes the intellectual fabric of Australian liberalism.

Others indispensable to this project are more fully acknowledged elsewhere. The MRC itself owes a particular gratitude to those who provided financial support for the endeavour, most notably to Tony and Rae McLellan of the McLellan Foundation.

Nick Cater
Executive Director, Menzies Research Centre
June 2021

FOREWORD

GOD AND MENZIES

How we see and engage the world is a product of the values and the truths we hold dear. It is driven by what we believe.

Our beliefs are formed in the nursery of our family, the classrooms of our experience and education, the fellowship of our community and the quiet spaces of reflection, where we confront our vulnerabilities and mortality.

It is also still true for the majority of Australians that what we believe is heavily influenced by where we come together to worship and pray.

Faith remains a powerful force in the lives of many Australians. This remains a good thing for our nation.

This was certainly true for Australia's longest serving Prime Minister (18-and-a-half years and seven election wins in total!), and founder and leader of the Liberal Party of Australia for twenty-five years, Sir Robert Menzies.

Dr David Furse-Roberts' work, *God and Menzies*, provides a valuable insight into the seasoning impact that faith had on the most significant political figure in Australia's history.

However, *God and Menzies* is not the story of Menzies the

political giant; it is the story of how the principles he believed in, 'drawn from a deep reservoir of faith' shaped him, the nation he led and the Party he founded.

Sir Robert described himself as a "simple Presbyterian". However, this underplays his deep, rich and layered understanding of the Judeo-Christian inheritance that he understood contributed so much to human freedom.

It also understates his clear sense of "calling" to Christian responsibility that fuelled a lifetime of service, noting 'every Christian citizen had the duty to live out their faith in public and, in so doing, would succeed in building a better world'.

He also saw the Scriptures not as a policy textbook, but a foundation stone for the values upon which a positive life and liberal democracy are built.

As David Furse-Roberts observes, though Menzies' world-view was secular in the classical sense, it was not conceived in a spiritual and moral vacuum.

Above all, Sir Robert's faith enlivened three core principles – the dignity of every human being "equal in the sight of God", the virtue and nurture of family and the responsibility of community.

In Menzies' liberalism, the individual uses his or her skills, talents, and efforts in the service of others. It was, in his words, "a selfless liberalism". Drawing from the biblical truths that informed his life, he said: "If we stand for anything as Liberals we stand for the inescapable responsibility of the individual, his dignity, his responsibility for every other individual. In that sense we are an individualist movement, not in the bad sense of saying 'Each for himself and the devil take the hindmost', but in the good sense of saying 'every man is his brother's keeper.'"

As Furse-Roberts observes, in Menzies' view, Christianity starts with the individual, not the society or the state. To transform society, you must first transform the heart, soul, mind and life of the individual believer. Likewise, it is the moral character and agency of individual Australians, rather than the collective state, that is the true driver of change, progress and renewal.

Menzies saw Christianity as both a bulwark against the godlessness of communism and the soullessness of materialism. Menzies believed in an enlightened and humane capitalism.

Wealth was not an end in itself, but a means to enrich others – "blessed to be a blessing" as some say, or in public policy terms "a strong economy to guarantee the essential services Australians rely on".

And he rejected the bitter sectarianism of his day, consistent with his inclusive view of responsible citizenship in a highly successful and diverse immigration nation: "Whether we be Catholic or Protestant, or Jewish or Muslim, the end remains clear: we have an overwhelming duty to serve our country on the highest level and to the best of our talents".

Recognising the important role of faith in the education of our children, Menzies would also end one of the longest running political debates in Australia, by extending Commonwealth funding to non-government schools.

In post-war Australia, Sir Robert was especially mindful of the strength and sufferings of Jewish Australians. He felt a kinship with Jewish people and their strong sense of family and community. He despised anti-semitism, declaring on Australia Day 1960, "there is absolutely no room in Australia for anti-semitism". His view was unequivocal: Jewish people were "not only in Australia, but of Australia".

This is a timely book produced by Dr David Furse-Roberts. It is a well-researched reflection on the faith of a great Australian and how that faith and moral character produced a principled but pragmatic Australian liberalism – a liberalism that sees the dignity and potential in the life of every person.

The work also provides a timely warning to protect against those forces that would seek to undermine the life of faith in Australia, so essential to our society, best expressed by Menzies himself in his 1954 Party Platform: "We believe that, under the blessing of Divine Providence, and given goodwill, mutual tolerance and understanding, energy and individual sense of purpose, there is no task which Australia cannot perform, and no difficulty which she cannot overcome".

Amen, Sir Robert.

The Hon Scott Morrison MP
Prime Minister of Australia

June 2021

Why God and Menzies?

O tto von Bismarck, Iron Chancellor of the Federal German Empire, once observed that "The statesman's task is to hear God's footsteps marching through history, and to try and catch on to His coattails as He marches past". Every national leader with a sense of divine providence has exhibited this sentiment in different ways, whether seeing themselves as God's "anointed" leader for "such a time as this", as was true of the patriarchs of biblical times, or whether they simply believe that statecraft involves observing and acting on the moral precepts of revealed religion. In the case of Australia's twelfth Prime Minister, Sir Robert Gordon Menzies, it was clearly a case of the latter as his political philosophy and vision was, to a large degree, informed explicitly by Christian principles.

By any historical reckoning, Menzies was a giant of Australian politics, with his record prime ministership from 1949 to 1966 following his first term as prime minister from 1939-41. As well as leading Australia into the Second World War and shepherding Australia's growth through the post-war years, his great legacy was founding the modern centre-right Liberal Party of Australia in 1944. The spiritual dimension of such a pre-eminent figure for modern Australia therefore merits serious exploration. For this self-described "simple Presbyterian", the spiritual impulses of Menzies derived from the Bible but were mediated through a variety of Christian traditions and experiences in his formative years.

The purpose of this book is to explore the religious faith and traditions that Menzies absorbed through his family background and church experiences, and then to explore how these shaped not only his political creed but his understanding of religious freedom, relationship with other faith traditions, and philosophy of education. With Menzies having a formative influence on the country he led, it is therefore a study of the real-life impact of these ideas on Australia.

In Australia's own history since Federation, Robert Menzies has been Australia's longest serving prime minister and one of its most consequential. On the international stage, he was also one of the great and enduring statesmen of the post-war world together with Konrad Adenauer of West Germany, Charles de Gaulle of France and Lee Kuan Yew of Singapore. Holding office as prime minister for a total of more than eighteen years, he helped lay the foundations for modern Australia in foreign affairs and defence, education, housing and economic reform that made the nation ultimately more secure and prosperous. As Josh Frydenberg recognised, however, "the most enduring aspect of Menzies' legacy was his conviction, his civility, and his principles". These sprang from his personal moral character and political philosophy, which, in turn, were moulded by a sincere yet often understated religious faith.

One of the tasks of this book is to explore this faith of Menzies in greater depth and to explain how it informed his guiding precepts of the "fatherhood of God and brotherhood of man", the immortality of the human soul, the equality of all human beings before God, the ethic of a selfless individualism, the notion that a citizen's duties preceded their rights, and the ideal for citizens in civil society to live as "members of one another". Such precepts mattered profoundly to Menzies as he believed that they were critical not only to his vision for a flourishing human society, but also to the very survival of liberalism and democracy itself. Indeed, he once warned that "If we are all tired democrats, eager beneficiaries but reluctant contributors, democracy would collapse under its own weight".[1]

Menzies' values assumed concrete form when he founded the Liberal Party of Australia late in 1944, but the religious background to these have thus far received scant attention. One of the probable

---

[1] Robert Menzies, "The First William Queale Memorial Lecture", Adelaide, 22 October 1954, Robert Menzies Papers, NLA, MS 4936, Box 260, Folder 61.

reasons for this is that liberalism in Australia and elsewhere has been widely assumed to be a secular philosophy emanating from the Enlightenment, but this overlooks the Christian origins of Western liberalism and, indeed, secularism itself.[2] The tradition of liberalism in Australia is no exception to this pedigree, supportive of a secular state yet eminently affirming of a flourishing religiosity in civil society. The emergence of the Liberal Party represented the revival of this Australian liberal tradition at large, yet, as "Menzies' child", it bore the additional imprint of its founder's own Liberal creed steeped in Judeo-Christian precepts. Much has been written about the philosophy of Australia's major political party on the centre-right, with political scientists and historians generally agreeing that the Liberal Party is comprised of a mixture of conservative, classical liberal and libertarian strands. Still others, such as the former Prime Minister, John Howard, have characterised the philosophical disposition of the Liberal Party as a combination of Edmund Burke's conservative emphasis on social order with John Stuart Mill's liberal ethic of individual freedom. In their respective studies of the Liberal Party, both Gerard Henderson and Judith Brett also recognised the links of the early Liberal Party to Australia's Protestant ascendency, but mostly along socio-economic lines. [3] This book, on the other hand, will probe deeper to explore the extent to which the founding philosophy of the Liberal Party was informed by Christian principles from both Protestant and Catholic streams of thought. In so doing, it will demonstrate that the modern Liberal Party, though secular in the classical sense of being non-ecclesiastical, was not conceived

---

[2] Larry Siedentop, *Reinventing the Individual: The Origins of Western Liberalism*, London: Penguin Books, 2014, pp 360-361. Siedentop argued that secularism, as properly understood, rested on the "central egalitarian moral insight of Christianity" which gave human individuals a sphere of "conscience and free action".

[3] See, for example, Gerard Henderson, *Menzies' Child: The Liberal Party of Australia, 1944-1994*, Allen & Unwin, 1994; Judith Brett, *The Australian Liberals and the Moral Middle Class: From Alfred Deakin to John Howard*, New York: Cambridge University Press, 2003 and *Robert Menzies' Forgotten People*, Melbourne: Melbourne University Press, 2007.

in a spiritual and moral vacuum but, on the contrary, was heir to a robust Judeo-Christian tradition affirming of individual dignity and freedom, strong families and subsidiarity, together with an ethical citizenship of neighbourly love, social justice and religious toleration.

With religious freedom becoming more of a contested issue in the public domain, both in Australia and internationally, this book offers a timely reminder that this was a key tenet of Menzies' philosophy and that of the Liberal Party as he conceived it. As will become evident, this was a conviction borne not only of his liberal philosophy but also of his Christian faith. Since Menzies' own time, there have been both continuities and changes to the essential place of religious freedom in Australian life. On the one hand, the recent Review into Religious Freedom (2018) revealed that the broad Australian community continues to cherish religious freedom as part of living in a diverse, vibrant and religiously plural society. In this vein, it is perhaps esteemed even more highly today than it was in Menzies' own time when sectarian prejudice and discrimination still lingered in the community. This led John Howard to observe in February 2021 that it was "not credible to say there is a frontal attack on religious freedom". At the same time, however, Howard noted that "there is a creeping intolerance in society towards faith-based schools" with attempts to put restrictions on them and that there was a "general attempt to diminish the impact of Christianity in our society". With the contemporary advance of secularism encroaching on some religious liberties, this book underlines the reality that religious freedom, whilst popularly cherished, can never be taken for granted, even in free societies such as Australia. It is a reminder that in the interests of unleashing the innate spiritual impulses of human individuals and maintaining a vibrant democracy, Menzies' principles of religious freedom remain eminently timeless and applicable.

The one religious and cultural variable that was markedly different in Menzies' own time to that of today was the standing of the churches and the cultural currency of Christianity. In contrast to the largely secular zeitgeist of the 2020s, the post-war Australia of the

Menzies years was one where Christianity and the church were very much in the ascendant, both spiritually and culturally. This broader context is essential to appreciating how Menzies, as prime minister, was able to address church congregations routinely, speak publicly about the Bible, make mention of Christ in his speeches, warn of pagan influences in education, and refer to Australia as a "Christian nation". In present day Australia, it would be almost unthinkable for a serving prime minster, even one of deep personal faith, to take such frequent and overt stands for Christianity, but in the Australia of the 1950s and early 1960s, it was unremarkable, and perhaps even expected from some quarters, for a national leader to speak publicly on occasions as the spiritual conscience of the nation. In his capacity as prime minister, Menzies certainly did much to amplify the "common Christianity" of Australians at large.

So how was the Australia of Menzies' time more expressly Christian in character and temperament than that of today? In what David Hilliard termed the "long 1950s", which began in the late 1940s and ended in about 1963-64, the Christian churches in Australia enjoyed a season of revival and expansion. Some 88-89% of Australians identified as Christian and three in ten attended church regularly.[4] Corresponding with Menzies' second term as prime minister, the long 1950s witnessed growth in the active membership of Protestant churches together with booming Sunday school enrolments that peaked early in the 1960s. This was matched by the visible presence of the churches in the public square where they were keen to be the leading voice, confident that religious values were universal and applicable to the whole of society.[5] Complementing the prominent role of the Anglican and Catholic Archbishops were senior ministers of the Protestant churches, eager to reach wide audiences through public addresses, radio broadcasts and newspaper articles.

[4] David Hilliard, "Church, Family and Sexuality in Australia in the 1950s", *Australian Historical Studies*, 27:109, 1997, p 135; "God in the Suburbs: The Religious Culture of Australian Cities in the 1950s", *Australian Historical Studies*, 24:97, 1991, pp 400-401.
[5] Ibid.

Such ministers were public figures in the community and included the Rev Irving Clarence Benson of Wesley (Methodist) Church in Melbourne, the Rev Alan Walker of the Central Methodist Mission in Sydney and the Rev Gordon Powell of St Stephen's Presbyterian Church, Macquarie Street, Sydney.[6] Irving Benson, of course, was a close personal friend of Menzies and their relationship typified the close ties between church and civic leaders. As a reflection of the community's vibrant religiosity, the 1950s were also the age of Alan Walker's Mission to the Nation (1953-56), Father Peyton's Family Rosary Crusade of 1953 and the Billy Graham Crusade of 1959.

The flourishing of religious life in the 1950s deeply affected the moral outlook of the age, with Christianity and its moral precepts considered to be the basis of a strong and healthy society. Drawing on this community consensus, church and community leaders alike stressed the connection between personal faith, divinely sanctioned moral values and a stable social order.[7] This was articulated most forcefully in the 1951 *Call to the People of Australia*, endorsed by a broad cross-section of church, civic and community leaders, including, not least, Prime Minister Menzies. To a large degree, this mindset was also informed by the Cold War where Australia and the West were seen as needing to stand firm for the traditional faith and moral virtues feared threatened by the menace of "godless communism". To bolster their case, church newspapers, parish magazines and sermons regularly impressed the importance of "Christian ideals" and "Christian moral standards" as the essential foundation for a democratic civilisation. Clergy and religious leaders cited the bloodbath of the Second World War as an example of what happened when civilisations ceased to observe God's moral law. In the post-war age, they warned a similar neglect would lead to "materialism" and the spiritual vacuum of irreligion would pave the way for communism. Such themes frequently found expression in the "Pleasant Sunday Afternoon" (PSA) addresses of Menzies to

[6] Hilliard, "God in the Suburbs", p 405.
[7] Ibid., p 410.

Benson's Wesley Church congregations during the 1950s and early 1960s. At these routine occasions, he alerted his audience to the dangers of both communism and materialism to a society based on a Christian conception of freedom.[8]

It was telling that, as prime minister, Menzies invoked Christian ideals and themes to a far great degree than any of his immediate Liberal successors, Harold Holt, John Gorton and William McMahon. The public records reveal that not only were his speaking engagements at church services and other religious events much more numerous and frequent, but also that he made many more allusions to religious terms such as "Christianity", "God" and "Scripture". In Menzies' own speeches, biblical aphorisms abounded, but in the speeches of his successors they were virtually non-existent. This, however, was not simply a manifestation of the relative strength of Menzies' own personal faith, but also a reflection of the reality that he was speaking in a far less secular age than the one to immediately follow in the late 1960s and 1970s. Similar to other Western nations, Australia experienced a "religious crisis" from the mid to late 1960s that saw church and Sunday school attendances plummet, the public authority of the churches weaken, and the disintegration of the old Judeo-Christian moral consensus. This rapid secularisation was attributable to multiple factors including the sexual revolution and the anti-Vietnam War counter-culture, the expanding reach of higher education, the popularisation of new technologies such as television and the motor car, growing general affluence and, not least, theological transformations within the churches themselves. Thus, by the time Menzies' successors came to office in the latter 1960s and early 1970s, they were already leading a more secularised Australia. They reflected the new spiritual temperament of the nation in a way that departed significantly from the palpably Christianised style and approach of Menzies that suited his time.

---

[8] Robert Menzies, Pleasant Sunday Afternoon (PSA) Address, Wesley Church, Melbourne, 3 September 1961, Robert Menzies Papers, NLA, MS 4936, Box 273, Folder 156.

The world-view of a conviction politician such as Menzies cannot be appreciated fully without considering religious faith and spiritual principles. With personal faith of one kind or another being typically foundational to an individual's character, behaviour, moral sensibilities and political outlook, it was arguably the case that Menzies' Christian faith formed the bedrock of his sustained Liberal philosophy. As well as being acknowledged by the biographies of Menzies, the Liberal philosophy of this Australian statesman was probed in some depth by the 2016 publication, *Menzies: The Shaping of Modern Australia*. In a chapter entitled "The Liberal Philosophy of Robert Menzies", the fundamentals of Menzies' Liberalism were duly acknowledged, including its affirmation of equal dignity for all, individual freedom, defence of democratic institutions and rejection of class warfare. Apart from noting Menzies' aversion to sectarianism, however, the scope of the chapter did not extend to explore the real spiritual basis for, or inspiration behind, such principles.[9]

The premise of this book is that the Christian faith of his boyhood and youth was fundamental to Menzies' Liberal philosophy and political convictions. This will give readers an appreciation that in a country often reticent about the role of religion in its politics and public life, Australia's longest-serving prime minister was a leader who drew his philosophy and principles from a deep reservoir of faith.

Elsewhere, this truth about national leaders of conviction appears to have been grasped with a number of published studies that explore the driving faith and spiritual impulses of transcendant leaders from Abraham Lincoln to Winston Churchill. Most published works of this kind first appeared in the United States, followed later by similar studies in Britain. Some of the tomes on the faith of US Presidents published included Allen C. Guelzo, *Abraham Lincoln: Redeemer President* (2002), followed by Mary Beth Brown, *Hand of Providence: The Strong and Quiet Faith of Ronald Reagan* (2005) and, more

---

[9] David Kemp, "The Liberal Philosophy of Robert Menzies", in J. R. Nethercote (ed), *Menzies: The Shaping of Modern Australia*, Brisbane: Connor Court, 2016, pp 1-26.

recently, Alan Sears, *The Soul of an American President: The Untold Story of Dwight D. Eisenhower's Faith* (2019).

In Britain, meanwhile, the publications of this type to appear include David Bebbington, *William Ewart Gladstone: Faith and Politics in Victorian Britain* (1993), Jonathan Sandys, *God and Churchill: How the Great Leader's Sense of Divine Destiny Changed His Troubled World and Offers Hope for Ours* (2016), and, most recently, Dudley Delffs, *The Faith of Queen Elizabeth: The Poise, Grace, and Quiet Strength behind the Crown* (2019).

These tomes vary in style and approach. Some are pitched to a broad popular readership while others are written for a specialist, academic readership. Some studies, such as Sandys's on Churchill, focus primarily on the inner personal life and experiences of their subject. Others, for instance, Bebbington on Gladstone, take the approach of examining their subject within the broader religious and political context of their time. What they have in common, nonetheless, is the underlying premise that the spiritual dimension of great leaders is noteworthy and merits close attention and study.

Australia is yet to produce an equivalent, standalone monograph on any one of its national leaders. *God and Menzies* is the first of its kind. Existing biographies of Menzies are generalist in nature and, as such, their narratives tend to provide a broad overview of both his political and personal life with limited coverage of his spiritual life or religious beliefs. The flagship two-volume biography by A. W. Martin made passing references to the religious beliefs of Menzies' father, James, and discussed some of young Robert's boyhood experiences of church life in Jeparit. Martin also mentioned Menzies' presidency of the Student Christian Union at Melbourne University in 1916, his pattern of church attendance in the 1920s, and made some references to the spiritual reflections from his 1935 diary of his first overseas trip to Britain.[10] As revealing as these glimpses were, however, Martin's

---

[10] A. W. Martin, *Robert Menzies: A Life, Volume I, 1894-1943*, Melbourne University Press, 1993, pp 9-10, 14, 22-23, 44 and 113.

biography provided no sustained commentary on either Menzies'
religious doctrines or personal piety.

Cameron Hazlehurst's earlier study, *Menzies Observed*, noted
aspects of Menzies' religiosity including his support for conscription on
Christian grounds and his preaching of a sermon at Kew Presbyterian
Church but, again, did not probe deeper into his religious thought and
practice.[11]Troy Bramston's very recent biography (2019) touched on
Menzies' well-known Presbyterian background and also reproduced
an insightful extract from an interview Menzies had with Frances
McNicoll, in which he expressly distanced himself from the narrow
sectarianism of his family. Drawing on this, Bramston observed
accurately that "Menzies never tolerated religious bigotry or prejudice"
but he otherwise did not touch upon Menzies' faith and practice.[12]

In addition to these valuable yet sparse insights offered by the
general biographies, the spiritual faith of Menzies has been investigated
elsewhere but in limited scope. In 2013, Roy Williams produced
a study of Australian prime ministers and their religious faith, *In
God they Trust? The Religious Beliefs of Australia's Prime Ministers*.
Williams devoted a chapter to each of Australia's prime ministers up
to Kevin Rudd. His nineteen-page chapter on Menzies provided an
account of his religious beliefs that was accurate, fresh and insightful.[13]
Importantly, Williams appreciated that Menzies' Presbyterianism was
not simply a cultural badge of his Scottish ethnic identity, but a genuine
faith that manifested itself in his patterns of speech and philosophy of
Australian Liberalism. As well as discussing the well-known Scottish
Presbyterian background and early upbringing of Menzies, Williams
acknowledged how Menzies' faith informed his abiding beliefs in
human equality before God and the law, the necessity of a moral
liberalism, the importance of education, and the value of home and

---

[11] Cameron Hazlehurst, *Menzies Observed*, George Allen & Unwin, 1979, pp
27, 33.

[12] Troy Bramston, *Robert Menzies: The Art of Politics*, Melbourne: Scribe, 2019,
pp 25-26.

[13] Roy Williams, "Robert Gordon (Bob) Menzies (1894-1978)", *In God they
Trust? The Religious Beliefs of Australia's Prime Ministers*, Sydney: Bible Society
of Australia, 2013, pp 120-138.

family life, together with his personal distaste of material greed and moral profanity. In what were fresh insights, Williams observed that Menzies' own Christianity was non-sectarian and ecumenical as well as being eminently practical. In his discussion of Menzies' faith, Williams drew mostly from the biographies of A. W. Martin and Cameron Hazlehurst, together with Menzies' own *Afternoon Light* and personal letters to his daughter, Heather Henderson. Taken on their own, however, the major biographies and memoirs of Menzies provide only brief and limited vignettes of his religious faith and outlook.

Williams's chapter on Menzies nevertheless provided much of the inspiration for the themes this book seeks to explore. In particular, this book takes up Williams's observation that Menzies favoured a moral form of Australian Liberalism by appraising the extent to which Menzies' Liberal philosophy adopted Christian presuppositions and ideals. This study extends Williams's references to Menzies' non-sectarian and ecumenical faith by exploring how he built bridges with Australia's Catholics to heal the sectarian rift. Menzies never conceded that the Catholic vote necessarily favoured Labor and was beyond attraction. The other facets to Menzies' faith alluded to by Williams, such as his moral temperament and the importance he accorded to education, are similarly explored at greater length in this study. As welcome a contribution as Williams's chapter has been, there were several crucial dimensions to Menzies' religious outlook that were either unmentioned or underexplored such as his theological dispositions, his opposition to communism, his warm rapport with Australia's Jewish community and his philosophy of religious freedom. These aspects will be explored in this book.

In addition to Williams's chapter on Menzies, Anne Henderson similarly wrote about Menzies for the edited publication, *Australian Jurists and Christianity*, edited by Geoff Lindsay and Wayne Hudson in 2021.[14] In keeping with the overarching theme of the

---

[14] Anne Henderson, "Robert Menzies (1894-1978)", Geoff Lindsay and Wayne Hudson (eds), *Australian Jurists and Christianity*, Sydney: Federation Press, 2021, pp 156-166.

volume, Henderson observed how aspects of Menzies' politics and jurisprudence were shaped by Christian principles. In particular, Henderson recognised his Presbyterian background and church attendance, biblical knowledge, Methodist connections with Irving Benson, support for church schools and opposition to communism on spiritual grounds. As with the aspects of his religious outlook raised by Williams, this book will take these key features of Menzies' Christianity identified by Henderson and explore them at greater length.

The other recent studies to touch on the religious faith of Menzies have been the academic works of Stephen Chavura and Greg Melleuish. In a journal article and, later, a monograph, they explored what they identified as the key philosophical, moral and spiritual ideas of Menzies exhibited in his public life. For them the key to understanding the thought of Menzies was appreciating his British streak of "cultural puritanism".[15] With political scientists and historians constantly debating whether Menzies was a "liberal", a "conservative", or, indeed, a hybrid of the two, Chavura and Melleuish argued that "Menzies may most helpfully be described as a "cultural puritan".[16] With this focus on Menzies' cultural puritanism, the religious beliefs of Menzies received welcome attention.

"Cultural puritanism" referred to the distinctive cultural habits of the puritans, the Elizabethan Calvinists who were the English cousins to the similarly Reformed Scots Presbyterians of Menzies' ancestry. To be sure, cultural puritanism had sixteenth-century origins, but its ideals were popularised by the Victorian age to which Menzies was heir. According to Chavura and Melleuish, cultural puritanism stressed decency and moral earnestness, independence, and a "disciplined, world-embracing sense of duty to improve society". By the example of his own personal life and the philosophy he espoused of a sturdy independence balanced with civic duty, Chavura and Melleuish regarded Menzies as a cultural puritan *par excellence*. The two authors

---

[15] Stephen Chavura and Gregory Melleuish, 'The Forgotten Menzies: Cultural Puritanism and Australian Social Thought', *Journal of Religious History*, 44(3), 2020, pp 356-379.

[16] Ibid., p 357.

reiterated this theme and developed it in *The Forgotten Menzies*.[17] Representing the first detailed study of the philosophical inclinations of Australia's longest-serving prime minister, *The Forgotten Menzies* argued that Menzies' thought, to a large degree, can be explained as a projection of both the cultural puritanism and British idealism prevalent in his formative years in early twentieth-century Melbourne.

As a well-researched study drawing extensively on original manuscript material, including Menzies' own speeches, *The Forgotten Menzies* provides the most sophisticated treatment thus far of his religious faith. The insights of Chavura and Melleuish into Menzies' cultural puritanism represented the first attempt to explain how his Scots Presbyterianism, as a close cousin to English puritanism, manifested itself in his moral outlook and political attitudes. Like Williams, Chavura and Melleuish understood that Menzies' Presbyterian identity was far more than a nominal label but a defining part of his whole temperament, character and world-view. The present volume is indebted to how *The Forgotten Menzies* both defined and analysed the outworking of Menzies' cultural puritanism and builds on this useful analysis.

With *God and Menzies*, however, representing a more specialised study of his religious beliefs, in contrast to a broader intellectual biography exploring both the religious and secular strands to his philosophy, this work traverses the wider theological contours of Menzies' faith. As well as appreciating the import of "cultural puritanism" through his Scots Presbyterian background and diet of Victorian English literature, this book will also engage with other Christian traditions that shaped Menzies' faith in its formative years. These included the Methodism of his schooling, the broad liberal Protestantism of his university years as well as the evangelical Protestant influences of C. H. Nash. Whereas *The Forgotten Menzies* focussed largely on the moral and cultural expression of Menzies' religious faith, this volume will probe deeper into the theological

---

[17] Melleuish & Chavura, *The Forgotten Menzies: The World Picture of Australia's Longest Serving Prime Minister*, Melbourne: Melbourne University Press, 2021.

doctrines of his Christian belief by exploring his views on God, Jesus Christ, the Bible and humanity.

With the religious faith and outlook of Menzies representing a largely fresh field of inquiry, the study behind this book has extended well beyond the biographies of Menzies and other published sources to draw extensively from Menzies' own papers, including his speeches, lectures, addresses, diaries and correspondence. The major newspapers and mainstream media occasionally covered stories with a faith significance, such as Menzies' address at the opening of Bible House in Canberra in 1960 and his address in 1964 to the Cardinal's dinner in Sydney, but it was in his own words that his spiritual sensibilities and faith were made most manifest. The public pronouncements of Menzies on matters spiritual were typically made not so much in formal contexts such as official state ceremonies or parliamentary proceedings, but at "lower key" community events such as school speech nights and church functions, in particular the "Pleasant Sunday Afternoons" (PSAs) hosted by Melbourne's Wesley Central Methodist Mission from the 1940s to the 1960s.

In more personal and intimate surrounds, Menzies perhaps felt less inhibition to speak from the heart about the deeper questions of life such as faith, spirituality and philosophy. It is accordingly Menzies' words from occasions of this kind that feature throughout this book. As well as his public utterances, Menzies would also express his faith in more private contexts such as in his personal diaries and correspondence. His 1935 diaries from his first visit to the United Kingdom, in particular, offer very frank and candid thoughts on religious matters from the style of services to the reading of the Bible. Meanwhile, his handwritten letters to concerned Catholic constituents about discrimination in his new Liberal Party also revealed his views on sectarianism and religious toleration. Without this wealth of manuscript material, an original study into Menzies' religious beliefs would have been impossible.

The first chapter of this book will explore the religious milieu into which Menzies was born. It will survey the Scots Presbyterian tradition personified by his father, James Menzies, and explain how this and its tradition of "cultural puritanism" influenced the young Robert in his childhood and youth. Appreciating faith as something that is by no means replicated in one's offspring, the chapter will address how Menzies' more liberal iteration of Presbyterianism differed from the stricter Calvinist form of his father. In addition, it will explore how Menzies was exposed to other critically influential Christian traditions especially the Methodism of Melbourne's Wesley College that he attended on a scholarship in the 1910s, the broad, liberal Protestantism of the Melbourne University Student Christian Union of which he served as President in 1916, and the evangelical Protestantism of the evangelist and preacher, Clifford Harris "C. H." Nash of the Melbourne Bible Institute.

The exposure to these various forms of Christianity evidently shaped Menzies' own religious disposition. The next chapter will examine his views on the key elements of Christian doctrine. By his own admission, Menzies was "no theologian", yet his genuine faith meant that he formed his own views on such themes as God and his "fatherhood", the humanity and divinity of Jesus Christ, the significance of the Cross, the nature of humanity, his appreciation of the Bible as the great repository of faith, and the Christian life as one of moral virtue and self-sacrifice. This all demonstrated that the Christianity of Menzies was not simply a cultural disposition but a confession of religious faith that sustained his philosophy and world-view. It also revealed that his theology, whilst assuming a definite form, was essentially broad and the product of a range of Christian traditions and influences. As such, this grasp of Menzies' broad theology helps to explain the essentially non-sectarian and ecumenical posture he took towards Christians of other denominations and schools of thought.

A critical dimension to the Christianity of Menzies was not only his theology but also his "churchmanship". His relationship with the institutional church, most notably, the Presbyterian and Methodist churches of his time forms the subject of chapter three. Although his Christian beliefs were very broad and non-sectarian, he made it little secret that he was proud to identify as a "Presbyterian". This chapter will explain both the cultural and doctrinal affinities he had with this Scottish, Calvinist strand of Protestant Christianity and the extent to which Presbyterianism moulded his own temperament and outlook. As one of this denomination's most eminent citizens, it will also locate Menzies within the Presbyterian Church of Australia and introduce some of the prominent Presbyterian clergy with whom Menzies identified, such as P J Murdoch and Fred McKay. As well as being a self-described "simple Presbyterian", it is also accurate to observe that Menzies was a "Methodist fellow-traveller" whose spiritual temperament and outlook exhibited many Methodist traits, owing both to his Methodist Sunday schooling and education at Melbourne's Wesley College. His affinity with Methodism was also evident in the warm friendship he shared conspicuously with Irving Benson, one of Melbourne's most prominent church leaders.

Having covered the essential terrain of Menzies' religious background and beliefs, and denominational loyalties, the book will turn to how Menzies brought his faith to bear on the major themes and issues of his time. Chapter four will address Menzies' abiding belief in the freedom of worship and religion, a conviction dear to both his Christian and liberal sensibilities. With liberal democracy fighting for its very survival in the midst of the Second World War, Menzies did not take this historically hard-fought liberty for granted and stressed its critical importance to a free and civilised society.

His dedication to preserving religious freedom sprang from a well of deep faith. His keynote broadcast on religious freedom in July 1942 helps to explain how his dedication to this principle was grounded in a long tradition of both Christian theology and liberal philosophy. Indeed, his principles of religious freedom remain eminently applicable to the present day and can thereby guide and inform contemporary debates on how this essential freedom should be protected. Menzies, moreover, was not simply committed to freedom of religion but also "freedom of political conscience", the freedom both for all Christians and others of faith to support the political creed and party of their choice.

Accompanying his dedication to religious freedom was a rejection of sectarianism, deploring it as repugnant to both liberal and Christian principles. Chapter five addresses Menzies' long track-record of seeking to mend the Protestant-Catholic divisions that had plagued the Australian social fabric, especially since the mid-nineteenth century. In part, his resolve to transcend this sectarian rancour was a reaction to the partisan Protestantism of his family background as well as according with his liberal instincts for religious toleration. In the post-war years of his prime ministership, the Protestant Menzies attempted to build bridges with Australian Catholics in several ways. First, by finding common cause with Catholics in the struggle against atheistic communism on the basis of affirming the shared moral and spiritual beliefs in God, family, human dignity and personal freedom from state tyranny. Second, Menzies made efforts to ensure that Catholics felt accommodated and enfranchised in his new Liberal Party. Indeed, long before, Menzies had made overtures to Catholics in his bid to bring Joseph A. Lyons into his side of politics in the 1930s.

Like its centre-right predecessors, the Liberal Party was predominantly Protestant in both its internal composition and support-base which meant that anti-Catholic prejudices occasionally flared at the local branch level. As leader, however, Menzies made it very clear that he would not entertain discrimination or sectarian bias against prospective Catholic members and, at the parliamentary level, sought to include Catholic MPs in his cabinets. Finally, and most significantly, Menzies addressed the longstanding grievance of Australian Catholics by supporting "state aid" to Catholic and independent schools from 1963, thereby helping to further diffuse sectarian tensions.

As well as forging closer ties with Catholics, Menzies enjoyed an excellent rapport with Australia's small yet influential Jewish community. Chapter six will explore Menzies' deep respect for the Jewish legacy and how he affirmed the important place of Australia's

Jews within the broader Australian community. The chapter will probe
some of the factors that accounted for Menzies' warm relationship
with Australia's Jews that included his reverence for the importance
to Christianity of the Hebrew Bible, his close personal contact with
individual Jews in Melbourne's legal fraternity, his admiration for the
loyalty of the Jewish community to Australia and its traditions and,
importantly, his respect for the faith and culture of Judaism itself.
Also addressed will be his staunch support for the State of Israel and
his strong stand against anti-Semitism in the community. Finally, the
chapter will explain how Menzies saw Australia's Jews as an integrated
yet distinctive part of the nation's post-war cultural tapestry.

Menzies' single greatest legacy was the founding of the Liberal
Party of Australia in 1944 from the remnants of the United
Australia Party. The birth of the Liberal Party signified the revival of
Australian Liberalism but, with the backdrop of fascism and Cold
War communism, it also represented the emergence of a post-war
liberal philosophy infused with humane, Christian ideals. Chapter
seven will examine the essence of this liberalism and how Menzies
articulated it in his keynote addresses, most notably, in the *Forgotten
People* broadcast of May 1942, before explaining how it formed the
philosophical basis of the new party. Whilst Menzies did not establish
the Liberal Party as a "Christian party" in the confessional sense,
its central principles of personal freedom, human dignity, family,
class harmony, subsidiarity, social justice and reliance upon "divine
providence" reflected the values of both Australia's Protestant and
Catholic traditions. The Party's principles were inspired by Christian
social thought but articulated in a way that could appeal to Australians
of all faiths or none. As a counterpoint to the liberalism championed
by Menzies, this chapter will also focus on the Cold War communism
that he so fervently opposed. It will appreciate that his opposition to
the Marxist ideology did not simply derive from political, economic
and security motivations, but was also stimulated by deep-seated
moral and spiritual sensibilities. By examining the key literature of
the communist movement and the relevant speeches of Menzies

on the subject, this chapter will explain how and why Menzies saw communism as anathema to his Christian beliefs and to a civilisation whose institutions and ethos were infused by Christianity.

Finally, with Menzies being Australia's pre-eminent "education prime minister", it is virtually impossible to understand his philosophy and approach to education without underlining the enormous importance he attached to religious faith. For Menzies, faith was deemed the essential foundation to the formation of moral character and citizenship in the pupil and the student. By analysing his keynote speeches on education, chapter eight will delve into Menzies' educational philosophy and explain how it was indebted to both the Judeo-Christian tradition and also the classical inheritance from the Greco-Roman world. Shifting to what this philosophy of education looked like at both the school and university level, this chapter will explain how Menzies saw faith-based schools, whether Catholic, Protestant or Jewish, as the great builders of personal moral character through an education informed by religion. From his own educational experience at Wesley (Methodist) College in Melbourne, Menzies appreciated that such schools not only fostered character in their pupils through religious instruction but also by practical means through leadership opportunities and extracurricular activities where pupils practised teamwork, responsibility and community service.

In light of this high premium Menzies placed on faith-based education, chapter eight will describe how his government supported church and independent schools in the post-war years. It will also explore how Menzies similarly saw universities as the incubators of moral character. For the prime minister and chancellor of Melbourne University, these seats of learning were not simply vocational training centres but great cultivators of civilisation. Whilst the public universities may not have had the same religious affiliation as faith-based schools, Menzies still envisioned them as schooling students in the "ancient virtues" inherited from the Judeo-Christian and classical traditions. From his days as a student editor during the Great War to his period as elder statesman in the 1970s amid rapid cultural change,

Menzies' philosophy of education, steeped in timeless principles, was essentially unchanged.

In a nation that is heir to a rich inheritance of Christian traditions, yet one where its citizens and public figures seldom wear their faith on their sleeves, a major study of the religious faith of an Australian prime minister may appear somewhat curious. Yet any thorough study of Menzies' speeches and pronouncements on a whole range of themes and topics will reveal that his philosophical instincts and world-view bore an unmistakable spiritual foundation that is worthy of further exploration. Characteristic of Australian leaders, Menzies was never given to ostentatious, public displays of his religiosity but nonetheless felt free to speak his mind on matters of spiritual significance, whether in a Pleasant Sunday Afternoon address at Melbourne's Wesley Church or at school speech nights. In so doing, he did not conceal the fact that his views on politics, culture and ethics were informed by Judeo-Christian precepts.

As the chapters of this book reveal, faith made a palpable contribution to his championing of religious freedom and challenging of sectarianism, to positive relations with the Jewish community, understanding of liberal democracy, opposition to communism, support for values-based education and emphasis on personal moral character. At a stylistic level, moreover, his public utterances were not infrequently seasoned with familiar, biblical turns-of-phrase, "my brother's keeper", "house of many mansions" and "the truth shall set ye free", suggesting that his own faith and piety were richly imbued with the Scriptures. With this evident spiritual thread running through Menzies' thoughts, pronouncements and policies, this book embarks upon the quest to explore the essence of this statesman's religious beliefs and how they informed his political philosophy and attitude to so many of the key issues in post-war Australia such as Cold War communism, private enterprise and initiative, self-reliance, welfare, sectarianism and education.

1

SON OF A PREACHER

FAMILY AND RELIGIOUS UPBRINGING

*Most of us inherit our religious faith, and
learn it in our early youth.*[1]

Menzies was born and raised in the period of Australian history
that the historian Stuart Piggin has characterised as the "high
noon" of Protestantism.[2] The period between 1870 and 1913 saw
unprecedented levels of church attendance. The cultural clout of the
Protestant ascendency in Australian public life was at its zenith. In
the 1901 census, 96.1 percent of the population claimed some kind
of Christian affiliation, which included 39.7 percent identifying
as Anglican, 22.7 percent as Catholic, and 33.7 percent as other
Christians.[3] It was an age where mainstream newspapers, such as *The
Argus, The Age* and *The Sydney Morning Herald* published sermons
and feature articles paying homage to Protestant figures like the
Scottish Presbyterian patriarch, John Knox.[4] With Menzies' birth and
early upbringing in this kind of religious climate, he was naturally
exposed to Protestant influences that laid the foundation for this

---

[1] Robert Menzies, Great Synagogue, Sydney, 28 April 1968.
[2] Stuart Piggin, *Spirit of a Nation: The Story of Australia's Christian Heritage*,
Sydney: Strand Publishing, 2004, p 49.
[3] Australian Bureau of Statistics (ABS), Chapter 12, Culture and Recreation,
Religious Affiliation, 1301.0 –Year Book of Australia, 2006.
[4] Stephen Chavura and Gregory Melleuish, "The Forgotten Menzies: Cultural
Puritanism and Australian Social Thought", *Journal of Religious History*, 44(3),
2020, p 360.

religious outlook. The Scots Presbyterianism and Victorian literature of his boyhood inculcated in Menzies the Puritan ethics of sturdy individualism, industry and moral earnestness. Added to this was the modernist evangelical theology of the Scottish Presbyterian, Henry Drummond (1851-1897), whose conceptions of God and the Christian life shaped those of Menzies. In adolescence and early adulthood, Menzies was exposed to yet further forms of Protestantism. These included: the Methodism of Jeparit and Wesley College to which he won a scholarship; the broad, ecumenical Protestantism of the Melbourne University Student Christian Union of which he served as President; and finally, the evangelical Protestantism of the evangelist and educator, C. H. Nash (1866-1958). These Protestant influences were disparate and, at times, conflicting in their theological premises and approach to the Christian life. Yet they each exerted a palpable influence in shaping the spiritual soul and mind of the young Menzies.

Fond of describing himself as a 'simple Presbyterian', Menzies had inherited a strong tradition of Scots Presbyterianism from his father's side of the family. In Ballarat, James Menzies was always a 'firm Presbyterian' who had served as an elder at Scots Church, Soldiers Hill. When James Menzies had settled in Jeparit with wife Kate in 1893, there was no local Presbyterian church so the elder Menzies joined the Methodist fold and became a trustee and lay preacher of Jeparit Methodist Church. Erected in 1891, the Methodist Church was the strongest non-Catholic worship community in the regional Victorian town. According to Menzies' biographer, James Menzies seemed to blend the strict Calvinism of Presbyterianism with the more emotional temperament fostered by Methodist teachings.[5] In essence, this meant that he would have held to a conservative interpretation of the Bible, the doctrine of predestination and a high moral standard together with the spirit-filled preaching, evangelism and personal holiness of Methodist tradition.

It was into this religious environment that Robert Menzies was

---

[5] Martin, *Menzies: A Life*, vol. 2, p 10.

James Menzies (1862-1945)

Presbyterian by upbringing, Menzies' father was a Methodist lay preacher in Jeparit. He seemed to blend the strict Calvinism of Presbyterianism with the more emotional temperament which characterised Methodism. (*Jeparit & District Historical Society*)

Elizabeth Menzies (neé Band) (1835-1911)

Elizabeth "Grandmother" Menzies lived in Ballarat, Victoria. When Robert Menzies attended school there, he lived with his paternal grandmother. Though not well educated, Grandmother Menzies had, in Robert's words, "the root of the matter in her". The only books allowed in her austere household were the Bible, the Presbyterian hymn book, *The Ingoldsby Legends* and *The Pilgrim's Progress*. According to Heather Henderson, when young Robert misbehaved, Grandmother Menzies would make him write out large slabs of the Bible as "punishment". As a result, Menzies learned much of the Bible "almost off by heart". (*Menzies Family Collection*)

born with regular church-going and Bible reading forming a part of his early upbringing. His memories of church in Jeparit remained with him for life. In *Afternoon Light*, he recalled "the pews in the church were of varnished pine... As a small boy, I can remember sitting forward after the sermon and disentangling my hair from the varnish with considerable difficulty!"[6] In the household of the young Menzies, the main books included *The Bible*, The *Presbyterian Hymn Book*, *The Ingoldsby Legends* (1837) written by the Church of England clergyman Richard Barham, and *The Pilgrim's Progress* (1678), authored by the English Puritan preacher, John Bunyan. Together with Scripture and Presbyterian hymnody, Bunyan's allegorical classic of the character, 'Christian', on his pilgrimage to the "Celestial City", arguably helped to furnish Menzies with what some historians have identified as his Puritan values.

The Puritans referred to the sixteenth and seventeenth century English and American followers of the Protestant Reformation leader and theologian, John Calvin. As such, they resembled close cousins of the Scots Presbyterians. In addition to confessing a Calvinist theology that stressed the sovereignty of God, the supreme authority of the Bible and the simplicity of church worship, the Puritans also stressed the virtues of moral earnestness, an independent and sturdy work ethic, thrift, frugality and family life centred around prayer and Bible reading. Whilst Menzies' broad and common Christianity did not mean he was a puritan in a strict doctrinal sense, perhaps like his father, James, his habits and attitudes were certainly typical of a *cultural* puritanism affirming of character, decency and moderation. That said, Menzies was no ascetic and his cultural puritanism was certainly not of the fanatical kind that spurned simple pleasures such as alcohol, dancing, theatre-going and club patronage.[7] It was defined more by what it stood for than what it opposed. According to Chavura and Melleuish, "Menzies' upbringing in a Presbyterian

---

[6] Robert Menzies, *Afternoon Light: Some Memories of Men and Events*, Melbourne: Cassell Australia, 1967, p 10.

[7] Menzies was a member of Melbourne's Savage Club.

household whose head was a small business owner did the most to instil the puritan virtues deep within Menzies psyche".[8]

Originating in the sixteenth century, the puritan movement appears chronologically remote from the Menzies of the twentieth century. It is important, therefore, to understand that the puritan values Menzies inherited were, in reality, mediated through the Victorian age to which Menzies was heir. Historians of the Victorian era recognise that "Victorian values", to a significant degree, were a product of the preceding eighteenth-century Evangelical Revival led by John Wesley and George Whitefield and, later, William Wilberforce and the Clapham Sect.[9] The prevailing narrative is that the Evangelicals succeeded in popularising the puritan virtues of moral earnestness, domesticity, industry, character and decency that, in turn, permeated the culture of the ensuing Victorian era. This impact was evident in both the politics and literature of the age. The Victorian English liberalism of figures such as William Gladstone emphasised independence and duty to others. Like the Australian Liberalism of Menzies, it struck a middle course between *laissez-faire* capitalism and state collectivism.[10] Victorian schoolbooks, likewise, were infused with the puritan and evangelical values of duty, domesticity, hard work and sturdiness.[11] Born in December 1894, some six years before the end of Victoria's reign, Menzies was a legatee of the Victorian age and its defining values left an indelible impression on his own temperament and outlook. As Chavura and Melleuish observed, the puritan-infused Victorianism of Menzies' early years looked not so much to traditional religious sources as to the great literature of the Victorian age and to the "prophets" who wrote it.[12] For Menzies, such

[8] Chavura and Melleuish, "Cultural Puritanism", p 360.

[9] For examples of literature discussing the influence of Evangelicalism on the Victorians, see Ford K. Brown, *Fathers of the Victorians: The Age of Wilberforce*. Cambridge: Cambridge University Press, 1961; Anne Stott, *Hannah More: The First Victorian*, Oxford: Oxford University Press, 2003; and Ian Bradley, *The Call to Seriousness: The Evangelical Impact on the Victorians*, Oxford: Lion Hudson, 2006.

[10] Chavura and Melleuish, *Forgotten Menzies*, p 28.

[11] Ibid., p 35.

[12] Ibid., p 28.

prophets would be Thomas Babbington Macaulay, the English Whig who wrote the celebrated *History of England,* and perhaps Samuel Smiles, the Scottish Liberal author who impressed the importance of character, duty and thrift in his writings.[13]

Menzies' own articulation of Victorian-derived puritan ethics came to the fore during his student days at the University of Melbourne. As editor of the student publication, *The Melbourne University Magazine,* the puritan tone of Menzies was evident. In an article for the October 1915 edition, entitled "An Evergreen Topic", he wrote:

> Remember, firstly, that we are not here to ape the "man of the world" and cultivate an easy acquaintance with vice. We are here, above all things, to fit ourselves by study and mental discipline for the calling of one or other of the great professions, and by so doing to help in the development of the highest intellectual and moral life both of ourselves and our country.[14]

Writing simply as a contributor, and not as the representative of a Christian group on campus, Menzies did not couch his message in doctrinally puritan or even Christian terms. It was simply a call to all fellow students, whatever their religious affiliation, to raise the moral tone of the academy. That said, the puritan inflexion of his message was unmistakable. Its warning not to "ape the man of the world" reflected the puritan call to live "holy lives" in the world but not of the world, and the reference to "the calling" of the "great professions" stemmed from the Calvinist doctrine that one's earthly vocation represented a "calling from God".

This last principle was particularly close to Menzies' heart. Like the Puritans, he believed very sincerely that all work, whether done inside or outside the church, had a "divine calling". Following the

---

[13] Samuel Smiles (1812-1904) wrote a number of books including *Self-Help* (1859), *Character* (1871), *Thrift* (1875), *Duty* (1880) and *Life and Labour* (1887). As well as promoting these virtues, Smiles railed against materialism and *laissez-faire.* Menzies was not on the public record for mentioning Smiles by name, but it was evident he exemplified the Victorian values he espoused.

[14] Robert Menzies, "An Evergreen Topic", *The Melbourne University Magazine* (hereafter *MUM*), Volume IX, No 3, October 1915, p 108.

teachings of Calvin, the Puritans taught that since God was sovereign over all of life and all of human activity, it followed that any vocation, whether that of a priest or a painter, a cleric or a carpenter, a minister or a miner, was done in the service of "God's world".[15] During his university days, he preached a sermon on this theme during his involvement with the local Church Bible Class at North Carlton and, later, at Kew. According to Cameron Hazlehurst, the title of the sermon was the "Sacredness of the Secular".[16] The sermon itself was not recorded and Hazlehurst did not provide any further details, but the topic suggested that Menzies preached a message to the effect that what is popularly termed, "secular work", in the professions and trades outside the formal domain of the church, is actually "sacred" as it is still performed in God's world.

In public life, Menzies returned to this puritan ethic of work when speaking in February 1944 on "The Christian Citizen in a New Era". Invited by a Presbyterian Church in Sydney to address their Sunday morning congregation, Menzies seized this opportunity to espouse an "all of life" Christianity. Lamenting the division of human capacities into "watertight compartments", he again affirmed the indivisibility between the sacred and secular:

> Certain things are sacred, certain things are secular, certain things may be done by the clergy, and certain things may be done by politicians. That is the kind of neat way in which we divide our lives up ... and "The Christian Citizen in a New Era" is really an answer to that subdivision because it starts off by reminding us that one cannot separate life in that way and that you cannot separate what is sacred from what is secular; and that you cannot above all things have any Christianity which begins only on Sunday morning and ends on Sunday night.[17]

---

[15] Michael Horton, *Calvin on the Christian Life: Glorifying and Enjoying God Forever*, Wheaton (IL): Crossway, 2014, pp 228-229.

[16] Hazlehurst, *Menzies Observed*, p 33.

[17] Robert Menzies, The Christian Citizen in a New Era, St Columba's Presbyterian Church, Woollahra NSW, 27 February 1944, p 1, Robert Menzies Papers, NLA, MS 4936, Box 253, Folder 13.

The overriding message was that in the post-war world, every Christian citizen had the duty to live out the ethics of their faith in public and, in so doing, would succeed in building a better world. According to Menzies, the four defining virtues of the Christian citizen were unselfishness, responsibility, honesty and courage. As was typical, Menzies' message was straightforwardly practical and did not delve deeply into any Scripture or puritan doctrine, yet it undeniably invoked the puritan philosophy of performing "sacred" work in the world by pastor and politician alike.

During Menzies' early life, the hallmarks of cultural puritanism in Australia and the English-speaking world were a disciplined, world-embracing sense of duty to improve society combined with self-reliance and individual endeavour. Doctrinally, however, such cultural puritanism was informed by a vague Protestantism rather than the Reformed Evangelical Protestantism of the original Puritans.[18] As would become apparent in his *Forgotten People* speech and other addresses during the early 1940s, this culturally Puritan-inspired sense of public duty would emerge as a defining tenet of Menzies' Liberal philosophy.

From his family background, this puritan ethic of public duty was closely attended by a very practical form of Christianity that also impressed his own faith. The practical evangelical Christianity of William Wilberforce and Lord Shaftesbury that had flourished in nineteenth-century England, with its proliferation of missions, charities and voluntary societies, from the RSPCA to the London City Mission, made its presence felt in the Victoria of Menzies' birth. Like London, Melbourne in the 1890s and early 1900s was home to a host of philanthropic organisations such as the "Ragged Schools" for destitute children and the Melbourne Central Methodist Mission founded in 1893. Menzies' own family had a direct involvement with such philanthropic endeavour as his father, James, served as President of the Milton Boys Home in 1926, a charity that succeeded the old Latrobe Street Ragged School and Mission to provide

---

[18] Chavura and Melleuish, "Cultural Puritanism", p 359.

residential care for homeless boys in Melbourne.[19] He was assisted by his wife, Kate, who actively worked on the women's auxiliary of the Home.[20] In honour of the Menzies' service, the Milton Boys Home was renamed the "Menzies Home for Boys" in 1943, and the family continued its involvement with Menzies' eldest brother, James Leslie Menzies, serving as President. As prime minster, Menzies visited the Home in 1958 and from 1961, the "Menzies Home for Boys" became the "Menzies Home for Children" to accommodate girls as well.[21] This practical Christianity embodied by his immediate family resonated with Menzies as he lauded the "practical Christianity" of the Salvation Army and that of the Central Methodist Missions.

As well as this example of his family, another important contributor to Menzies' iteration of Christianity were the writings of the Scottish Presbyterian minister and theologian, Henry Drummond (1851-1897). Together with his education at Wesley and involvement in the Student Christian Union, the influence of Drummond helped to explain why Menzies developed a broader and more liberal Christian outlook than the "narrow Calvinism" of his father. In his memoirs, Menzies recalled being brought up on a "melange of books", and he singled out "the writings of Henry Drummond for evangelistic fervour".[22] Born in 1851, Drummond was educated in Edinburgh and eventually promoted to a professorship in theology by the Scottish Free Church. Originally subscribing to a traditional evangelical theology, Drummond shifted to a more modern, liberal evangelical position that still emphasised redemption through Christ but with a greater emphasis on human reason and scientific thought.[23]   The

[19] Minton Boys Home, Find & Connect, History about Australian orphanages, children's homes and other institutions; URL: https://www.findandconnect.gov.au/guide/vic/E000396 (Last updated: 30 October 2018).

[20] Obituary, Mrs James Menzies, *The Argus*, 1 July 1946, p 4.

[21] The Menzies Home for Boys (1943-1961), Find & Connect, History about Australian orphanages, children's homes and other institutions; URL: https://www.findandconnect.gov.au/guide/vic/E000397 (Last updated: 30 October 2018).

[22] Menzies, *Afternoon Light*, p 9.

[23] Geoffrey Treloar, *The Disruption of Evangelicalism: The Age of Torrey, Mott, McPherson and Hammond*, London: Inter-varsity Press, 2016, p 29

liberal evangelicalism of Drummond and others has been described as "a confident, inclusive style of evangelicalism arising from a conviction that history was on its side, that society and progress were its debtors" and that the Bible should be understood in ways that made it compatible with respectable, modern scholarship.[24]

In works that would have been familiar to Menzies, such as his addresses published in *The Life of Henry Drummond* (1899), Drummond enunciated doctrinal principles that evidently resonated with Menzies in later life. In softening the strict Calvinism of his earlier years, Drummond emphasised God more as father than judge, Christ more as friend and exemplar than as advocate and saviour, and sin more as specific aberrations of conduct than a state of "fallenness". More attention was given to the life of Christ than the atonement and redemption, an emphasis which in turn required a change of personal character more than a change of status from 'unsaved' to 'saved'.[25] As such, those who rejected Christ were regarded not as "eternally damned", but rather as missing out on living "life to the full". Like Drummond, Menzies similarly drifted from the staunch Calvinism of his background to a Christianity that placed greater emphasis on fostering moral character and brotherly love than on the traditional doctrines of sin, judgment and salvation.[26]

In a practice that would later be adopted by Menzies as prime minister, Drummond was fond of delivering addresses to school and college students with a spiritual and moral message to inspire the growth of character. In these addresses, Drummond touched on familiar Christian themes that Menzies would invoke in his own addresses, albeit in less specifically doctrinal terms. In an address on "Temptation", Drummond implored his listeners to "walk in the spirit". In so doing, he appealed to them to: "Expand and enrich the higher life. In all ways and in every way expand. In music, in the arts, in literature, in poetry, in religion – anything which is stimulating to

---

[24] Piggin, *Spirit of a Nation*, p 50.

[25] Treloar, *Disruption of Evangelicalism*, p 29.

[26] Menzies, The Christian Citizen in a New Era, pp 1-6.

the man".[27] With Menzies' own frequent pitches to students to pursue learning in English literature and the liberal arts, and to cultivate the spiritual side to human nature, he underlined Drummond's ideal of a spiritually-nourished citizenry. In a speech on Australian universities, Menzies told the House of Representatives that:

> civilisation in the true sense requires a close and growing attention, not only to science in all its branches, but also to those studies of the mind and spirit of man, of history and literature and language and mental and moral philosophy ...[28]

Speaking at the time that his government had commissioned the Murray Report on Australian Universities (1957), Menzies had an ideal of Australian higher education fostering greater study of the humanities which he saw as so essential to enriching the mind and spirit.

In another address on what he called "The Bread of Life", Drummond reminded his students that individuals are also members of a community who must live for others - another theme Menzies was keen to impress. Drummond told his audience: "No man liveth or worketh for himself. Live for others. Work for others. Work unitedly as members of His body".[29] This principle of selfless interdependence was derived from the teaching of the Apostle Paul in his first epistle to the Corinthians, chapter 12, verse 12, where he spoke of the church being "one body with many parts". In Drummond's own paraphrase of the Apostle, he said:

> I think, of more comfort than that we are all, as members of the body of Jesus Christ, of some use; and made by Him especially for His work in the world. If you have not discovered your function, depend upon it, that is something out of the ordinary.[30]

In retirement, Menzies articulated the same principle inspired

---

[27] Henry Drummond, "Addresses to Students", in George Adam Smith, *The Life of Henry Drummond*, London: Hodder & Stoughton, 1899, p 482.
[28] Robert Menzies, The Australian Universities, House of Representatives, *CPD*, 28 November 1957.
[29] Drummond, "Addresses to Students", p 497.
[30] Ibid., p 498.

by the same passage of Scripture. In a 1974 address to accept the Freedom to the City of Kew, Menzies reflected:

> You know, I think it was the Apostle Paul who said that "we are all members of one another". It is a lovely phrase, you know. It is a lovely expression. It means that no man lives to himself, that every man who lives in a community is a member of that community. He shares his membership with other people in it and, political friend or political foe, he owes them every good thing that he can contribute to the life of the country.[31]

In his twilight years, Menzies lamented what he saw as the supersession of individualism by selfishness, even greed, in modern society, but was optimistic this moral malaise could be arrested if people returned to this biblical ideal of selfless community. As with the other principles Menzies espoused, this had also been a key tenet of Drummond's thought. There is little doubt that among the various Christian traditions and influences which shaped Menzies' religious outlook, the theological literature of Henry Drummond made a perceptible contribution.

In addition to the religious qualities of his homelife, Menzies' formal education had a marked impact. At school he was exposed, most notably, to the Methodist tradition of Melbourne's Wesley College. Later at university, he experienced a broad, ecumenical Protestantism through the Student Christian Union.

Following his education in Ballarat at both state and private schools, Menzies won a scholarship to Wesley College in 1910. In the face of his father's preference that he attend Scotch College, Menzies opted for Wesley, following his peers from Ballarat. Established by the Methodist Church in 1866 as one of Melbourne's Associated Public Schools, Wesley stood for many of the ideals of its eponym, John Wesley, the eighteenth-century English evangelist and founder

---

[31] Robert Menzies, Speech at the conferral of the Freedom of the City of Kew, 11 August 1974, p 272, cited in Heather Henderson (ed), *Letters to My Daughter: Robert Menzies, Letters, 1955-1975*, Millers Point, NSW: Murdoch Books, 2011, p 272.

of Methodism. The College's crest symbolised these with the pale blue cross representing the Wesleyan Methodist Church; a lion, representing vigilance and constant progress; the book, signifying learning and wisdom; the Bible, recognising the school's Christian ethos; a lamp, signifying the light necessary to guide the student in the path of wisdom; and a lion's head, asserting that in struggle, royal courage is a ruling element. With John Wesley's own personal courage and character, together with his preaching from the Bible, wide reading of sacred and secular literature, premium attached to the gaining of wisdom, and faith in human progress under God, the College expressly recognised the Methodist founder as the fountainhead of its ethos. Much of this ethos influenced Menzies in later life, both spiritually and culturally, as he would likewise stress the fundamental importance of the Bible,[32] the value of wisdom,[33] the importance of courage to moral character,[34] and education as the key to human progress.[35]

In Menzies' period at Wesley College from 1910 to 1912, the Headmaster was Lawrence Adamson. Serving at the helm for 30 years from 1902, Adamson was widely regarded as the most important and influential figure in the College's history. A practising Anglican associated with St Paul's Cathedral, Adamson's influence on the Methodist College and its pupils was pronounced. At regular school assemblies, he would stress the importance of good manners, community service, music, sporting achievement and, in particular, the cultivation of a corporate school spirit.[36] At Wesley College, Menzies

[32] Robert Menzies, Bible House, National Memorial Opening, Canberra, 13 February 1960, Robert Menzies Papers, NLA, MS 4936, Box 269, Folder 124.

[33] Robert Menzies, "Education and its Application", Australia Today – Man to Man Series, Broadcast, 17 March 1954, Robert Menzies Papers, NLA, MS 4936, Box 257, Folder 45.

[34] Robert Menzies, Speech at Cranbrook School, 10 December 1960, Robert Menzies Papers, NLA, MS 4936, Box 271, Folder 144.

[35] Robert Menzies, "Australian People and Government", Australia Today – Man to Man Series, Broadcast, 4 November 1953, Robert Menzies Papers, NLA, MS 4936, Box 257, Folder 42.

[36] M. A. Clements, "Adamson, Lawrence Arthur (1860-1932)", *Australian Dictionary of Biography* (hereafter *ADB*), Volume 7, Melbourne University Press, 1979.

is justifiably remembered for his academic achievement, especially in literature and history, but it is also noteworthy that the Headmaster's stress on serving the community and cultivating good manners made its mark upon him. In Menzies' spiritual journey, it is likely that the College provided a segue into his subsequent involvement with the Student Christian Union at Melbourne University. After the Union was founded in 1896, it established branches, or "Christian Unions", at many of Melbourne's private schools including Caulfield Grammar, Scotch and Wesley, for students preparing to matriculate to university.

Menzies maintained his religiosity during his years at the University of Melbourne from 1913 to 1916. In conjunction with involvement in the Student Representative Council, the Melbourne University Rifles, and the editing of the *Melbourne University Magazine*, Menzies joined the University's Student Christian Union (SCU) which he eventually served as President in 1916. Menzies himself had little to say about his involvement in the SCU and it is mentioned only in passing by his biographers. Yet this sphere of his early adulthood had a significant influence in shaping his Christian outlook and it is worth exploring in greater detail. As Renate Howe appreciated, the SCU movement was "a powerful influence theologically, socially and politically", and this was certainly the case with Menzies.[37]

The SCU of Melbourne University was part of the broader Australian Student Christian Movement (ASCU) established in 1896.[38] The ASCU, in turn, represented the Australian offshoot of the World Student Christian Fellowship (WSCF), founded by the American evangelist, John R. Mott, in 1895. A convert to Methodism, Mott founded the WSCF as an international Christian missionary movement to bring a lay-driven, ecumenical and socially engaged Protestantism to university campuses around the world. By reaching

---

[37] Renate Howe, *A Century of Influence: The Australian Student Christian Movement*, Sydney: UNSW Publishing, 2009, p 19.

[38] Renate Howe and Brian Howe, "E. H. Sugden and civic liberalism in Melbourne", Renate Howe (ed), *The master: the life and work of Edward H. Sugden*, Uniting Academic Press, Parkville, Vic., 2009, p 89.

students such as Menzies, Mott's vision and strategy was to raise up the next generation of Christian leaders to influence society and public life. The ethos of the Melbourne SCU owed much of its inspiration not only to Mott but also to the Methodist clergyman and educationist, Edward H. Sugden, Master of Queen's College from 1887 to 1928. During his long tenure at the Methodist residential college, Sugden embodied a liberal, ecumenical theology which saw faith as being relevant to the whole of people's lives and recognised the importance of Christians being involved in public affairs.

In the tradition of Sugden, the SCU subscribed to a pan-Protestant identity that drew Methodists, Presbyterians, Anglicans, Baptists, Congregationalists and other Nonconformists into its fold.[39] The theology of the SCU was accordingly broad yet orthodox in the period leading up to, and during, the Great War. Its doctrinal basis affirmed the deity of Jesus Christ, regeneration by the Holy Spirit, the reality and efficacy of prayer, the Bible as God's most complete revelation of himself and its indispensability for Christian life and, finally, giving all people an opportunity to know Jesus Christ.[40] In contrast to more evangelical Protestant movements, however, the SCU promoted a modernist approach to study of the Scriptures, whereby the Bible was interpreted through the lens of modern science. In this vein, the SCU reflected the influence of Henry Drummond who was already familiar to Menzies.[41] As with Menzies' own thought, Drummond was critical to informing the theology of the Melbourne SCU. The Union's forerunner, the MU Christian Alliance, had invited the Scottish theologian to Australia as a guest lecturer in 1890, so his teachings on reconciling Christianity with natural science were part of the SCU's received doctrine.[42]

With implications for the development of Menzies' own theological outlook, the SCU entered a transitional phase during

[39] Howe, *Century of Influence*, p 53.
[40] Ibid., pp 59-60.
[41] Ibid., p 32.
[42] Ibid., p 171.

the Great War when it was pulled two ways between the broad, evangelical theology of its founder Mott and an emerging, liberal Protestant "social gospel" movement.[43] The primary emphasis of the former was on evangelism and commitment of individuals to Jesus Christ. The latter focussed more on practical application of Christian ethics and transformation of human society to resemble the kingdom of God. This tension was indeed emblematic of Protestant Christianity at large in the English-speaking world where a rift arose in the 1910s and '20s between the hitherto intertwined missions of 'winning souls' and changing the world. When the SCU was born in the 1890s, this Protestant synthesis was still largely intact, the Union being committed both to evangelising individuals and applying Christian principles to society. According to Piggin and Linder, the SCU "maintained its evangelistic thrust in the decade before the Great War, but incipient liberalism was increasingly evident".[44]

By the time Menzies became involved with the SCU during the Great War, it was evident that the pre-eminent focus was now on Christian ethics although the traditional deference to the Bible had not faded entirely. A report on the SCU in the May 1916 edition of the *Melbourne University Magazine* provided a glimpse into its outlook when Menzies was President:

> It is to enable men by mutual helpfulness to maintain and develop this spiritual side [to character] that the Christian Union exists. Our concern is less for Theology and Philosophy as such than to bring home to men the fundamental facts of Christ, their bearing on life, with the obligations they carry of right thinking and right acting; in a word, the ideal of serving through our fellow-men Him whose whole life served men.[45]

Therein lay some of the roots to Menzies' uncomplicated, practical religiosity. His Christianity at university did not spring

---

[43] Stuart Piggin and Robert D. Linder, *The Fountain of Public Prosperity: Evangelical Christians in Australian History 1740-1914*, Clayton [Vic]: Monash University Publishing, 2019, pp 501-502.

[44] Ibid., p 502.

[45] Robert Menzies, "Men's Christian Union", *MUM*, Vol X, No I, May 1916, p 25.

from a richly theological tradition, as was the case with the Puritans or some of his Scots Presbyterian forebears, but from a simple appreciation of Christ's life, death and resurrection. The mission of Menzies' SCU, therefore, was not to probe deep into studying theological doctrines, but to apply the precepts of Christ to everyday living. This essentially reflected the SCU's general shift in emphasis to ethics, practical Christianity and the teachings of the human Jesus.[46] For Menzies, the chief lesson to draw from Christ and apply to contemporary living was his supreme example of sacrificial service. He became fond of invoking this impulse of Christianity. In an address to a Presbyterian church service in 1961, he reminded the congregation that "The capacity for sacrifice, the whole idea of sacrifice is at the very root of the Christian faith".[47]

At the same time as adopting this new outlook, it was evident the SCU of Menzies' time maintained some of its older preoccupations. The report in the *Magazine* made mention of CSU groups meeting "in suitable places to discuss the Bible and subjects allied with it, such as Missions or Social Service".[48] Whilst it may have been interpreted in more modern ways, Scripture continued to be acknowledged as the inspiration for much of the SCU's activity, including mission. It is also important to recognise that for all of Menzies' openness and embrace of the SCU's new outlook, he stopped short of adopting, wholesale, what became known as the "social gospel" after the Great War. This was partly because the social gospel movement did not make its full impact on the SCU until after Menzies' time, but also because its precepts and approach would have conflicted with Menzies' outlook.

Formulated in the writings of American Protestant theologians such as Josiah Strong and Walter Rauschenbusch, the social gospel movement emphasised the social significance of the Christian message. Rauschenbusch's works, *The Social Principles of Jesus* (1916)

---

[46] Howe, *Century of Influence*, p 172.
[47] Robert Menzies, Civic Service, Presbyterian Church, Cheltenham [Vic], 4 April 1965, Robert Menzies Papers, NLA, MS 4936, Box 282, Folder 222.
[48] Menzies, "Men's Christian Union", *MUM*, p 25.

and *Christianity and Social Crisis* (1917), for instance, concentrated on public morality in contrast to the traditional Protestant emphasis on private morality. For Rauschenbusch and other proponents of the social gospel, the essential purpose of Christianity shifted to the transformation of human society into the Kingdom of God by regenerating all human relations and reconstituting them in accordance with the will of God. With its preoccupation to transform the structures of society as opposed to reforming the individual, the social gospel movement attracted large numbers of Anglicans and other Protestants with more social democratic political sympathies. Amongst these was H. V. Evatt, a High Anglican and active member of the Sydney University SCU, and future leader of the ALP. Another was the future Labor Prime minister, Bob Hawke, son of a Congregational Minister who involved himself in the University of Western Australia SCU before abandoning his Christian faith early in adulthood.

For both political and spiritual reasons, the social gospel would have had little appeal to Menzies. Whilst he certainly did not subscribe to a narrowly individualistic form of Protestantism and was committed to a public-spirited Christianity dedicated to advancing the common good, Menzies believed essentially that Christianity *started* with the individual and not with society or the state.

For Menzies, Christianity or, indeed, any other religious faith, was something that began with transforming the heart, soul, mind and life of the individual believer before it could have the desired effect on society to bring about righteousness, peace and justice for all. In a speech to the evangelical-based Salvation Army, he told his audience that "Christianity is an individual matter. It may bring us all – as it has brought the Salvation Army – into an acute sense of social responsibility, but at base it is an individual thing".[49]

Certainly, in this respect, Menzies stood closer to the traditional evangelical Protestant position than that of the modern social

---

[49]   Robert Menzies, "Speech by the Prime Minister at the Salvation Army Citizens' Rally", Melbourne, 22 March 1959, Robert Menzies Papers, NLA, MS 4936, Box 268, Folder 117.

Clifford Harris Nash (1866-1958)

An English-born Evangelical Anglican clergyman who founded the Melbourne Bible Institute. Menzies never forgot his address at Melbourne University, holding up a little black book, a Greek New Testament, and saying "In this book is all I know of Jesus Christ and all I need to know of what God has in store for me".

gospellers. In later life, Menzies expressed his discomfort and frustration with church leaders who placed what he saw as too much faith in the state to bring about the desired transformation of society. Speaking in 1943 Menzies sought to impress the importance of reviving individual responsibility after the Second World War. He took issue with public figures such as the wartime Archbishop of Canterbury, William Temple, who were talking about a post-war "world in which the state runs everything".[50] He quipped "that all the talk that is going on makes you think that all we need is to be completely socialistic and the millennium will come in". In his stress on individual agency in the Christian life, Menzies' understanding of faith was analogous to his broader philosophy of Liberalism. In both cases, he saw not the collective state but individual men and women as the true drivers of change, progress and renewal.

The primacy of personal transformation over societal renewal was not the only principle Menzies derived from traditional evangelical Protestantism. In his own Christian life, his practice of regular Bible reading was typical of evangelical piety.[51] In addition to the influence of his parents and his dogmatically Presbyterian paternal grandmother with whom he lived in Ballarat for some years, Menzies' reading of Scripture was impressed upon him by the evangelical preacher, Clifford H. Nash. An Anglican clergyman of the evangelical tradition, Nash was founder of the interdenominational Melbourne Bible Institute, but it was at an evangelistic address he gave at the University of Melbourne where he crossed paths with Menzies. The then law student was part of Nash's congregation and, thirty years later, the evangelist again encountered Menzies who was now prime minister. Nash recalled:

---

[50] Robert Menzies, The Individual in the New Order, City Hall, Brisbane, 21 January 1943, Robert Menzies Papers, NLA, MS 4936, Box 253, Folder 13. In his influential book, *Christianity and Social Order* (1942), Archbishop Temple had envisioned a significant role for the state in the coming post-war order.
[51] Stuart Piggin, "The Bible says and so say all of us: Decades of Equipoise or Entropy? Evangelical Currents in Australia, 1946-65", *Lucas: An Evangelical History Review* 2.6, December 2013, p 19.

...The Prime Minister of Australia, Mr Menzies, came to me at a meeting and said, "Did you give a lecture in Melbourne in a classroom there many years ago? I said, "Yes I went several times". He said, "Did you have a little black book in your hand, and did you hold it up and say, 'In this book is all I know of Jesus Christ and all I need to know of what God has in store for me?' I said, "Yes", and produced the Book from my pocket – my Greek Testament. Mr Menzies said, "I was one of those who heard you and I have never forgotten the effect that your words had on me."[52]

Menzies later testified to another evangelist, Dr Leyland Wang, that, since this encounter, "he never gave up reading the Bible".[53] Indeed, Heather Henderson has recalled that when attending church together as family in Melbourne, Menzies would even bring his French Bible so they could follow the readings in French.[54]

Indeed, Menzies not only valued reading the Bible for himself, but encouraged others to do likewise. When, as prime minister, he opened the new headquarters of the Bible Society in Canberra in February 1960, he said of the sacred book: "It is the great source of faith, and of course that is why we ought to read it. That is why so many of us who are credited with light minds, like myself, constantly do read it!"[55] Though his less literal interpretation of Scripture was more characteristic of liberal evangelicals such as Henry Drummond than that of traditional evangelicals such as C. H. Nash, Menzies regarded regular Bible reading as integral to the Christian life and, in this vein, he reflected the outlook of evangelical Protestantism at large.

Following his university years, Menzies embarked on his career at the Melbourne Bar. During that time, he married Pattie Leckie on 27 September 1920 at Melbourne's Kew Presbyterian Church.

---

[52] Darrell N Paproth, *Failure is Not Final: A Life of C H Nash*, Sydney: Centre for the Study of Australian Christianity, 1997, p 127.
[53] Ibid., p 128.
[54] Henderson, "Robert Menzies", p 156.
[55] Robert Menzies, Bible House Opening, 13 February 1960.

Pattie was similarly of Scottish Presbyterian stock, and together they worshipped occasionally at Kew Presbyterian Church. As A. W. Martin noted, however, "they took no part in wider church activities and Sunday was a day for reading, and occasional picnics and outings".[56] According to Heather Henderson, Menzies' active churchgoing declined somewhat as he dedicated much of his time to his successful career at the Bar and his young family. It was suggested that he may have been "over-burdened with religion" in his early life and "churched out".[57] Henderson remembers that, when growing up in Melbourne, the local family church was the West Hawthorn Presbyterian Church, and during their stays in Canberra, it was the Presbyterian Church of St Andrew.[58] Whilst Menzies, in his more mature years, may have shown signs of waning religious observance in his private life, his Christian convictions remained firm and they were frequently made manifest in his public life. Accordingly, his views of God, the Bible, the church, and the Christian life merit further attention.

---

[56] A W Martin, *Menzies: A Life*, p 44.
[57] Williams, *In God they Trust?*, p 124.
[58] Henderson, "Robert Menzies", p 156.

2

THE FATHERHOOD OF GOD AND BROTHERHOOD OF MAN

THE THEOLOGY OF MENZIES

*Christianity connotes faith in a Divine
Creator expressed by a willingness for
sacrifice embodied by its highest symbol, the
Cross of Crucifixion.*[1]

True to his own epithet as a 'simple Presbyterian', Menzies' personal brand of Protestantism was theologically uncompli-cated. Like the twentieth-century Anglican writer and apologist, C. S. Lewis, Menzies would have viewed himself as an exponent of 'mere Christianity' which rejected atheism to affirm the Christian basics of a Trinitarian God, a divinely inspired Bible and personal redemption through Jesus Christ. Described by Chavura as "moral and aesthetic, with little reference to credal dogma", Menzies seldom dwelt on doctrinal specifics.[2] In part, this was because he saw Chris-tianity as laying pre-eminent emphasis on deeds rather than creeds, and also because he was cognisant of the historical fact that churches had fought bitterly over the meaning, interpretation and application of various doctrines and was therefore studious to avoid inflaming sectarian tensions of any kind. Nevertheless, Christian beliefs were still important to Menzies and his theology had definite origins in a number of denominational and theological traditions.

---

[1] Robert Menzies, Communism and Christianity, 1946.
[2] Stephen Chavura, "The Christian Social Thought of Sir Robert Gordon Menzies", *Lucas: An Evangelical History Review*, 2.12, December 2018, p 24.

From his birth in Jeparit in 1894 to his graduation from the
University of Melbourne in 1916 (LL.B) and 1918 (LL.M), the
Presbyterian and Puritan inheritances of his boyhood, the Methodism
of Wesley College, the broad Protestantism of the SCU, and the
conservative evangelical ideas of Nash each contributed to Menzies'
emerging religious identity and outlook. As such, the Christian
beliefs of Menzies were too varied and nuanced to be summed up
in one single classification as being either simply "Presbyterian" or
"Methodist", "broad Protestant" or "evangelical", or, indeed, "liberal"
or "conservative". The reality was that he exhibited characteristics of
each to varying degrees, depending both on the nature of the occasion
at which he was speaking and his audience. In some contexts, such as
his Christmas Message to the nation in 1943, he spoke the language of
liberal Protestantism, in others, such as the speech in 1960 to the Bible
Society, he channelled the spirit of evangelical Protestantism; while
in a Pleasant Sunday Afternoon address to a Methodist audience,
he spoke proudly of his Presbyterian identity.[3] As prime minister,
however, of a majority Christian nation with an increasingly diverse
post-war community of Catholics, Anglicans, multiple Protestant
denominations, and a small but growing Eastern Orthodox presence,
the faith he most frequently invoked was that of a broad, common
Christianity which was denominationally nondescript and eminently
practical with an emphasis on self-giving service. Behind this common
Christianity, nonetheless, Menzies held to distinctive theological
principles and denominational loyalties that are worth exploring in
more depth. Menzies is on record articulating his position on basic
Christian doctrines such as the character of God and Jesus Christ, the
nature of humanity, the value of the Bible, and the hallmarks of living
a Christian life.

Fatherhood of God

Menzies saw God first and foremost as a "father". There were no doubt
many other attributes he could have ascribed to God such as "creator",

---

[3] Robert Menzies, PSA Address, Central Methodist Mission, Melbourne, 7
September 1958, Robert Menzies Papers, NLA, MS 4936, Box 265, Folder 103.

"provider", "ruler", "sovereign", or "judge" but, in the tradition of Henry Drummond and many liberal Protestant theologians in the late nineteenth and early twentieth century, it was God's "fatherhood" that was the defining characteristic. When touching on spiritual matters in speeches, Menzies was fond of invoking "the fatherhood of God and the brotherhood of man".[4] In a speech to Sydney's St Joseph's College in 1961, Menzies reminded the students that "men … should be united in a brotherhood which is the inevitable result of the fatherhood of God".[5] The aphorism was actually popularised, if not coined, by the German liberal Protestant theologian, Adolf von Harnack (1851-1930). In his major work, *What is Christianity?* (1901), von Harnack wrote that the essence of Christianity is the "fatherhood of God, the brotherhood of man, and the infinite value of the human soul". There is no evidence that Menzies was necessarily a devotee of von Harnack, yet von Harnack's teachings proved to be very influential throughout the broader liberal Protestant movement to which Menzies was exposed during his formative years in the Melbourne University Student Christian Union.

For Menzies, the concept of the fatherhood of God appeared universal. God was deemed to be the father of all human beings whatever their gender, race, nationality, religion or station in life. In accordance with orthodox Christian belief, Menzies believed all human beings were created in the image of God. It was therefore axiomatic in Menzies' eyes that every person was a child of God, whether or not they consciously acknowledged Him or worshipped Him as their father in heaven. If every male and female individual was created by God in His own image, then there was simply no cause to doubt that he or she was God's child. This universalist conception of God's fatherhood was characteristic of liberal Protestantism at large and differed from more traditional, Calvinistic

---

[4] See for example, Robert Menzies, "The Communists", Broadcast, 2 July 1943, Robert Menzies Papers, NLA, MS 4936, Box 253, Folder 13; and Robert Menzies, Opening of Science Block, St Joseph's College, Sydney, 16 July 1961, Robert Menzies Papers, NLA, MS 4936, Box 272, Folder 152.

[5] Menzies, St Joseph's College, 16 July 1961.

forms of Protestantism. Traditional Calvinists, such as conservative Presbyterians, Congregationalists and other Reformed Protestants, agreed that all people were created in God's image and that every human life was sacred, but held that only those who came to faith in God through Jesus Christ could be truly regarded as sons or daughters of God. This was because a person's relationship with God had been severed by sin, and it was only by accepting Christ as Saviour and Lord that they could be restored to a right relationship with God their father. As in other areas of Christian belief, Menzies' view of God aligned more with the liberal Protestantism of his young adulthood than the Presbyterian Calvinism of his father, James.

Jesus Christ and the Cross

As to the figure of Jesus Christ, whom all branches of Christianity confess to be "God the Son" together with "God the Father" and "God the Holy Spirit" as part of the triune God, Menzies' views appeared to be fairly orthodox in that he affirmed both the divinity and humanity of Jesus. In his Christmas broadcast of 1953, Menzies spoke on the theme of human greatness and told his listeners that Christmas pointed to the greatest man in history:

> The one man, for he was human as well as divine, whose memory holds no blemish, whose influence has grown for nearly two thousand years, whose birthday is the occasion for rejoicing for hundreds of millions of men and women, was and is Jesus Christ. There is a deep inspiration in this historical fact. The recollection of it encourages men and women the world over to go forward in faith, in hope and in charity.[6]

In contrast to the proponents of radical liberal theology in some of the mainline denominations, Menzies did not subscribe to revisionist views of Jesus as simply a "great man" esteemed for his ethical teachings. His divinity was part of who Christ was and this was a fact of human history as recorded by the gospel accounts in

[6] Robert Menzies, "Christmas Message", Australia Today – Man to Man, Broadcast, 23 December 1953, Robert Menzies Papers, NLA, MS 4936, Box 257, Folder 44.

Scripture. In other places, Menzies did not make his views known on the historicity of the miracles or the bodily resurrection of Christ, but in accordance with mainline Protestant thought of his day, it is likely he accepted the resurrection of Jesus as true, even if his reading of the miracles was not invariably literal.

For all Christians, the focal point of Jesus' life was his crucifixion, or passion, on the cross, where the "Son of God" was believed to have borne the sins of the world for the salvation of human beings. Christians recognise Christ's crucifixion as sacrificial, because if He had not died on the cross, then all of humanity would perish from sin. On a couple of occasions, Menzies made reference to the cross of Christ and its significance. In his Christmas broadcast of 1942, in the midst of the Second World War, Menzies spoke on the theme of "sacrifice". Appreciating the large number of Australian troops who had sacrificed their lives in Europe, Menzies noted that "The Cross which is the symbol of the Christian faith is itself the figure of sacrifice."[7] Whilst the focus of Christmas is typically on the incarnation, the birth of Christ, Menzies singled out the cross as the defining feature of the Christian faith. For him, the cross epitomised the greatest Christian virtue, "sacrifice".

In a 1946 speech that contrasted Christianity with communism, Menzies explained what Jesus' sacrifice on the cross actually meant:

> Christianity connotes a faith in a Divine Creator expressed by a willingness for sacrifice embodied by its highest symbol, the Cross of Crucifixion; not crucifixion of the enemy, which is the expression of hatred and revenge, but of ourselves, which is the expression of unselfishness and universal love. For all Christians the Cross, after nineteen hundred years, remains the symbol of the freely accepted sacrifice for others.[8]

---

[7] Robert Menzies, Broadcast by the Rt Hon R. G. Menzies KC MP on Christmas Night, Friday, 25 December 1942, Robert Menzies Papers, NLA, MS 4936, Box 252, Folder 12.

[8] Robert Menzies, Communism and Christianity, Broadcast, 1946, Robert Menzies Papers, NLA, MS 4936, Box 256, Folder 35.

Describing the passion as the "expression of unselfishness and universal love", Menzies appreciated that the overriding impulse of Jesus' suffering and death was love, and a universal one at that. It accorded with the message in the Gospel of St John that "God so loved the world, that he gave his only begotten Son" on the cross for the salvation of all who believed.[9]

Menzies did not delve into the theological mechanics of how the cross of Christ worked to bring atonement and redemption to every believer, but acknowledged that it was the symbol of the "freely accepted sacrifice for others". Accordingly, Menzies reflected the Christian understanding that Christ died on the cross not because he was forced to by human authorities, but did so sacrificially as a free offering out of his great love for the world. By referring to the crucifixion of "ourselves", Menzies believed that people walked in the footsteps of Christ if they likewise sacrificed themselves for the sake of others, though such sacrifice need not take the form of death.

Human nature

As to the nature of ordinary human beings, Menzies' firm belief in the *imago Dei* (image of God) naturally informed his Christian doctrine of humanity. In contrast to atheistic or naturalistic belief systems that regarded human life as a random freak of nature and existing solely by chance, Menzies saw an inherent dignity, worth and purpose to every human life bestowed by a divine creator. In terms of understanding humanity better, the *imago Dei* was the most important attribute to appreciate. Menzies told an audience at the Australian College of Education in 1961 that:

> We must recapture our desire to know more, and feel more, about our fellowmen; to have a philosophy of living; to elevate the dignity of man, a dignity which, in our Christian concept, arises from our belief that he is made in the image of his Maker.[10]

---

[9] St John 3:16.

[10] Robert Menzies, The Challenge to Education, Australian College of Education, 19 May 1961, Robert Menzies Papers, NLA, MS 4936, Box 272, Folder 149.

Speaking in an age where humanities disciplines such as English literature, history, philosophy and anthropology were becoming increasingly secularised, Menzies was eager for educators in the academy to be impressed with the importance of recognising and affirming the *imago Dei*. For Menzies, this was not only fundamental to appreciating the unique nature and dignity for the human race, but critical to fostering greater respect and affection for our neighbours. In light of the two diabolical world wars of the twentieth century, Menzies saw such an ideal as never more important than in the early 1960s.

Belief in the divine origin of human beings gave Menzies a fairly optimistic view of human nature. Since God was deemed perfectly good, it followed that human beings created in His own image also bore remarkable, God-like qualities and were capable of achieving great good. Unlike some of the earlier free thinkers shaped by the Enlightenment, however, he did not believe in human perfectibility. The human barbarism of the twentieth century, alone, had emphatically discredited such fanciful thought and Menzies was all too aware of the baser human proclivities of greed, selfishness and malice. Speaking to a Presbyterian congregation in 1961, he expounded what it meant for humans to be created in the image of God:

> When God made man in His own Image, He wasn't creating something necessarily that had a physical resemblance to Him. He was creating something that had the God-like elements in the spirit and in the character. This is it. If we are in His image, it is because we have within us a capacity for rising to great heights of pure virtue, side by side with a capacity for sinking to the lowest level of selfishness and bitterness; but these God-like elements in the human character, sometimes twisted, sometimes ignored, I believe survive and blossom and develop as life goes on.[11]

Whilst not blind to the reality of human fallenness, Menzies believed that God endowed humanity with the innate capacity to

---

[11] Robert Menzies, Civic Service, Presbyterian Church, Cheltenham, Victoria, 4 April 1965.

realize its full goodness despite the disfigurement of sin and vice.

His sanguine outlook on humanity was as much indebted to his liberal instincts as it was to his Methodist sympathies. Consistent with the Victorian English liberalism of the Whig historian, Thomas Babbington Macaulay, whom he quoted approvingly, Menzies essentially subscribed to the Whig narrative of human progress.[12] Notwithstanding the cataclysmic effects the two world wars had in stunting human progress through the first half of the twentieth century, he essentially believed that with the necessary preconditions of freedom and democracy, human beings had the potential to flourish and become better people. As he expressed it in a Pleasant Sunday Afternoon Address, it was about "the freedom to do our best and to make that best better".[13]

In his reflections on the *imago Dei*, it was also true that Menzies was articulating an inner Methodism even if the congregation was Presbyterian. Subscribing to Wesley's faith in human progress under God, Menzies' vision of "rising to great heights of pure virtue" had far more in common with the doctrine of sanctification preached by the Wesleys than with the doctrine of "total depravity" emphasised by Calvinists.[14] To many Christian believers the two were by no means mutually exclusive but, to Menzies, the Methodist focus on becoming holy, or more God-like in character, was eminently more congenial to his spiritual sensibilities than Calvinist preoccupation with the fallen state of human sinfulness. When Menzies spoke of how the "God-like" elements in the human character "survive and blossom and develop as life goes on", his message essentially resembled

---

[12] Robert Menzies, "The Achievements of Democracy, in *The Forgotten People and other Studies in Democracy*, Sydney: Angus and Robertson, 1943, pp 181-182. In this speech, Menzies quoted a lengthy extract from Macaulay's *History of England from the Accession of James the Second* (1848).

[13] Robert Menzies, "PSA Address, Bond or Free", Wesley Church, Melbourne, 7 September 1947, Robert Menzies Papers, NLA, MS 4936, Box 253, Folder 17.

[14] John Wesley's views on sanctification, that is, becoming more and more like God, were propounded in *A Plain Account of Christian Perfection*, published in 1777. The Calvinist doctrine of "total depravity" teaches that every human being is totally enslaved to sin as a result of their fallen nature.

that of the Methodists who stressed individuals cultivating a more Christian character as they journeyed closer towards God in their lives on earth. Whilst Menzies' Scots Presbyterian inheritance was profoundly influential in other areas, it was the Methodist ethos of Wesley College, and perhaps the Methodist church in Jeparit, that provided the spiritual wellspring for his liberal philosophy of human progress.

The Bible

For Menzies and the church at large, the Bible represented the great source of doctrine on God, Jesus and humanity. In Menzies' own Scots Presbyterian upbringing, it was the great spiritual resource, together with *The Pilgrim's Progress* and the *Presbyterian Hymnal*. In young adulthood, the importance of reading Scripture regularly was impressed upon him by both the liberal Protestant SCU and the conservative evangelical clergyman, C. H. Nash. In his ensuing career in public life, his reading of the Bible remained a constant, even when his church-going ebbed and flowed. As the phraseology of his speeches attested, Scripture was seldom far from Menzies' mind and his explicit thoughts on the Bible were matters of public record. On two occasions as Prime Minister, he addressed the Bible Society. The first was during his first term when he addressed the British and Foreign Bible Society (Victoria) in July 1940. The second was in his lengthy post-war prime ministership when, in February 1960, he spoke at the opening of the Bible Society's new headquarters in Canberra. What, then, were Menzies' views of the Christian holy book and why did he think it was so important?

Praising the Bible as "this great and immortal book", Menzies esteemed it as both a literary masterpiece and a sacred text of faith. Taking the linguistic quality of the Bible first, Menzies cherished the traditional King James Bible as the jewel in the crown of English literature. Together with the Book of Common Prayer of 1662, the works of Shakespeare, the poetry of Donne and Keats, and perhaps the works of Milton and Shelley, the Authorised Version of Scripture formed part of the great canon of literature that had gifted the English-speaking people with their language. In his 1940 address to the Bible Society in Victoria, Menzies remarked that "this great Book has given to us, more than any other book and more than any other man, the language that we speak ... This is the great repository of our tongue."[15] Such was the pervasive influence of Scripture on the English lexicon that he suggested that even somebody unacquainted with Christianity would "still need to read the Bible if they wanted to understand the speech of the English people".[16]

As well as its cultural omniscience, Menzies revered the King James Bible for the rhythm and cadence of its prose and the felicity in its turn-of-phrase. In his 1960 speech to open the Bible Society headquarters, he declared:

> ... This is the greatest piece of literature in the history of man. Unbelievably great! I am an old-fashioned Tory reactionary myself, as everybody knows. And therefore I like the Authorised Version, and will undertake to say that anybody who wants to understand English at its best ought to read from the Authorised Version every week and if possible every day ...
>
> In the Bible you have this noble simplicity, this illustration of the most complete command of English. Because you either have command of words or words have command over you. And that is the difference! And in the language of the Bible, its superb eloquence based upon superb simplicity, you have what I will always believe to be the greatest piece of literature in the world.[17]

Viewing the Bible as the gold-standard of English literature, Menzies lamented what he saw as the deterioration of modern political speech. With the tendency for modern politicians and

---

[15] Robert Menzies, British and Foreign Bible Society Centenary Thanksgiving Meeting "The Oldest Book with the Newest Message", Victoria, 15 July 1940, Robert Menzies Papers, NLA, MS 4936, Box 252, Folder 6.

[16] Ibid.

[17] Menzies, Bible House Opening, 13 February 1960.

bureaucrats to use lengthy, cumbersome language, he appealed to the "superb simplicity" of the Bible as the lodestar to recovering the clarity and eloquence of everyday speech.

Like Abraham Lincoln, for whom he had considerable admiration, Menzies exhibited his love of biblical verse in his own spoken and written language. From his early pieces of the 1930s to his last in the 1970s, his speeches, addresses, lectures, presentations and orations were peppered with biblical aphorisms, idioms, phrases and quotations. One of his first public speeches, "Freedom in Modern Society", was illustrative.[18] In this speech, in which Menzies defined the broad meaning and essence of human freedom, quotes or paraphrases from both the Old and New Testaments abounded. To imply that a free body also needed to be inhabited by a free spirit, Menzies spoke of the human body as a "temple of the spirit".[19] Emphasising the truth that a free mind and free spirit were bound together, he intoned that "ye shall know the truth, and the truth shall make you free".[20] Sounding caution about the smug complacency of Australians to compare their freedom favourably with that of others, he warned against the temptation to say, "We thank Thee, Lord, that we are not as other men".[21] Urging a proactive commitment to freedom, he noted that "Faith without works is vain".[22] Drawing attention to the duties of citizens towards each other, he reminded his audience that "I am my brother's keeper".[23] Inveighing against the materialistic attitudes of the age, he reminded his audience that "Man does not live by bread alone".[24]

Menzies valued these passages of Scripture for more than just

---

[18] Robert Menzies, "Freedom in Modern Society", circa early 1930s, cited in Robert Menzies, *Speech is of Time: Selected Speeches and Writings by The Right Honourable Robert Gordon Menzies*, London: Cassell & Company Ltd, 1958, pp 209-224.

[19] 1 Corinthians 6:19 quoted by Menzies, "Freedom in Modern Society", p 211 .

[20] John 8:32 quoted by Menzies, Ibid., p 212.

[21] Luke 18:11 quoted by Menzies, Ibid., p 213.

[22] James 2:20 quoted by Menzies, Ibid., p 213.

[23] Genesis 4:9 quoted by Menzies, Ibid., p 221.

[24] Deuteronomy 8:3 quoted by Menzies, Ibid., p 221.

their pithiness or rhetorical flourish. For this regular reader of the Bible, they contained important kernels of moral truth, wisdom and insight that were pertinent to all of life. Indeed, they were not only applicable to the private devotional life of the Christian believer but to the whole of life in the wider world. For Menzies, these biblical principles of care for the body and soul, pursuit of truth, humility, integrity matched by deeds, brotherly concern and affection for the spiritual above the material, went to the heart of his ideal of a flourishing, healthy and free society. In this vein at least, his view of the Bible accorded with the Calvinist teachings of his Scots Presbyterian background. The Reformed Protestant tradition affirmed Scripture as divinely inspired and thereby applicable to all spheres of life over which God was deemed sovereign.

Accordingly, he saw the Bible as much more than a brilliant literary masterpiece but as the great repository of enduring truth, wisdom and faith. In his first speech to the Bible Society in 1940, he had credited the Bible for weaving the "existence of God" and the value of "moral judgment" into the English character. Twenty years later, in his second speech, he extolled the spiritual riches of Christian Scripture. To Menzies, these surpassed even its literary or historical qualities:

> In the second place, and of course in the greatest place, the Bible is the repository of our faith and inspiration. Never out of date, always up-to-date, always difficult of application and therefore stimulating to thoughtful people. It is the great source of faith, and of course that is why we ought to read it…
>
> Let's seek the fountainheads - it's all there! The story is there, the great history is there, the great gospel is there, the whole spirit of Christianity is there.[25]

In the Old Testament books of law, history, prophecy and wisdom, together with the New Testament Gospels, Acts of the Apostles and Epistles, Menzies was able to see the whole narrative of God's

---

[25] Menzies, Bible House Opening, 13 February 1960.

redemption of the world, the gospel of Jesus Christ and the birth of Christianity. These represented the "fountainheads" of Christian belief and the Bible contained them in their entirety.

Menzies' choice of the image, "fountainheads", was key to understanding his view of the Bible as the basic source of all Christian doctrine. As somebody who had encountered a variety of Christian traditions and denominations, he was well aware of the existing differences in doctrine and worship between various churches and the tensions this often brought. Whilst appreciative of the reality that such age-old divisions could never be easily concealed or erased, Menzies' anti-sectarian instincts gave him an abiding desire for Christian unity. With all churches and branches of Christianity deferring to Scripture in various ways, the Bible thereby represented a focal point for Christian unity in an age where sectarianism still lived. As such, it was "better for the ordinary layman at any rate, like most of us, to go to it than to be taken up too much with theological refinements".[26] To illustrate, Menzies employed the Latin maxim, "*melius est petere fonts quam sectare rivulos*" ("it is better to seek the fountainhead than to divide up the little streams"). So, instead of being preoccupied with theological divisions between different denominations, it was eminently better for Christians to affirm their common faith in the Bible.

With Menzies regarding the Bible as the primary repository of Christian belief, it was evident he also viewed it as the supreme authority. Indeed, he drew an analogy from his background in the law where Australian legal theory holds the Constitution of Australia to be the supreme and overriding authority in the construction (or interpretation) of the law:

> I remember many years ago I was reading in the Chambers of a very eminent constitutional lawyer. When a case for an opinion on the Constitution of the Commonwealth came in, he would always say, "Now, Menzies, the first thing we ought to do before we become too involved in the decision given by the courts is to read the Constitution again". We always

---

[26] Ibid.

sat down and read it from beginning to end so that we might
not miss the elements of the problem by being led on to the
side issues which occasionally do find their way into judicial
interpretation.[27]

Appreciating the parallels between the legal art of statutory
interpretation and the theological discipline of hermeneutics,
Menzies believed that when it came to matters of deciding Christian
theology, it was always wise to consult the Bible and defer to it as
the ultimate authority. Just as a diligent barrister would return to the
Constitution, the serious Christian would seek the "fountainheads"
of Scripture. Again, the Scots Presbyterian influence on Menzies was
evident as that tradition affirmed Scripture as the supreme and final
authority in its *Scots Confession of Faith* (1560).

With Menzies' making his high view of Scripture known, what
was his actual reading of the Bible? Owing to both the influence of the
liberal evangelical Henry Drummond and the liberal Protestantism
of the Melbourne University SCU, it appeared that Menzies while
taking the Scriptures seriously did not necessarily interpret them
literally. This was evident from a diary entry recording his first travels
to Britain in 1935. On Sunday 30 June, he attended a service at the
Church of England Parish of Chevening, St Botolph's, in Kent, and
wrote approvingly of the Vicar's approach to the Bible:

> The old vicar mumbles the service in the usual meaningless
> way, but preaches quite vigorously, his statement that the
> literal interpretation of the Bible was now abandoned "by all
> intelligent men, including most of the bishops" being much
> appreciated by me.[28]

Menzies here was reflecting the views of many mainline
Protestants in the interwar years who had welcomed the advance of
biblical "higher criticism" in denominations such as the Church of
England. "Higher Criticism", also known as "modernism", essentially

---

[27] Ibid.
[28] Robert Menzies, Diary for Overseas Journey – 19/2/35-9/9/35, 30 June 1935,
p 97. Robert Menzies Papers, NLA, MS 4936, Box 572, Folder 5.

referred to a re-reading of the Bible where the more supernatural elements of Scripture, such as the miracles, were reinterpreted in light of modern science and the modern mind. Such a movement had been well underway since the nineteenth century and reached the high point of its ambition and influence following the Great War.[29] With Menzies himself shaped by the liberal theology of both Henry Drummond and the Student Christian Union, he found the approach of the Chevening vicar to his liking.

While Menzies may not have read the Bible as literally as more conservative Protestants such as his father James, or C. H. Nash, there is little doubt he took the Bible seriously as the revelation of God and as "the repository of our faith and inspiration". On his same travels in 1935, he made his high views of Scripture known in his diary. Attending a service at the Church of the Middle Temple in London, he expressed his irritation that the Bible reader "would say *Epistle, Apostle* and *knowledge* and had no conception that the words of Isaiah's prophecies meant anything!".[30] On another occasion he felt that the reading of the Bible in church was perfunctory at best and sacrilegious at worst. He took aim at the reader in St Giles' Cathedral, Edinburgh, where "the one who does the reading is so pleased with his own appearance that he falls into the vain and blasphemous error of considering that the Bible means nothing and should be read accordingly".[31] Menzies suggested that "the best ways to fill the churches" would be "to arrange that the Bible should always be read with intelligence and power". He said that "it would be worth more than all the pretty essays (miscalled sermons) which have been intoned today!"[32] With little time for ceremonial trappings and rituals for ritual's sake, Menzies clearly favoured worship where the Bible was read and preached with sincerity and conviction.

---

29 Treloar, *Disruption of Evangelicalism*, p 177.
30 Menzies, *Diary for Overseas Journey*, 2 June 1935, p 80.
31 Ibid., 21 July 1935, p 114.
32 Ibid.

Believing that the Bible should be taken seriously rather than literally, the Christian faith for Menzies was more concerned with the *spirit* of the Word than the *letter* of the Word. Invited by a Sydney Presbyterian church to speak on "Christianity and Law" at their Sunday night forum, Menzies told the congregation:

> It would be a barren theologian who thought that the religion of Christ was concerned with the letter. It is concerned exclusively with the spirit. It issues its orders not to the mind of man but to the conscience of man, to that immortal part of man which does not depend upon final interpretation but which depends upon its adjustment to the laws of God and its adjustment to the rights, the interests, properly understood, of all other human beings. So I venture to say that it is easy to obey the law and that it is hard to be a Christian.[33]

To illustrate that Christianity was concerned not so much with the law as with the spirit, Menzies pointed to Christ's Sermon on the Mount from the Gospel of St Matthew. He observed that "the whole essence of the Sermon on the Mount is that you must be prepared to do more than the law commands, and that means that you are not to concern yourself only with the letter but concern yourself with the spirit". In the Sermon on the Mount, Jesus had rebuked the Pharisees for their adherence to the letter but their wanton neglect of the spirit. In contrast to the example of the Pharisees, Christ called his followers to walk in the spirit of the law by honouring God with their hearts and minds as well as their lips and hands. For Menzies, a faith of the heart, mind and spirit, was more the essence of what it meant to be Christian than outward observance of laws.

Hallmarks of living the Christian life

Given his views on the nature of God, Jesus, humanity and the Bible, Menzies had a definite idea of what it looked like for people to live the Christian life in the world. In common with all Christians, Menzies

---

[33] Robert Menzies, Address on Christianity and Law, St Stephen's Forum, 15 December 1946, p 3, Robert Menzies Papers, NLA, 4936, Box 1, Miscellaneous Folder.

believed that following in the footsteps of Christ and living by the Bible led to a transformation of one's life. Although Menzies did not employ theological vocabulary such as "sanctification", or becoming more "holy", he had a similar idea in mind of the Christian believer becoming more God-like in personal character. In the Christian life, the importance of reforming one's character far surpassed that of performing "religious obligations". Menzies noted that "if we think of Christianity only in terms of intention, of going to church, or even of making a handsome subscription to the collection, then we have not got very near to it".[34] It was the renewed heart of the believer that most mattered, and the personal character which that brought forth. Speaking in 1944 to a Presbyterian congregation on "The Christian Citizen in a New Era", Menzies outlined what he saw as the hallmarks of living the Christian life.[35] He maintained that if "real Christianity were applied to the ordinary life of the world", it would bring forth the following four attributes of character in the individual Christian, namely, unselfishness, responsibility, honesty and courage.

From his career in politics Menzies certainly understood the disposition of human nature towards selfishness, remarking that the "majority of our citizens will approach the problem of politics with one question in mind – 'What will this be worth to me?'" Turning this impulse on its head, Menzies observed that Christianity "begins its teaching by imposing on every citizen the obligation of unselfishness, of thinking of the interests of his neighbour before his own, and regarding himself as his brother's keeper".[36] Put another way, it was about exercising the second limb of Jesus' Great Commandment to "love one's neighbour as one's self". Recognising how intertwined selfishness was with greed, Menzies continued: "if there is one social vice to which Christianity directs itself with all its force, it is the commonest vice, the vice of sheer selfishness, especially the devotion to material self-interest". Accordingly, the unselfish character of the

---

[34] Ibid.
[35] Menzies, Christian Citizen in a New Era, 27 February 1944, p 2.
[36] Ibid.

Christian citizen would be marked by generosity and love for one's neighbour.

The living of a selfless life would also include "responsibility", which, for Menzies, was the second great hallmark of the Christian character: "It is a great and a Christian virtue, you know, to accept responsibility; and if ever a man stood on earth and faced responsibility with courage, it was the Founder of our Faith".[37] With Christians believing that Jesus was sent to earth by his heavenly Father to redeem humanity, the founder of Christianity took on tremendous responsibilities with courage by proclaiming the Kingdom of God in the face of stiff opposition from the religious teachers of the day, and by bearing the sins of the world upon the cross.

For ordinary people, accepting responsibility would not come at such a grave cost, but in taking it upon themselves to deal with something instead of leaving it to their neighbour, they would be following Christ. Menzies warned that if Christian citizens in Australia failed to take responsibility seriously, then "Australia will continue to be what it is now, a cheerfully irresponsible, pagan community".[38] Although an overwhelming majority of Australians would have identified as Christian in 1944, Menzies was under no illusion that a near-universal "cultural Christianity" implied that Australia, at large, was a nation of active Christian observers. [39]

Turning to "honesty" as the other great virtue of the Christian life, Menzies pointed to two types of honesty. The first was the "common" honesty of refraining from lying, stealing or cheating. The second was "honesty of mind", which he saw as the rarer of the two. This quality referred to the ability of individuals to speak, think or act on the basis of the facts of a problem and not merely on what they thought best suited them. In essence, it was about reaching a solution that put the greater good, or interests of others, ahead of one's own

---

[37] Ibid., p 3.

[38] Ibid.

[39] According to the 1947 Census, 88 percent of Australian respondents identified as Christian. This compared to 86.4 percent in the previous Census of 1933.

self-interest. As with the quality of unselfishness, it was integral to the Christian call to love one's neighbour. Emphasising the importance of this attribute, Menzies concluded that "if the Christian citizen is to be a dominating force in the new era, then the Christian citizen will need to discover and practice this great Christian virtue of honesty not only of the hand, but of the mind and of the heart".[40]

The final quality of the Christian life for Menzies was, indeed, "courage". By courage, he was not referring so much to the physical courage, commonly displayed by athletes and adventurers, but to the "moral courage" to do what was right even when it was costly, difficult or unpopular. With Menzies referring to Christianity as the "greatest minority movement in human history", he was all too aware that this would be a common predicament for Christians whose allegiance to God called frequently for moral courage to be displayed. Menzies saw this virtue as lacking in contemporary life and lamented that "this great absence of moral courage disfigures Australia even more than physical courage adorns it". Speaking of the political world he inhabited, Menzies conceded that this virtue was often a difficult one to practise as by doing what was right, it was "awkward", in many contexts, to be "out of fashion", "divorced from your friends" or "nonconformist" in a world that demanded uniformity. Of all the Christian virtues, Menzies cherished moral courage as "the most important in the world".[41]

A Christian life exuding the qualities of unselfishness, personal responsibility, honesty and courage, for Menzies, was an authentic one. It not only resembled the character of Christ but gave flesh and blood to his Great Commandment to "Love the Lord thy God with all thy heart, soul and mind, and to love thy neighbour as thyself".[42] Menzies may not have quoted this Great Commandment verbatim in his pronouncements, but it certainly informed his understanding of what he saw as the greatest objective in life for every individual.

---

[40] Menzies, Christian Citizen in a New Era, 27 February 1944, p 4.

[41] Ibid., p 4.

[42] St Matthew 22:37-39.

In the "Christian Citizen" address of 1944, he reflected that: "The greatest problem of the world is … to expand the heart and nature of man, and how you may extend your duties to another man, and how above all, we may understand our duty to our maker".[43] As prime minister in 1954, he reaffirmed similar sentiments in a radio broadcast to the nation:

> The most important thing in the world, may I say for myself, is man's relation to his maker: his relation to the divine and spiritual law. The second most important thing is man's relation to man, with all that it implies of brotherhood and understanding and fair play and responsibility.[44]

Whilst inspired by the Great Commandment of Christ from the New Testament, Menzies couched his pronouncement in non-doctrinally specific language; these principles were applicable to citizens of all faiths. As somebody with universalist conceptions of the Christian faith, particularly with regard to the "fatherhood of God and the brotherhood of man", he regarded Christian teachings, principles and virtues as embracing all of humanity.

---

[43] Ibid., p 5.
[44] Robert Menzies, "Education and its Application", 17 March 1954.

3

A SIMPLE PRESBYTERIAN
MENZIES' CHURCHMANSHIP

*How proud we ought to be of the history of
our Church. How proud we ought to be to
consider its roots in Scotland, its flourishing
and growth in Australia, its vast missionary enterprises, the clarity of its thinking, its
concentration upon the essence.*[1]

Menzies' Christianity was very broad and non-sectarian but, in public, he made little secret of his pride in identifying as a Presbyterian for both cultural and ecclesiological reasons. In a 1958 Pleasant Sunday Afternoon address to Melbourne's Central Methodist Mission, he referred to his "deep-seated Presbyterianism" as he appreciated the broadmindedness of his Methodist hosts.[2] Speaking at a Jewish function in February 1960 to open a War Memorial Hall,[3] he made light of his "outsider" status as an "unblushing Presbyterian", and it was as a "simple Presbyterian" that he spoke to the Australia Club in March 1961.[4] Many of his references to his Presbyterianism were made in a typically light-hearted fashion, especially when in

[1] Robert Menzies, St Andrew's Church Centre, Box Hill, Victoria, 20 March 1960

[2] Robert Menzies, Pleasant Sunday Afternoon Address, Wesley Central Methodist Mission, Melbourne, 7 September 1958, p 1.

[3] Robert Menzies, Jewish War Memorial Hall Opening, Waverley, NSW, 7 February 1960, Robert Menzies Papers, NLA, MS 4936, Box 269, Folder 124.

[4] Robert Menzies, Speech to the Australia Club Dinner, London, 20 March 1961, p 4.

the company of Christians from other denominations, yet they still pointed back to his distinctive religious identity.

As a proud Scottish Australian, Menzies saw his Presbyterianism as integral to his cultural identity in much the same way that many Irish and German immigrants respectively viewed their Catholicism and Lutheranism. Dating back to the Protestant reformer and great father of Presbyterianism, John Knox (1514-1572), who himself had been a student of John Calvin in Geneva, Presbyterianism had been deeply woven into the Scottish cultural fabric with the Church of Scotland, or the "Kirk", the national church of the land. The 1706 Act of Security had entrenched Presbyterianism as Scotland's national religion and the national Kirk and its General Assembly, at least in symbolic terms, appeared to act as a de facto parliament for Scotland to represent the will of the Scottish people.[5] The Kirk had played a leading role in provision of universal education in Scotland, owing to its teaching that all should be able to read the Bible. Until the onset of secularism in the 1960s, Presbyterian Scotland was one of the great biblically-literate cultures of the world.

Especially through his father James and his Scottish forebears, this Scottish Presbyterian tradition formed part of Menzies' cultural inheritance. Along with Anglicanism, Roman Catholicism and Methodism, Presbyterianism was one of the four great faith traditions of early modern Australia and contributed richly to both the religious and civic life of the nation through its churches, charities, educational institutions and influential networks of professionals and public figures. Opening a new Presbyterian Church centre in Melbourne in 1960, Menzies spoke of his pride in what the Presbyterian Church had brought to Australia:

> How proud we ought to be of the history of our Church.
> How proud we ought to be to consider its roots in Scotland,

---

[5] Ryan Mallon, "A Church for Scotland? The Free Church and Scottish Nationalism after the Disruption?", *Scottish Church History*, 49:1 (2020), p 5.

its flourishing and growth in Australia, its vast Missionary enterprises, the clarity of its thinking, its concentration upon the essence. This is something to be proud of.[6]

Drawing from the same Calvinist font as Puritanism, Scottish Presbyterianism not only brought a Reformed variety of Protestantism to Australia but did much to contribute to the evolving national psyche. With its early commitment to representative democracy dating back to Sydney's formidable Presbyterian divine, Dr John Dunmore Lang of the Scots Church, and its balance of sturdy individualism with civic responsibility, it helped to forge the Australia that Menzies' cherished as part of his Liberal vision.

In "The Power of Presbyterianism" for the Melbourne-based newspaper, *The Argus*, Menzies articulated his conception of the principles of Presbyterianism:

> The history of Presbyterianism embodies truths and experiences that are as significant in the twentieth century as they were in the sixteenth ...
>
> The principles of personal liberty, independence and tolerance, for which lives, fortunes, and untiring effort were spent gladly, are still the great fundamental issues upon which rest the destiny of nations ...
>
> The impress left upon Australia by the many thousands of men and women who have passed through Presbyterian institutions is a factor in the life of the State and of the Commonwealth the value of which is inestimable. Their ideals of citizenship, their acceptance of personal responsibilities to the community in which they were reared, their record of social service of diverse kinds are a monument to principles which no civilised community can afford to disregard.[7]

Menzies exemplified these principles in both his personal life and in the espousal of his creed of Australian Liberalism. As a

---

[6] Robert Menzies, St Andrew's Church Centre Opening, Box Hill, Victoria, 20 March 1960, Robert Menzies Papers, NLA, MS 4936, Box 269, Folder 125.
[7] "The Power of Presbyterianism", *The Argus*, 16 September 1933, p 22.

student and later lawyer at the Victorian Bar, Menzies impressed the importance of civic duty and contributing to the community. Later, as prime minister, he affirmed personal liberty, independence, citizenship and the acceptance of personal responsibilities to the community as the great drivers of democracy and progress.

Having appreciated Menzies' cultural Presbyterianism, what *doctrinal* beliefs of Presbyterianism, based on the *Westminster Confession of Faith* (1647) and the *Westminster Shorter Catechism* (1647), did Menzies then espouse? Menzies was certainly acquainted with the *Shorter Catechism*, used typically by Presbyterian churches and families to catechise children and new believers in the faith. He knew its opening line well: "Man's chief end is to glorify God and enjoy him forever". In various speeches he used it at the expense of his political opponents, light-heartedly but sarcastically, to expound a key message. "… the chief end of the State becomes man";[8] "… the chief end of men is to glorify science and enjoy it forever";[9] and "… the chief end of totalitarianism is to glorify power and enjoy it forever".[10]

Second only to the Bible itself as the supreme standard of faith for Presbyterianism, the *Westminster Confession of Faith* encapsulated the Calvinist theology John Knox had brought to Scotland. As well as affirming beliefs common to all Christians such as the Trinitarian God, the birth, death and resurrection of Christ, the divine inspiration of Scripture and the *imago Dei*, the Confession enunciated such Calvinist doctrines as predestination, the "total depravity" of all humanity and the salvation of the "elect". Given Menzies' own broad and general form of Christianity, he had, at various times, confessed the more foundational Christian beliefs about God, Jesus and humanity, but was either non-committal or silent on the more explicit Calvinist doctrines of traditional Presbyterian belief for two main reasons.

---

[8] Robert Menzies, "The Nature of Democracy", *The Forgotten People*, p 172.
[9] Robert Menzies, "Modern Science and Civilisation" (1958) in *Speech is of Time: Selected Speeches and Writings*, London: Cassell, 1958, p 245.
[10] Robert Menzies, "Freedom in Modern Society" (1935/6)", Robert Menzies Papers [4936], Series 6, Box 251, Folder 4.

First, Menzies' own form of Presbyterianism was eminently simple and doctrinally minimalist. For his part, he was happy to go straight to the Bible to draw his Christian beliefs and leave finer points of doctrine for theologians to probe and expound. As Menzies himself acknowledged, he was "no theologian" and therefore not disposed to much preoccupation with what he called "theological refinements". As a Presbyterian layperson serving in public life as distinct from a cleric in the ministry of the church, his chief business was not so much to study doctrine closely, and preach it, as it was to give practical effect to broad Christian principles in his personal and pubic life. By all means, he was willing to speak publicly on Christian beliefs and values in a generalist vein at the appropriate occasion, but as prime minister for all Australians, whether Presbyterian or Methodist, Protestant or Catholic, Christian or otherwise, he was content to leave theological specifics to the churches.

Besides, Menzies' broad Christianity could hardly be described as strictly Calvinist in a way that conformed with all the teachings of the Westminster Confession. On the one hand, it is true the Presbyterian Menzies assented to Calvin's teachings on the sovereignty of God, the divine inspiration of Scripture, the *imago Dei*, and the rejection of a false dichotomy between the "sacred" and the "secular", not to mention Menzies' own habits of industry, discipline and thrift reflecting Calvinist ideals. On the other hand, however, there were various points of Calvinist doctrine with which he felt uncomfortable owing to a combination of both Methodist and Enlightenment liberal sympathies. For one thing, Menzies had a too high and too optimistic view of human nature to have subscribed to the Calvinist doctrine of "total depravity" which held men and women to have no innate capacity for good apart from God's grace. As Melleuish appreciated, Menzies' liberal views of human nature stood more comfortably with the Anglophiles of the Scottish Enlightenment than with the dour doctrines of the Calvinists.[11] In addition, Menzies'

---

[11] Greg Melleuish, "Sir Robert Menzies and Australian Education", J R Nethercote (ed.), *Menzies: The Shaping of Modern Australia*, p 260.

universalist conception of God's fatherhood would not have sat well with the Calvinist doctrine of "limited atonement", the idea that God sent Christ to die only for the "elect", leaving the rest of humanity "damned". Whilst Menzies did not proffer specific views on the nature of the atonement, he would have warmed more to the Wesleyan Methodist understanding that Christ's death on the cross was for all of humanity and not just the elect. Thus for all his Presbyterian identity and familiarity with the *Westminster Confession* and *Shorter Catechism*, much of his theology was, indeed, more Methodist than Calvinist.

Given the essence of Menzies' Presbyterian theology, which was sufficiently orthodox on the Christian fundamentals yet too broad and liberal to be classified as conventionally Calvinist, he perhaps occupied something of a "middle ground" within the Presbyterian Church of Australia itself. Typical of mainline Protestant denominations in post-war Australia, Presbyterianism was a very broad church with conservative, Bible-believing evangelicals occupying one end of the spectrum and radical social gospelers with revisionist theologies at the opposite end. On the one hand, Menzies would not have been closely aligned with the Reformed evangelicals who adhered strictly to the *Westminster Confession of Faith* and focused primarily on "saving souls" through gospel preaching and evangelism. Yet, on the other, he would not have felt at home with the radical theological revisionists, such as Allan Dalziel, a member of Dr Evatt's staff, and Keith Dowding, who preached a gospel of social justice and agitated for a range of progressive causes from nuclear disarmament and opposition to the Vietnam War, to abortion and homosexual law reform.[12]

Instead, Menzies represented an older-style, broad-church Presbyterianism that still valued the gospel essentials yet favoured a practical Christianity stressing moral character and good works. Channelling this form of Presbyterianism, Menzies once remarked,

---

[12] David Hilliard, "The Religious Crisis of the 1960s: The Experience of the Australian Churches", *Journal of Religious History*, Vol. 21, No. 2, June 1997, pp 223-224.

The Rev Patrick Murdoch (1850-1940)

The father of Sir Keith and grandfather of Rupert, the Reverend Patrick Murdoch regarded prime ministers Andrew Fisher, Alfred Deakin and Menzies as friends. Murdoch belonged to the Liberal Free Church tradition of Presbyterianism. He distanced himself from literal interpretation of the Scriptures, acknowledging there were "imperfections and mistakes" but they nonetheless conveyed "the truth about God". (*The Argus*)

"I've always maintained that we Scots Presbyterians have a very practical outlook".[13] Tending to be politically and socially conservative, such Presbyterians emphasised personal integrity, service to the community and the moral transformation of individuals more than the restructuring of society. This strand of Presbyterianism was well represented by leading clergy such as the Rev David John Flockhart, who served as Moderator-General of the Presbyterian Church of Australia (1957-59). Like Menzies, Flockhart combined social conservatism with theological liberalism and ecumenism. Disdainful of radical policies, he urged a return to God and Christian moral principles to counter economic and social ills.[14] In very familiar language, he affirmed that "the doctrine for the world in our day, with its moral decadence, its social unrest, its demand for security is the Fatherhood of God and the Brotherhood of Man".[15]

The other two Presbyterian Church figures of this broad-church tradition, whom Menzies had occasion to acknowledge expressly, were John Laurence Rentoul and Patrick John Murdoch. In his 1960 speech to open the St Andrew's (Presbyterian) Church Centre at Box Hill, he praised Rentoul for his engaging, gospel-based preaching and, likewise, Murdoch, "a magnificent preacher" who was also "a great scholar with all the tradition of scholarship that we have in this Church". [16] Rentoul described his own theological position as "the liberal faith of an evangelical broad churchman".[17] Although committed to the historic Christian gospel, he sought to interpret Christianity in the light of recent biblical criticism and

[13] Robert Menzies, Speech to Knox Grammar School, Sydney, 15 December 1960, p 1.

[14] Joan Mansfield, 'Flockhart, David John (1889–1964)', ADB, National Centre of Biography, Australian National University, http://adb.anu.edu.au/biography/flockhart-david-john-10205/text18035, published first in hardcopy 1996, accessed online 3 October 2020.

[15] Quoted by Peter Barnes, "NSW Presbyterianism in the 1950s and 1960s", Lucas: An Evangelical History Review, Series 2, No 15, June 2020.

[16] Menzies, St Andrews Church Centre Opening, 20 March 1960, p 5.

[17] Stuart Macintyre, "Rentoul, John Laurence (1846-1926)", ADB, Vol 11, MUP, 1988.

The Rev Dr Frederick McKay (1907-2000)

Menzies enjoyed a personal friendship with Fred McKay, a Presbyterian clergyman who succeeded the Rev Dr John Flynn as head of the Australian Inland Mission in 1951. Together with Flynn, McKay pioneered the Royal Flying Doctor Service. McKay officiated at Menzies' funeral in May 1978. (*Portrait by Esme Bell*)

to accommodate the tenets of his faith to scientific knowledge.[18] Notwithstanding, his high view of the Bible led him to campaign vigorously for the teaching of Scripture in government schools. In an outlook not dissimilar to that of Menzies, he dismissed as "twaddle" the notion that mere secular training could restrain the passions.

Of similar ilk was the Melbourne clergyman, Patrick John Murdoch, who regarded prime ministers Andrew Fisher, Alfred Deakin and Menzies as his friends or admirers. Murdoch was father of the journalist and newspaper proprietor, Keith Murdoch, and the grandfather of Rupert Murdoch. As a young man, Menzies encountered Murdoch through his preaching ministry at Trinity Presbyterian Church, Camberwell, in Melbourne's inner east.[19] A theologian of the liberal Free tradition of Presbyterianism, Murdoch published several works including *The Central Doctrines of the Christian Faith* (1915).[20] In this book, Murdoch affirmed the orthodox Christian teachings on God, the trinity, sin and the Scriptures, but maintained "that doctrine should be in every age verified and justified in the experience of Christian men".[21] On the Bible, he believed that it contained the gospel which was "the history of God's redeeming work for men" culminating in Jesus Christ.[22] He also appeared, however, to distance himself from a literal interpretation of the Bible, acknowledging that there were "imperfections and mistakes" in the Scriptures even as they still conveyed "the truth about God to us in the most impressive and convincing way".[23] As such, Murdoch's theology and views on the Bible aligned closely with those articulated by his admirer, Menzies.

With Menzies' own preference for a practical Christianity, he also identified closely with Presbyterian clergy such as John Flynn

---

[18] Ibid.
[19] Menzies, Knox Grammar School Speech Night, 15 December 1960, p 1, Robert Menzies Papers, NLA, MS 4936, Box 271, Folder 144.
[20] Neil Gunson, "Murdoch, Patrick John (1850-1940)", *ADB*, Vol 10, MUP, 1986.
[21] Patrick John Murdoch, *The Central Doctrines of the Christian Faith*, Melbourne: Lothian Book Publishing, 1915, p 4.
[22] Murdoch, *Central Doctrines*, p 108.
[23] Ibid., p 109.

and Fred McKay. In 1912, Flynn had started the Australian Inland Mission and subsequently founded what became known as the Royal Flying Doctor Service. Like Menzies, Flynn favoured ecumenicalism and, accordingly, placed more emphasis on practical outreach than on creed in his outback ministries.[24] Laying the Foundation Stone for the John Flynn Memorial Church in Alice Springs on 26 June 1954, Menzies paid tribute to Flynn's vision and "executive ability to get things done", likening him to "a modern Apostle Paul".[25] It is not known whether Menzies was personally acquainted with Flynn, but he certainly knew his successor at the Royal Flying Doctor Service, Fred McKay. Regarding McKay as a personal friend and spiritual confidant, he admired the clergyman as a "good, practical Christian". McKay would feature at important points in Menzies' own life, assisting in the conduct of his daughter's wedding, taking his son Ian's burial service and officiating at his own State Funeral at Melbourne's Scots Church in May 1978. In McKay's last meeting with Menzies before his death, he clasped Menzies' hand and said, "God be with you, Bob". To which Menzies replied with the Aaronic blessing from Numbers 25:6, "And with you, and may He make His face to shine upon you, and be gracious unto you". It was said that this final exchange "was their deep moment of truth, and an appropriate farewell" between friends of kindred faith.[26] During his time in Canberra, Menzies also valued the ministry of Hector Harrison, the minister at Canberra's Presbyterian Church of St Andrew, for the "splendid and dignified way" he conducted the worship at commemorative public services.[27]

A Methodist fellow traveller?

For all his professed identity as a Presbyterian, many features of Menzies' religious temperament and outlook actually resembled

---

[24] Piggin and Linder, *National Soul*, p 161.

[25] Maisie McKenzie, *Outback Achiever: Fred McKay successor to Flynn of the Inland*, Brisbane: Boolarong Press, 1997, p 109.

[26] McKenzie, *Outback Achiever*, pp 180-181.

[27] Roger C. Thompson, *Religion in Australia: A History*, Melbourne: Oxford University Press, 2002, p 103.

Kate Menzies (née Sampson) (1866-1946)

Menzies' mother was the daughter of immigrants from Cornwall, a stronghold of Methodism often visited by John Wesley. Menzies considered Wesley "a great man [who] put life into the body of the church". After marrying James, Kate became involved with the work of Kew Presbyterian Church and the Menzies Home for Boys at Frankston. (*Jeparit & District Historical Society*)

Methodism. Together with the Scottish Presbyterianism of the Menzies lineage, the Cornish Methodism of his mother's side coursed through his veins. His mother, Kate, later identified with the Presbyterianism of her husband, James, but her Sampson family background was of Methodist origin. Her father, John D. Sampson (1834-1913), hailed from Gulval, Cornwall, and her mother, Mary Jane Sampson (1831-1871), was born in the Cornish town of Penzance. Dating back to the eighteenth-century Evangelical Revival, Cornwall had represented a Methodist stronghold with John Wesley visiting the county no less than thirty-two times.

In many respects, Robert Menzies' own form of Protestantism, with its belief in human freewill, optimistic view of human transformation and emphasis on the practical, was more in keeping with the Methodist spirit of John Wesley than with the Presbyterian tradition of John Knox. In one sense, this was not surprising given his upbringing in the Jeparit Methodist Church and his secondary education at Wesley College. Yet he self-identified as Presbyterian and has almost always been classified as such by historians and biographers. Passing reference to his Methodism, however, was made by Roger Thompson who claimed that Menzies had "long abandoned the staunch Methodism of his childhood"; Stephen Chavura thought that "Menzies' childhood Christianity was a fusion of Methodism and Presbyterianism", but that "Menzies only ever identified with the latter owing to his aversion to religious enthusiasm and his enthusiasm for his Scottish heritage".[28]

It was certainly true that Menzies identified publicly as Presbyterian rather than Methodist, including at functions where a large Methodist audience was present, and that he was not a Methodist churchgoer beyond attendance at chapel services at Wesley College. Yet far from fading into obsolescence, the Methodism of his childhood and adolescence continued to infuse the flavour of his Protestantism well into his riper years. In the most

---

[28] Thompson, *Religion in Australia*, p 103; Stephen Chavura, "Christian Social Thought", p 22.

apparent sense, this was evident in the high praise he accorded
the founder of Methodism, John Wesley (1703-1791). With the
possible exception of Edmund Burke, there were few figures of the
eighteenth-century that Menzies admired more, and he invoked
the name of Wesley in a way that he had not done with other pre-
eminent church figures such as John Calvin, or even John Knox, the
father of Scottish Presbyterianism.

On at least two public occasions, Menzies spoke of his affection
for the Methodist founder. In a speech to open a new building at
the Methodist-run Lincoln College of the University of Adelaide,
he noted that John Wesley had attended a college of the same name
at Oxford. He praised Wesley as "one of the very great men of the
eighteenth century" and "one of the immortals of English history".[29]
Previously, at a "Salvation Army Citizens' Rally" in March 1959,
Menzies had expressed what he saw as the reason for Wesley's
"greatness":

> ... Anybody who looked back over modern history would
> come to the conclusion that in the eighteenth century –
> great century it was in so many ways – the outstanding man
> – certainly one of the few outstanding men, the few men
> who just leap to the mind – was John Wesley. And he was a
> great man of the eighteenth century, because he founded a
> form of evangelism which was destined to put life into the
> body of the church.[30]

For Menzies, the greatness of Wesley lay not simply in his status
as a historical figure but in his spiritual legacy of reviving the life
of the church. Through energetic preaching and evangelism, John
Wesley and his followers were widely credited with breathing life
into a spiritually lethargic and stagnant eighteenth-century Church
of England. Menzies, to be sure, was no religious enthusiast or
evangelical revivalist in the mould of a Billy Graham, but nonetheless

---

[29]   Robert Menzies, Opening of Keith Murray Building, Lincoln College,
University of Adelaide, 1 September 1963, Robert Menzies Papers, NLA, MS
4936, Box 277, Folder 186.
[30] Menzies, Salvation Army Citizens' Rally, 22 March 1959.

appreciated a Christianity that exuded spiritual life. In the diary of his travels in Britain in 1935 where he attended some churches, including Canterbury Cathedral, he lamented the "cold mechanical tone so chronic in English services" and observed that the "Church of England seems to lack all evangelical fire".[31]

In the spirit of Methodism, Menzies believed church services should be less about perfunctory ceremonies of simply going through the motions of the liturgy than about heartfelt worship and gospel preaching. In the Box Hill address of 1960 to open a church centre, Menzies drew attention to the importance of preaching the gospel. He recalled, as a schoolboy, listening to a sermon by the liberal evangelical clergyman, John Laurence Rentoul, and remarked that even though it lasted 50 minutes, "he had never heard a shorter sermon". This "was because he wasn't playing to the gallery; he wasn't doing anything else but concentrating his powerful and clear mind on the preaching of the gospel".[32] In addition to preaching the central message of Christianity, Menzies regarded worship of God as the primary focus of church life. In a letter to his friend, the Rev Irving Benson, of Wesley Church in Melbourne, he affirmed that "worship is the great foundation of the Church" even while Benson's church ran many other worthwhile activities such as the PSA forums to discuss social problems.[33] Thus when it came to church worship, Menzies took his cue more from the historic Methodist tradition of Wesley than from the prevailing practice of denominations such as the Church of England in his day.

As well as finding this vibrant spiritual dimension of Methodism appealing, Menzies also found its relative confidence in human reason and progress eminently agreeable to his own liberal temperament. With the Methodist movement emerging as it did in the eighteenth-

---

[31] Robert Menzies, Diary for Overseas Journey, 15 June 1935, p 88.

[32] Menzies, St Andrew's Church Centre Opening, Box Hill, 20 March 1960.

[33] Robert Menzies, letter to The Rev Sir Irving Clarence Benson, CBE, 29 August 1963, Irving Benson Papers, NLA, MS 7695 (2 Boxes).

century, it was permeated by British Enlightenment influences.[34] The first of these was the compatibility of faith and reason, the notion that it was possible for devout people of faith to embrace critical thinking and engage with the new intellectual currents of the age. Wesley himself believed in the marriage of faith and reason. He once stated that "religion and reason go hand in hand" and that to "renounce reason is to renounce religion".[35] Accordingly, his beliefs in religious tolerance, freewill and anti-slavery were identified as the outworking of both Enlightenment thinking and evangelical Christianity. Menzies likewise affirmed the compatibility of faith and reason, pointing to the value of Methodist educational institutions, such as Adelaide's Lincoln College, for being able to "fuse ultimately the feelings of pure intellectualism and the feelings of pure religious learning and faith".[36]

The Methodist movement also imbibed the Enlightenment's faith in human progress, both individual and social, which was yet another feature of Menzies' outlook. The Scottish Enlightenment thinkers of the eighteenth-century believed that humanity had great potential for improvement. This was the age that saw the idea of progress emerge, the conviction that human beings were gradually becoming wiser and therefore better as they enlarged their knowledge and understanding.[37] Combining this eighteenth-century optimism with their Arminian theology of human freewill, Wesley and the Methodists believed that humanity, by God's universal grace,

---

[34] As John Gascoigne and Gertrude Himmelfarb have observed, the British Enlightenment had a decidedly more Christian inflexion than either the secular French Enlightenment, or the radical deistic strand of American Enlightenment thought represented by Thomas Jefferson and Thomas Paine. See Gertrude Himmelfarb, *The Roads to Modernity: The British, French and American Enlightenment*, New York: Vintage Books, 2005; and John Gascoigne, *The Enlightenment and the Origins of European Australia*, Cambridge: Cambridge University Press, 2006.

[35] John Wesley to Dr Thomas Rutherforth, 28 March 1768, Letters, ed. Telford, Vol 5, p 364, cited in David Bebbington, *Evangelicalism in Modern Britain: A History from the 1730s to the 1980s*, London: Unwin Hyman, 1989, p 52.

[36] Robert Menzies, Opening of Keith Murray Building, 1 September 1963.

[37] Bebbington, *Evangelicalism in Modern Britain*, p 60.

could usher in a period of progress on earth marked by increased evangelism, missionary endeavour, philanthropy and humanitarian social reforms, such as the abolition of slavery. The Methodists also preached reason, tolerance, and liberty, both civil and religious, all foundational to liberalism.[38] With Methodism providing spiritual inspiration for such liberal ideals, it was a religious tradition with which Menzies had affinity.

In 1958, the Prime Minister was invited by Sydney's Methodist Wesley Mission to speak at the farewell of its long-serving Superintendent, Frank Rayward. After paying tribute to Dr Rayward, Menzies explained how his government's recent reforms to aged care had represented social progress of the "Christian kind" championed by the Methodist movement. Referring to how the *Aged Persons Homes Act* (1954) had given subsidies to churches and charities to build new, more personalised aged-care facilities, Menzies remarked:

> Why is it, Sir, that we are so proud ... of this great matter of homes for aged people? It isn't because they are institutions; it's because they are homes; it's because they set out to reproduce for the individual – the old man, the old woman – living in them, not the sense of institution (like the asylums that one used to walk by as a boy) but a home with friendliness in it, administered with loving kindness, the maintenance of friendships, the sense of personal identity and of personal dignity. This is one of the great revolutions of all time: that we should have been able to convert the old ideas into new ideas of an infinitely more Christian kind.[39]

Menzies' quest to advance human dignity through social reform was not only true to his liberal ideals but accorded with the Methodist narrative of progress envisioned by Wesley and his followers. In the tradition of the nineteenth-century Methodist, Quaker, evangelical

---

[38] Bernard Semmel, *The Methodist Revolution*, New York: Basic Books Inc, 1973, p 198.

[39] Robert Menzies, PSA Address, Farewell to Dr Frank Rayward, Wesley Mission, Sydney, 30 March 1958, p 4, Robert Menzies Papers, NLA, MS 4936, Box 265, Folder 99.

and liberal reformers who had agitated for more humane prisons, hospitals and asylums, Menzies believed that the drab, institutionalised nature of aged care he had been unhappily familiar with as a boy stood in need of similar reform. Marvelling at how more senior Australians were able to live in greater dignity and comfort amongst friends and loved ones, it represented a more Christian ideal of human existence where the divine gifts of community, family, friendship and, indeed, life itself, could be enjoyed to the full.

A philosophical fellow traveller of Menzies who similarly blended Methodist impulses with liberal ideals was the Australian lawyer, politician and writer, Frederic Eggleston (1875-1954). Born into a Melbourne Methodist family, Eggleston esteemed the values of hard work, self-sacrifice, thrift and duty.[40] Despite abandoning Methodism and institutional Christianity early in adulthood, he retained the Christian social vision of his Methodist youth. It informed much of his liberal philosophy. In *Search for a Social Philosophy*, Eggleston envisioned a liberal society defined by what he called the "Christian ethic". Inspired by Wesley's teaching of a "social holiness", Eggleston's "Christian ethic" preached the importance of selfless citizenship by being a "good neighbour".[41] For Eggleston, the ideal liberal society was one where "communities should develop into brotherhoods in which the members behave towards each other in such a way as to produce the happiest social relations".[42] Like Menzies, Eggleston believed that liberalism and democracy could be saved by its leaders and citizens "sacrificing themselves for the common good".[43]

Menzies esteemed Methodism's emphasis on a practical

[40] Warren G Osmond, *Frederic Eggleston: An Intellectual in Australian Politics*, Sydney: Allen & Unwin, 1985, p 1.

[41] Frederic Eggleston, *Search for a Social Philosophy*, Melbourne University Press, 1941, p 325.

[42] Eggleston quoted by Gregory Melleuish, *Cultural Liberalism in Australia: A Study in Intellectual and Cultural History*, Cambridge University Press, 1995, p 168.

[43] Eggleston, *Search for a Social Philosophy*, p 325.

Christianity of good works. In short, a Christianity of *doing* as well as *believing*. In common with other Protestant traditions, Methodists saw good works as not so much a means to salvation as a visible demonstration of God's love for the world. Wesley, again, was an exemplar of this practical Christianity. In addition to his vocation of preaching and proclaiming the gospel message, Wesley performed works of mercy, whether it was scattering coins to beggars or wading through snow in old age to raise money for relief of the poor.[44] Succeeding generations of Methodists followed Wesley's example of practical Christianity by establishing central missions in major cities to provide charitable relief. Placing greater emphasis on the practical outworkings of faith was, indeed, a distinctive trait of Methodism. As the Australian historian of Methodism, Glen O'Brien, has observed:

> Methodists have not squabbled over the finer points of doctrine to the same degree as some other Protestant traditions. They have been kind of "sleeves rolled up", getting on with the business of helping others and letting your Christianity be shown in your deeds and in your actions.[45]

Menzies similarly believed that it was infinitely more constructive for the Church, as a whole, to preach a common gospel and seek to enrich the community through good works than to be inwardly preoccupied with settling finer points of doctrine. He had a particularly high regard for the practical Christianity of churches such as the Salvation Army and the Central Methodist Missions of Melbourne and Sydney.

The Salvation Army, in particular, attracted the admiration of Menzies. Founded by the firebrand Methodist preacher, William Booth (1829-1912), in London's East End in 1865, it represented an offshoot of Methodism and carried on that movement's emphasis on both evangelism and practical Christianity. For Menzies, Booth represented the natural nineteenth-century successor to Wesley.

---

[44] Bebbington, *Evangelicalism in Modern Britain*, p 70.
[45] Glen O'Brien, Interview with John Cleary, *Sunday Nights with John Cleary*, ABC Radio, 4 October 2015.

And so, in the nineteenth century, I venture to say that the name of Booth will be looked back on by the historians as the name of a man who has founded something of the highest evangelistic quality, of the most attractive and devoted service, which has made its mark on almost every country in the world

Admiring the Salvation Army for its relief of poverty and destitution by "holding out a kind hand to individuals", Menzies remarked that this was something no law or government department could compel a person to do as it came from the impulses of the human heart ignited by religious faith. For Menzies, the practical expression of Christianity was precisely what made the church all the more attractive to the surrounding world. He observed that "the practical Christianity of the Salvation Army is, I believe, the great element in it which has brought to it an army of admirers – whether they are Protestant or Catholic or Jew or Gentile, it does not matter". When churches like the Salvation Army put the very Christianity they professed into practice, they enriched not only their own flock but contributed to the common good of all, regardless of belief. Like the wartime Archbishop of Canterbury, William Temple, Menzies believed that the church was a "society that exists for the benefit of those who are not its members".

It was also evident that Menzies absorbed traditional Methodist teachings on stewardship of money and material goods. Presiding as prime minister over a nation that enjoyed record levels of economic growth during the post-war years, material prosperity was something he welcomed, yet, at the same time, he harboured a lifelong disdain of greed and materialism.[46] Like Wesley, he regarded material riches as a blessing, but recognised they could become a curse if used by people for selfish ends. In a land of plenty such as Australia, the great antidote to materialism, therefore, was not so much asceticism but generosity with the selfless giving of one's wealth to others in need. Wesley articulated this attitude in a sermon on "The Use of Money"

---

[46] In his 1935 "Speech on Freedom in Modern Society", Menzies wrote that "materialism is not enough. Man does not live by bread alone. A slavery to the gods of material wellbeing is a degrading slavery. We have inherited great spiritual traditions of unselfish service."

in which he coined the maxim, "earn all you can, save all you can and give all you can". It was a sentiment familiar to Menzies. When officiating at the opening a new aged care facility in 1962, he paid tribute to its benefactors, remarking:

> It's a wonderful thing to see a man going along in life who has money, who has worked for it, who has accumulated some money, who finds his highest pleasure in giving it away; and giving it away in circumstances that will produce the maximum of pleasure for as many people as possible.[47]

Notwithstanding a hint of utilitarianism in seeking the "greatest happiness for the greatest numbers", the manifestation of Wesley's ethic was unmistakable. Menzies' own creed of civilised capitalism held that the earning and accumulation of wealth was never an end in itself, but always a means to the more noble end of enriching others.

Methodism may also have helped inform Menzies' views on women, particularly through movements such as the Australian Women's National League (AWNL).[48] Declaring his own thoughts on the capabilities of women in 1943, Menzies remarked that "there is no reason why a qualified woman should not sit in parliament or on the bench or in a professional chair, or preach from a pulpit, or, if you like, command an army in the field".[49] His specific reference to women "preaching from a pulpit" was particularly telling. In contrast to other Protestants of more conservative traditions who held that the Bible did not allow women to preach, Menzies evidently affirmed

[47] Robert Menzies, Montefiore Jewish Home Opening of Cecil Rosenbaum Memorial Wing, Hunters Hill, NSW, 19 August 1962, Robert Menzies Papers, NLA, MS 4936, Box 275, Folder 170.

[48] The Australian Women's National League was founded in 1904 as a grassroots organisation to mobilise women to campaign against socialism, and to promote loyalty to the Crown and the interests of women and families. In its objective to educate women of their political responsibilities, the League had links to first wave feminist and suffragette organisations such as the Women's Christian Temperance Union, particularly through figures such as Jessie Ackermann and Eleanor Glencross. In 1944, the League merged into Menzies' new Liberal Party.

[49] Robert Menzies, Women for Canberra, Canberra, 29 January 1943, Robert Menzies Papers, NLA, MS 4936, Box 575, Folder 28.

The Rev Sir Irving Benson (1897-1980)

The long-serving Superintendent of the Central Methodist Mission in Melbourne (1933-67). A close friend of Menzies who frequently spoke at Benson's Pleasant Sunday Afternoon ministry. For Benson, Christianity essentially started with spiritual renewal of individuals rather than restructuring society.

(*Uniting Church Archives*)

this critical role for women within the church. Historically, this accorded most with the Methodist tradition where the prominent role of women was a distinguishing feature of Wesley's movement. In Methodist churches, it was fairly normative for women to take the lead in prayer, counselling and exhortation. Even more notable was the large proportion of female preachers who had the same status and enjoyed the same respect as men.[50] With the sizeable number of Methodist and Nonconformist women active in early twentieth-century movements such as the AWNL, this egalitarian church culture undoubtedly shaped the character of Menzies' Liberal movement and its decided openness to female involvement in both the organisational and parliamentary wings.

As to Menzies' connections with the Australian Methodist Church following his education at Wesley College, his closest ties were with Irving Benson, the long-serving Superintendent of Melbourne's Central Methodist Mission at Wesley Church. Trained in the evangelical tradition, the Yorkshire-born Methodist served as the Superintendent of the Central Methodist Mission from 1933 to 1967. Presiding over a large and flourishing congregation, he was best known for his Pleasant Sunday Afternoon (PSA) ministry. Presented live and on radio, Benson's PSA ministry became a "national institution", featuring public figures who would speak on current issues from a typically moral and spiritual angle.[51] PSA's were essentially services but, instead of conventional sermons, the address had a broader range. It was through the PSA that Menzies became acquainted with Benson as a friend, and was among the most regular guests on the PSA's platform (Richard Casey was another).[52] Benson, whose ministry had started at Toorak, made contact with members of the Melbourne establishment. Menzies nominated him as a member of the Savage Club.[53]

---

[50] Himmelfarb, *Roads to Modernity*, p 128.
[51] Renate Howe, "Sir Clarence Irving Benson (1897-1980)", *ADB*, Volume 13, Melbourne University Press, 1993.
[52] Ibid.
[53] Renate Howe & Shurlee Swain, *The Challenge of the City: The Centenary History of Wesley Central Mission*, Hyland House, pp 112-113.

The Prime Minister and the Methodist Superintendent not only bonded over their common affection for Britain, Winston Churchill and the monarchy, but also shared a similar religious temperament. As admirers of Wesley, Menzies and Benson appreciated the far-reaching social implications of the Christian message but recognised that Christianity started essentially with spiritual renewal of individuals, not restructuring of society. They were both suspicious of the post-war collectivist vision for a more just society achieved through a planned economy and interventionist state. Benson, for his part, saw the key to a better world as lying with the spiritual and moral transformation of people by the power of the Christian gospel:

> The word Reconstruction denotes an outward mechanical process; the putting together of the parts of a building or a machine. But life develops from within … Our Lord never said that society must be reconstituted, or the world must be rebuilt. What he said was, Man must be born again – born of the Spirit.[54]

Menzies likewise held Christianity to be an "individual matter", a faith that began in the heart, mind and soul of the individual.[55] It was a view that accorded with his ideal of individual men and women, more than the state, as being the true agents of reform and progress in society.

In common with the more traditional Methodism of Benson, Menzies was primarily preoccupied with the building of personal moral character rather than with remedying structural injustice when it came to Christian engagement with society. Like the Presbyterian Church in the 1950s and 1960s, the Methodist Church was also divided between its traditional focus on moral issues such as marriage, divorce, sexual propriety, gambling, alcohol and sabbatarianism, and its growing concern for new social justice issues such as income inequality, indigenous disadvantage, nuclear disarmament and racial equality.[56] For many younger Methodists, such as Alan Walker of Sydney's Wesley

---

[54] C Irving Benson, "Remaking the World", Sermons, Ms 1493, State Library of Victoria, quoted in Ibid., p 116.

[55] Menzies, Salvation Army Citizens' Rally, 22 March 1959.

[56] Glen O'Brien (ed.), *Methodism in Australia: A History*, Farnham, Surrey and Burlington, VA: Ashgate, 2015, p 164.

Mission, these emerging priorities were not mutually exclusive, but for more conservative leaders such as Benson, the focus remained on personal morality.[57] Benson emphasised work, the stewardship of time, talent and money, the guarding of moral integrity through control of gambling and alcohol, and the importance of home and family life; each underpinned by the ethic of personal responsibility.[58]

In sharing the conservative, middle class Protestant outlook of Benson, Menzies similarly stressed these moral sensibilities, yet it would be very misleading to characterise him as a "wowser". As somebody not only fond of the occasional cigar, but partial to a good drink himself, Menzies was no teetotaller and certainly no proponent of prohibition. In a wartime broadcast addressing "The Drink Problem", he conceded there was a problem but believed that the antidote to this "extravagance" lay not necessarily in banning alcohol, as some Methodists and others advocated, but in commercial incentives to encourage frugality and moderation.[59] On the question of gambling, meanwhile, Menzies was in step with much of Methodist opinion with his distaste of gaming venues such as casinos. Towards the end of his life, Menzies wrote a strong letter to protest against the proposal to establish a casino in Canberra. He said that he was "horrified" and feared that a new casino would "convert Canberra into a sort of Las Vegas", concluding that "nothing could be more inconsistent with the existence of a dignified National Capital".[60] To be sure, his chief reasons for opposing a new casino in Canberra may well have been aesthetic, with a glitzy casino appearing incongruous amongst the stately monuments of a capital city. But it is equally probable that his opinion was informed by a moral aversion to gambling. It was a practice he would have regarded as inimical to

---

[57] Alan Walker, for example, addressed traditional Methodist concerns about sexual morality, drinking and gambling, but was also very prominent in opposition to national service and the Vietnam War.

[58] Howe & Swain, *Challenge of the City*, p 119.

[59] Robert Menzies, "The Drink Problem", *Forgotten People*, p 119.

[60] Robert Menzies, Letter to Mr Bradbury, 1 July 1977, reprinted in *The Canberra Times*, Tuesday, 29 March 1988, p 1.

his deep-seated habits of industriousness, thrift and prudence, together with his sincere belief in honest work for honest gain.

With Menzies drawing from both Presbyterian and Methodist traditions, each rich and diverse, his Protestantism was broadly cast. The Scots Presbyterian tradition had imbued him with a sturdy individualism balanced with social responsibility, a recognition of God's sovereignty over all spheres, and an appreciation of the sacredness of the "secular". Added to this, the Wesleyan Methodist movement had given Menzies his belief in human free will, his faith in human progress under God, and his ethic of unselfish capitalism. With these strands of belief being shared by a whole range of Protestant churches, they were exclusive to neither Presbyterianism nor Methodism, and thereby contributed to the ecumenicalism of Menzies' Protestantism. While his Protestant faith exhibited a Scots Presbyterian identity and was nourished from the well of Methodism, it was wide-ranging and essentially minimalist when it came to confessions of faith. Deferring to the Bible as its basic source, it downplayed the significance of differences between the denominations and branches of Christianity. In a speech to a Salvation Army citizens rally in 1959, Menzies told his audience:

> I know that in the course of history there have been divisions in the Christian Church, and for some reason that seemed good to somebody or other, we are among Protestants, Anglicans or Presbyterians or Methodists or Congregationalists or Baptists. And no doubt we all have some differences among ourselves in terms of governments; sometimes in some points of doctrine. But I always like to feel that underneath all this there is one Bible; there is one message; and that the nearer we get to that, the less will we be concerned with dogma of any kind.[61]

Well aware of the lingering differences between the Protestant churches in theology and ecclesiology, not to mention the even greater sectarian rift between Protestants and Catholics in Australia during the 1950s, Menzies was eager to project a common Christianity that appealed to the Bible as the foundation of faith for all believers.

[61] Menzies, Salvation Army Citizens' Rally, 22 March 1959.

4

FREEDOM OF RELIGION AND FREEDOM OF POLITICAL CONSCIENCE

We are a diversity of creatures, with a diversity of minds and emotions and imaginations and faiths. When we claim freedom of worship, we claim room and respect for all.[1]

Proud of his Scottish Presbyterian roots and committed to nourishing Australia's Christian life, not least of all its church schools, Menzies recognised the diversity of the nation's faith communities and therefore advocated religious freedom and tolerance in Australia. The faith composition of Australia remained overwhelmingly Christian throughout the entirety of Menzies' time in public life. In the census of 1947, the proportion of Christians was 88 percent. By the time Menzies retired in 1966, the percentage of Australians identifying as Christians in the census that year was slightly higher at 88.2 percent after peaking at a post-war high of 89.4 percent in 1954. During the same period, the percentage of Australians identifying respectively with either 'other religions' or 'no religion' was at 0.5 percent and 0.3 percent in 1947, and 0.7 percent and 0.8 percent in 1966.[2]

While Menzies took it as "a given" that the default spiritual dis-

---

[1] Robert Menzies, Freedom of Worship, Broadcast, 3 July 1942.
[2] Australian Bureau of Statistics (ABS), Chapter 12, Culture and Recreation, Religious Affiliation, 1301.0 - Year Book of Australia, 2006.

position of most Australians was Christian of one kind or another, he especially appreciated Australia's small yet influential Jewish community.[3] In addition to communities of Jews residing mostly in Melbourne and Sydney, post-war Australia was also home to small numbers of Buddhists descended largely from nineteenth-century Chinese gold prospectors and Muslims related to the Afghan cameleers who had arrived in Australia from the 1860s. Indeed, in his speech to the Cardinal's Dinner in 1964, Menzies acknowledged the place of Muslims in Australia when he said that "whether we be Catholic or Protestant or Jewish or Muslim, the end remains clear: We have an overwhelming duty to serve our country on the highest level and to the best of our talents".[4]

Menzies' dedication to religious freedom for all was most forcefully articulated in a speech on "Freedom of Worship" delivered on 3 July 1942. Menzies took this theme directly from the "four freedoms" enunciated by the United States President, Franklin D. Roosevelt, in the State of the Union Address to Congress on 6 January 1941. Roosevelt declared that "we look forward to a world founded upon four essential human freedoms". In a world he saw as under siege from the anti-democratic and tyrannical forces of Nazism, fascism and communism, where the very survival of human freedom was at stake, the leader of the free world held that the following four freedoms needed to be reaffirmed: the freedom of speech; the freedom of worship; freedom from want; and freedom from fear.

Aside from mentioning that the second freedom was about the "freedom of every person to worship God in his own way – everywhere in the world", Roosevelt did not venture into any further detail as to what this freedom implied or entailed. Accordingly, when Menzies adopted this theme as his own in July 1942, he was able to explain its significance and meaning to his Australian audience.

[3] See chapter six for an account of Menzies' relationship with the Jewish community in Australia.

[4] Robert Menzies, Cardinal's Dinner, Catholic Committee Associated, Sydney, 30 July 1964, p 2, Robert Menzies Papers, NLA, MS 4936, Box 279, Folder 202.

Like the American President, Menzies believed that the spectre of the Second World War provided the opportune moment to reassert the fundamentals of human liberty, which he did with a broadcast on each of the four freedoms enunciated by President Roosevelt.

When he came specifically to the "Freedom of Worship", however, it was not only the contemporary context of the Second World War that was relevant to Menzies but also Australia's unhappy history of sectarian strife against which he felt the need to assert the primacy of religious freedom for all. For Menzies, sectarian rancour between Australia's Protestants and Catholics was not only contrary to the gospel virtue of neighbourly love but also anathema to the principle of religious freedom. To illustrate, Menzies opened his "Freedom of Worship" broadcast with a story from his time as Attorney-General of Victoria when an "earnest partisan" upbraided him for not using his powers to ban a Catholic Eucharistic procession through the streets of Melbourne. When Menzies questioned why this person wanted the procession banned, he remonstrated that his ancestors had "fought for religious freedom" and that the procession was "an affront to every Protestant", presumably regarding the procession as symbolic of what had, in his eyes, been an authoritarian church. Whilst Menzies similarly appreciated the religious freedom ideals of his Scottish Presbyterian ancestors, he did not see this as any justification to deny anyone else their religious freedom in the present age, be they Catholic, Protestant, or otherwise. He well understood that a commendable enthusiasm for one's own faith could all too often, but by no means always, lead to suppression of another's faith.

As such, Menzies himself identified as a Protestant but stressed that freedom of religion was "freedom for all, Catholic or Protestant, Jew or Gentile, and that to deny it was to go back to the dark ages of man".[5] He said that such freedom "must mean freedom for my neighbour as well as for myself". This was a principle he had long practised, telling his own father that being the young Member for

---

[5] Robert Menzies, "Freedom of Worship", *Forgotten People*, 3 July 1942, p 22.

East Yarra meant "being the Member for the lot" – for "Presbyterians, Anglicans, Roman Catholics, [and] Brahmins for all I know".[6] For Menzies, the freedom of belief also meant the freedom of unbelief. It encompassed not only people of all faiths but also those of no faith, such as naturalistic sceptics, atheists and agnostics. As unappealing as atheism may have been to Menzies as a belief system, he nonetheless affirmed the freedom "to worship or not to worship". Of atheists and agnostics, he remarked: "There have been honest and indeed noble men in this world who have never been able to find a God. Are we to deny them their place?"[7] Menzies' commitment to religious freedom was based not simply on a sense of fair play but also on his appreciation of human diversity, not least in faith and worship. He observed that "we are a diversity of creatures, with a diversity of minds and emotions and imaginations and faiths. When we claim freedom of worship, we claim room and respect for all". He concluded by affirming that "each of us has his own faith, and no mortal man may compel it or suppress it. That is, I believe, a freedom worth fighting for".[8]

Amid this spiritual diversity, Menzies also appealed for human unity, holding that: "the things which unite us as human beings are deeper and more lasting than the things that divide us as members of different creeds. They should be a source of harmony and unity, not of discord and strife; of tolerance and generosity not of intolerance and bigotry". In affirming this, Menzies was not seeking to diminish the very real differences existing between faiths or, indeed, the disparate strands within a particular faith such as Christianity or Judaism. He was, instead, reminding citizens that for all their spiritual differences, concord on universal human values was still possible and indeed essential. A free and civil society could be comprised of people who were either happily Protestant, Catholic, Jewish, Muslim or agnostic,

---

[6] Frances McNicoll interview with Robert Menzies, 11 May 1972, cited in Bramston, *Robert Menzies*, p 26.
[7] Menzies, "Freedom of Worship", p 23.
[8] Ibid., p 25.

yet still be committed to the virtues of charity, justice, kindness, generosity, patience, temperance and humility. For this formula to work, Menzies held that tolerance was an essential ingredient. By "tolerance", however, Menzies did not imply acceptance of every belief and practice as morally neutral or equivalent, as the word is frequently interpreted to mean in today's post-modern parlance. It is, on the contrary, a recognition that every other honest person "who, hating the same evil, will see a different road by which to come against it". Elsewhere, Menzies asserted similarly that:

> Tolerance does not mean flabbiness. Tolerance of each other does not mean that we condone evil things or that we are not prepared to fight against evil things. Tolerance is mutual understanding, forbearance, a desire to assemble ourselves every time there is a common cause to be served.[9]

Applied to religious freedom in Australia, this meant that citizens could entertain their own differing conceptions about God and other things spiritual, yet still share a degree of consensus on what was good and evil and thereby work together in the furtherance of common causes in civil society. Menzies had witnessed an example of this in Australia's private education realm where Catholic, Protestant and Jewish schools each shared a vision for inculcating the rising generation of citizens with moral character and faith in something greater than themselves.

As a Presbyterian, Menzies took particular pride in what he saw as the contribution of his spiritual ancestors, the "Scottish Covenanters".[10] He remarked that "the religious freedom for which the Scottish Covenanters fought was freedom for all, Catholic or Protestant, Jew or Gentile". By recalling the spirit of the Scottish Covenanters, Menzies evidently drew upon a hard-fought battle for religious liberty. Committed to the Calvinist theology of John Knox, the Covenanters had fought bitterly for their freedom to practice what they regarded as a purified Protestant faith over and above the

---

[9] Menzies, Cardinal's Dinner, 30 July 1964, p 2.
[10] Menzies, "Freedom of Worship", p 22.

imposition by the English King of the more catholicised Christianity found in the Church of England. As such, their battle cry was for everybody to have the "liberty to utter and declare his mind with knowledge to the comfort and edification of the Church".[11] In their struggle for religious freedom, the Covenanters were fond of invoking Knox's dictum: "Take away the liberty of Assemblies and you take away the liberty of the evangel".[12] Like so many other religious movements of the early modern era, however, the religious liberty credentials of the Scottish Covenanters are decidedly mixed. On the one hand, their quest for religious liberty for *themselves* was undoubtedly sincere, and this was the aspect of their legacy that Menzies much admired and valued. On the other, however, their willingness to afford religious freedom to *others* was questionable. As W. Landels noted, the Covenant, "though right in spirit, and originally a protection to liberty, became hostile to liberty when subsequently they sought to enforce it to the letter".[13] Whilst the Covenanters fought doggedly for the right to practise their own faith, they were not open to conceding that same freedom to others of differing faiths. In this historical sense, therefore, the Scottish Covenanters fell short of Menzies' estimation of them as the great exemplars of religious freedom.

In reality, Menzies' attitudes to religious freedom aligned more closely with the enlightened, liberal outlook of English Nonconformity, the class of dissenting Protestants from the Church of England whom Timothy Larsen termed the "friends of religious equality".[14] Borne of their own experience of persecution by the Established Church of England in the sixteenth and seventeenth centuries, the Nonconformists emerged as early advocates of

---

[11] J. D. Douglas, *Light in the North: The Story of the Scottish Covenanters*, Grand Rapids [Mich]: Eerdmans, 1964, p 191.

[12] Douglas, *Light in the North*, p 194. The term "evangel" meant "Gospel".

[13] W Landels, "The Scottish Covenanters", in Exeter Hall Lectures, 1861, p 38, cited by Douglas, *Light in the North*, p 192.

[14] See Timothy Larsen, *Friends of Religious Equality: Nonconformist Politics in Mid-Victorian England*. Woodbridge, UK: Boydell, 1999.

religious liberty, supporting both Catholic and Jewish emancipation as well as religious equality under the law. Through his mother's Cornish Methodist lineage, Menzies had some historical links to eighteenth and nineteenth-century English Dissent, and the close ties of these Protestants to the English Whig/Liberal movements helped to explain how their religious liberty-affirming ideals made their way into the consciousness of a twentieth-century Australian Liberal such as Menzies.

Best exemplified by the likes of Edmund Burke and T. B. Macaulay, each of whom Menzies was fond of quoting, English Whiggism, at least in its political party form, dated back to the First Earl of Shaftesbury (1621-1683). Lord Shaftesbury founded the Whig Party in 1679 and was patron of the English Whig philosopher, John Locke (1632-1704). It was in this Whig stream of thought from which Menzies drew his ideas on religious freedom. As supporters of religious liberty, Locke, Shaftesbury and the early Whigs were advocates for the rights of dissenters and sceptical of all forms of clerical authority. In accordance with Nonconformist thought, Locke reasoned that religion was a spiritual matter. In the *First Tract on Government* (1660), he opined that "the great business of Christian religion lies in the heart", not in external behaviour.[15] Menzies, likewise, held that religion was essentially a matter of the heart, observing that "in the heart of every man, whatever he may call himself, is that instinct to touch the unknown, to know what comes after, to see the invisible".[16] This arose from Menzies' guiding premise that every human being is a "spiritual animal".[17] Following on from Locke, Menzies stood in the Whig tradition of Burke who similarly championed religious liberty to achieve a broader toleration for Roman Catholics and Protestant Dissenters from the established church. Appealing to the primacy of conscience, Burke once stated that if ever there was anything to

---

[15] Wilken, Liberty in the things of God, p 170.
[16] Menzies, "Freedom of Worship", p 24.
[17] Robert Menzies, "Freedom and the Call to Action", Lecture to Junior Chamber of Commerce, 4 August 1947.

which, from reason, nature, habit, and principle, I am totally averse, it is persecution for conscientious difference in opinion".[18]

Menzies' conception of religious freedom was moreover indebted to the later Victorian-era liberalism of figures such as John Stuart Mill (1806-1873). Menzies' own philosophy of Liberalism differed from that of Mill in some important respects, most notably in being non-utilitarian, grounded in tradition and informed by a theistic, Christian world-view. Nonetheless, he enthusiastically embraced the Victorian philosopher's zeal for the basic human freedoms of thought and expression that were relevant to religious faith. Praising Mill's seminal essay of 1859, *On Liberty*, as still "full of freshness and truth",[19] Menzies applauded Mill's assertion that an individual not only had the freedom to hold an opinion but also the freedom to have that opinion challenged. Menzies thus quoted Mill:

> Complete liberty of contradicting and disproving our opinion is the very condition which justifies us in assuming its truth for purposes of action, and on no other terms can a being with human faculties have any rational assurance of being right.[20]

Given the competing claims of different faiths in society, this meant that one's personal belief was poorly founded and weakly held if it was not able to resist the onset of another person's critical mind. Elsewhere in Mill's essay, Menzies would have agreed with the philosopher's assertion that an individual's liberty of conscience and religious belief was essentially unbounded:

> This, then, is the appropriate region of human liberty. It comprises, first, the inward domain of consciousness; demanding liberty of conscience, in the most comprehensive

---

[18] Edmund Burke, *Reflections on the Revolution in France*, p 87 (Hackett, 1987) (J. G. A. Pocock, ed.) (originally published 1790) (*Reflections*), cited in Michael W. McConnell, "Establishment and Toleration in Edmund Burke's Constitution of Freedom," 1995 *Supreme Court Review* 393 (1995), p 395.

[19] Menzies, "Freedom of Speech and Expression", *Forgotten People*, p 13.

[20] John Stuart Mill, *On Liberty*, Second Edition, Boston: Ticknor and Fields, 1863 (originally 1859), p 40 quoted by Menzies, "Freedom of Speech and Expression", *Forgotten People*, p 14.

sense; liberty of thought and feeling; absolute freedom
of opinion and sentiment on all subjects, practical or
speculative, scientific, moral or theological.[21]

His outlook on the freedom of worship may have had its roots in
the Whig liberalism of John Locke, but it was the nineteenth-century
classical liberal thought of John Stuart Mill that contributed to its full
flowering.

Following the "Freedom of Worship" broadcast, Menzies again
came to the defence of religious freedom during the referendum
campaign to amend the Australian Constitution. To facilitate post-
war reconstruction, the Curtin Labor Government had proposed
to enlarge and expand the Commonwealth's reach under the
Constitution. One of the proposals put to referendum on 19 August
1944 included extension of section 116 of the Constitution to cover
the states. Commonly known as the religious freedom "guarantees",
section 116 in its existing form applied only to the Commonwealth.
It provided that:

> The Commonwealth shall not make any law for establishing
> any religion, or for imposing any religious observance, or for
> prohibiting the free exercise of any religion, and no religious
> test shall be required as a qualification for any office or
> public trust under the Commonwealth.

The rationale for extending the ambit of this provision to the states
was to buttress basic freedoms deemed fundamental to survival of
democracy. The Attorney-General, Dr H. V. Evatt, told the House
of Representatives that while "freedom of speech and freedom of
religion seemed securely established in the modern democracies",
the "rise of modern dictatorships in Europe had shown that rights
can be swept away and that the consequences can be disastrous."[22]
The Attorney-General's justification for extending section 116 to the

---

[21] Mill, *On Liberty*, pp 27-28.
[22] Commonwealth of Australia, *Parliamentary Debates* (Hansard), House of
Representatives and Senate, First Session of the Seventeenth Parliament, 1943-
1944, p. 1153.

states was that the existing limitation of 116 to the Commonwealth was "anomalous"' particularly because the plenary legislative powers of the states were 'the more likely to involve the risk of interference with religious freedom'.[23]

In principle, Evatt's affirmation of religious freedom accorded with Menzies' own approach to the matter. Indeed, Attorney-General Evatt had himself invoked the "four freedoms" enunciated by President Roosevelt to defend his stance on extending the religious freedom guarantees of the Constitution to the states. Where Menzies differed from his opponent, however, was that codification of religious freedom at the state level, by extending section 116 of the Constitution, was deemed unnecessary for preserving this essential liberty. In a November 1942 broadcast on "Constitutional Guarantees", that expressly addressed the Curtin Government's referendum proposal to extend section 116, Menzies asked rhetorically:

> First the freedom of religion: Has there been any attack on religious freedom in Australia? Has any Parliament been meditating on bringing in some Bill to establish a religion or to prohibit the free exercise of a religion, or to impose religious tests? Of course not. Dr Evatt is defending us with sword and buckler against a non-existent enemy.[24]

Menzies, aware that neither sectarian prejudice in the community nor the anti-religious movement of communism did the cause of religious freedom any favours, was not convinced that this liberty faced some existential threat in Australia. In contrast to some of the fragile democracies of interwar Europe that had succumbed to Nazism or fascism, Australia was a robust enough democracy of self-governing citizens to be able to safeguard this freedom without resorting to any further constitutional machinery. In his words, "to ask the people of Australia ... to put into a Constitution some written guarantee of a principle which every intelligent person accepts seems to me to be

---

[23] Ibid.

[24] Robert Menzies, "Constitutional Guarantees", Broadcast, 27 November 1942, p 1, Robert Menzies Papers, NLA, MS 4936, Box 256, Folder 33.

almost fantastic".[25] Revering the Australian Constitution as the "most fundamental and the most sacred" of all laws, Menzies understood that only the people, and not the Parliament, were its masters with the power to change it through a referendum.[26] Therefore, the proposal to alter the religious freedom provision of section 116 could only be justified if there were a mood for change among the people, an appetite Menzies clearly could not sense at that time. He nevertheless conceded that if religious freedom were threatened, "I should hope to be among the first to act promptly to destroy that threat".[27]

In his broadcast, Menzies warned that the modern-day proclivity to "put things into writing" ran counter to "the whole genius of our people". He reminded his audience that "we don't live under codified laws and we have always distrusted codified ideas. There is nothing truer than that 'the letter killeth'." Menzies borrowed the phrase, "the letter killeth", from 2 Corinthians 3:6, where the Apostle Paul wrote: "Who also hath made us able ministers of the new testament; not of the letter, but of the spirit: for the letter killeth, but the spirit giveth life." Like St Paul, Menzies appreciated that faith was a matter of the human soul and not something that could be either compelled or suppressed by the letter of the law, a principle affirmed in Christian thought from the early church fathers to the English Nonconformists. When it came to codification of laws in general, Menzies believed the legal truism that "less meant more", whereby fewer codified laws and rules actually implied greater freedoms for the people. Accordingly, when it came to religious freedom, he held that the love of this and other liberties sprang not from "Acts of Parliament or blue books or dusty records", but from "the hearts of the people themselves".[28]

While Menzies rejected any further codification of religious

---

[25] Ibid., p 1.
[26] Robert Menzies, The Law and the Citizen, Broadcast 3AW, 12 June 1942, Robert Menzies Papers, NLA, MS 4936, Box 256, Folder 32; also R. G. Menzies, The Forgotten People, Angus & Robertson, 1943, pp 165-68.
[27] Menzies, "Constitutional Guarantees", p 1.
[28] Ibid., p 2.

freedom in the law, he held that it was important for such a principle to be affirmed explicitly in the platform of the new Liberal Party. The third objective of the October 1944 platform provided that "We will strive to have a country in which an intelligent, free and liberal Australian democracy shall be maintained by freedom of speech, religion and association".[29] The subsequent November 1954 platform went a little further, containing two objectives pertaining to religious freedom. The thirteenth affirmed that "We believe in the great human freedoms: to worship; to think; to speak; to choose; to be ambitious; to be independent; to be industrious; to acquire skill; to seek and earn reward". This was followed by the fifteenth which stated that "We believe in religious and racial tolerance among our citizens".[30] The objectives of both platforms embodied the principles that Menzies had articulated in his "Freedom of Worship" broadcast. For the manifesto of a party committed to championing the fundamentals of liberal democracy, freedom of worship and religion represented a non-negotiable article of faith.

Campaigning for the Liberal Party at the 1949 election, Menzies again affirmed his new party's dedication to religious freedom. Reiterating the basic principles of liberal democracy, Menzies declared:

> The real freedoms are to worship, to think, to speak, to choose, to be ambitious, to be independent, to be industrious, to acquire skill, to seek reward. These are the real freedoms, for these are of the essence of the nature of man.[31]

---

[29] "Name and Objectives", *Forming the Liberal Party of Australia*, Canberra, 16 October 1944, p 14, Robert Menzies Papers, NLA, MS 4936, Box 410, Folder 1.

[30] Robert Menzies to William H. Anderson, *We Believe* (Liberal Party Platform), 3 November 1954, Robert Menzies Papers, NLA, MS 4936, Box 410, Folder 6. Menzies co-drafted this statement with Anderson, the Federal President of the Liberal Party of Australia. In religious outlook, Menzies and Anderson were close bedfellows. Like Menzies, Anderson was a Presbyterian layman with firm Christian convictions yet one with broad sympathies. In the midst of the 1954 Labor Party split, Anderson supported the Catholic-oriented ALP industrial groups and deplored sectarian prejudice.

[31] Robert Menzies, "Election Speech", Melbourne, 10 November 1949, Robert Menzies Papers, NLA, MS 4936, Box 575, Folder 28.

The context for this pronouncement was his campaign against the socialist agenda of the Labor Government. With the principle of religious liberty so firmly embedded in the spirit of the Australian people, Menzies did not necessarily fear that this freedom would be swept away with re-election of the Chifley Labor Government, but made it known that the ideology of socialism, at large, was less congenial to this and other basic human freedoms. This was because the inherent statism of socialist doctrine resulted in government assuming more power and control not only over the economy but also the life choices of ordinary citizens. This approach was evidently taken to its extreme in countries such as the Soviet Union, where citizens were persecuted for their religious faith. Menzies did not believe that such a fate would befall Australia, but he was convinced that the election of a government unequivocally committed to liberal democratic ideals would provide the optimum climate for religious freedom to thrive in post-war Australia. Some years into his post-war prime ministership, Menzies remarked at a 1961 naturalisation ceremony on how new immigrants to Australia were able join a country where such freedom abounded:

> ... to come to a country where freedom will be defended by everybody, whatever political party he may belong to, whatever religion he may profess, where everybody is agreed that we are free people, free ... to pray as we want to pray, to speak as we want to speak, to assemble as we want to assemble.[32]

Addressing his audience of new citizens, a large proportion of whom had fled European countries oppressed by either fascist or communist dictatorships, he celebrated Australia as a beacon of freedom for all, whatever the religious beliefs or otherwise of its people.

To be sure, Menzies' pronouncements on religious freedom had a definite historical context in President Roosevelt's declaration of the

---

[32] Robert Menzies, Speech at Naturalisation Ceremony, Perth, 24 July 1961, Robert Menzies Papers, NLA, MS 4936, Box 272, Folder 152.

"four freedoms" in 1941, followed by the United Nations Universal Declaration of Human Rights in 1948. The UN Declaration had made the following provision for religious freedom in Article 18:

> Everyone has the right to freedom of thought, conscience and religion; this right includes freedom to change his religion or belief, and freedom, either alone or in community with others and in public or private, to manifest his religion or belief in teaching, practice, worship and observance.

The Declaration essentially embodied the principles that Menzies had consistently articulated throughout his public life. Together with the UN and the leaders of the free world, Menzies was dedicated to championing religious liberty in an era when such liberties had been under grievous assault from Nazism and fascism, together with communism. It was the ideal of Western leaders such as Roosevelt and Menzies that religious freedom for all would form one of the great pillars of the new liberal international order.

Freedom of political conscience

Menzies also affirmed his belief in the "freedom of political conscience", which essentially referred to the freedom for Christians and others of faith to support the political party or creed of their choice. In a March 1958 address to farewell the long-serving superintendent of Sydney's Wesley Mission, Menzies declared that "there is room in every political party for Christian men and women of all schools of Christian thought".[33] He urged his audience not to forget the oft-repeated maxim of Jesus from St John's gospel that "In my Father's house there are many mansions".[34] This meant, for example, that either a Roman Catholic, a Baptist or some other Christian could each find their niche in either the Labor, Liberal or Country parties. For Menzies, there were no false conceptions that the ALP was a "Catholic party" or that the Liberal and Country parties were somehow "Protestant Parties". On the contrary, they

---

[33] Menzies, Farewell to Dr Rayward, p 4.
[34] John 14:2 quoted by Menzies, Ibid., p 4.

were each political movements steeped in values and principles that could appeal to Christians of all kinds, as well as to others of different faiths or, indeed, no faith. For all the differences in ideology and approach between the political creeds of liberal democracy, social democracy and agrarianism, he recognised that all of Australia's major parties adhered to the central precepts of human dignity, freedom, family, social and industrial justice as well as sharing a commitment to realising the common good, though differing in their policy pathway towards this goal. The obvious exceptions to this rule, however, would have been political parties of either a communist or fascist disposition whose anti-democratic, totalitarian ideologies ran counter to such objectives.

Believing in a faith that transcended political creeds, Menzies' conception of Christianity was avowedly non-partisan. He remarked that: "It would be a poor day if we got to the stage of believing that in our particular church everybody must subscribe to a particular political party or feel that he is running counter to the views of the church".[35] He warned against the temptation for Christians to express their faith in party-political terms, but insisted that this was different from expressing one's politics in Christian terms:

> Therefore, it's right that we should all, in a country like this, constantly test our politics, constantly try our political faith by seeing that we express it in Christian terms – but that doesn't mean that we can't disagree about politics; that doesn't mean that to be a good Christian you have to be a good Liberal or a good Country Party man or a good Labor man – I'm saying exactly the opposite – to be a good Liberal, to be a good Labor man, to be a good Country Party man, you'd be all the better if you are a good Christian.[36]

Menzies' point was that instead of a person's faith being informed by their political ideology, their political creed should be informed by their faith. This was because he believed that, as important

---

[35] Ibid., p 5.
[36] Ibid.

as political ideas were, a religious faith such as Christianity was of even greater and overriding importance. With faith being of primary importance to the individual and political philosophy being secondary, Christians and others of faith had every liberty to support the politics of their choice, providing that the political ideas embraced were not repugnant to the guiding precepts of one's faith.

In contrast to many contemporary proponents of religious pluralism, Menzies' unwavering commitment to both religious freedom and freedom of political conscience was not simply borne of a postmodernist world-view affirming of moral and religious relativism. On the contrary, it was a disposition that had deep historical roots in both the Christian tradition and in liberal thought. As a Christian believer himself, Menzies regarded religious freedom as an expression of the neighbourly love his own faith preached, but not necessarily always practised. In Menzies' own words, religious freedom "must mean freedom for my neighbour as well as myself".

For Menzies, religious freedom in the true sense was not simply about an individual claiming the right to practise his or her own personal faith, but about affording that same freedom to one's fellow citizen, whatever their faith or creed. The ideal of religious liberty stemmed from the classical Christian notion that faith was a matter of personal choice and individual conscience that could never be oppressed or compelled from the outside. As Robert Wilken observed, "liberty of conscience was born, not of indifference, not of scepticism, not of mere open-mindedness but of faith".[37] Complementing this Christian stream of thought was the philosophy of liberalism, developed over centuries by figures from John Locke to John Stuart Mill, that affirmed the primacy of toleration, not least religious toleration, in a free society.

To Menzies, freedom of worship and religion was a pillar of his own Liberal philosophy as well as a fruit of his religious faith.

---

[37] Wilken, *Liberty in the things of God*, p 6.

5

MEMBERS OF ONE ANOTHER

TRANSCENDING AUSTRALIA'S

SECTARIAN DIVIDE

Whatever branch of the Christian Church
we may belong to, we must all thank God
that the work of the Church goes on.[1]

Throughout his life, Menzies sought to heal the Catholic-Protestant rift that had long blighted Australian society. Born into a decade where deep divisions festered between predominantly Irish working-class Catholics and middle class Protestants, Menzies was all too familiar with the sectarian rancour that simmered in the community. With the Great War breaking out during his formative years at university, Menzies witnessed the acrimonious conflict over conscription between the Prime Minister, Billy Hughes, and Daniel Mannix, the Catholic Archbishop of Melbourne. Out of loyalty to the British Empire, the Protestant prime minister had campaigned strongly for introduction of conscription which was opposed vehemently by Mannix. Polarising public opinion, this squabble only served to exacerbate existing sectarian divisions. Years later, Menzies reflected on this reality of his early life:

> My youth was lived in a period of Australian social history
> when there was much religious intolerance. Sectarianism
> was not engaged in solely by one side; but from my earliest
> days it nauseated me. The ecumenical movement had not

---

[1] Robert Menzies, Opening of Dominican Sisters Training College, Canberra, 24 March 1963.

been heard of (at least in my circle). There were bitter publications, masquerading as religious literature. Prelates and divines sought and obtained the courtesy of the Press to preach the gospel of love – with grave exceptions.[2]

Raised as a Protestant by devout parents, Menzies nevertheless felt an instinctive revulsion of sectarianism from an early age. First and foremost, he saw the spectacle of different Christians at bitter loggerheads as flagrantly at odds with the message of Christ for fellow believers to love one another. He went so far as to deplore sectarian strife as "the denial of Christianity and not its proof".[3] He would have been familiar with the Gospel teaching that "all men know that ye are my disciples, if ye have love one to another".[4] For Menzies, this was the behavioural litmus test of what it was to be an authentic Christian.

To be sure, Menzies recognised the tremendous diversity of the universal Christian church and recognised that there would always be differences amongst Christians over theology, church government, worship, liturgy, and numerous other matters. He regarded sectarianism, however, as having much less to do with conscientious disagreements between Protestants and Catholics over points of doctrine than with a mutually hostile, cultural tribalism that he regarded as unchristian, illiberal and corrosive to the social fabric. Menzies alluded to this on his wartime visit to Ireland where sectarianism was even more pronounced, especially in the troubled region of Ulster. Referring to the animosity of Northern Irish Protestants towards the predominantly Catholic South, he remarked: "Protestant and Presbyterian as I am, I long since learned that there are some Protestants whose Protestantism is an expression of hostility rather than of faith".[5] For such sectarian warriors, their Protestantism represented more of a defensive battle flag against the Catholic "enemy" than a stream of life-transforming faith drawn from the Bible and the preacher's pulpit.

---

[2] Robert Menzies, *The Measure of the Years*, Melbourne: Cassell Australia, 1970, pp 91-92.

[3] Menzies, "Freedom of Worship", *Forgotten People*, p 23.

[4] St John 13:35.

[5] Menzies, *Afternoon Light*, p 38.

Menzies' distaste of sectarianism also sprang from his exposure to a broad, "common Christianity" in his early life. First, from the new community of Jeparit where denominational boundaries amongst Protestants were relatively fluid; and, second, from his student years with the pan-Protestant SCU at Melbourne University. Through the SCU, the primary preoccupation was with the basics of Christian doctrine on which adherents of all denominations could agree, such as the nature and person of Jesus Christ and not so much finer points of doctrine such as predestination or human freewill, modes of baptism or eschatology. The more ecumenical outlook of the SCU contrasted with the sectarian, anti-Catholicism of his father James, and Menzies noted this aspect of his family background in an interview with Lady Frances McNicoll:

> I was born in a household of people whose memories I revere but they were the most bigoted people in the world, and for Robert to be seen on the same platform as that man Mannix was an unthinkable offence. My father was violently upset, my mother was, my uncles were, they had a family gathering about it ...[6]

Menzies was referring to the adverse reaction of his family when, as a newly-elected Member for the province of East Yarra in the Victorian Legislative Council in 1928, he had attended the opening of a Catholic school in his electorate where Archbishop Mannix was also present. As his political career progressed in the 1930s, he continued to confront religious intolerance when, in his capacity as the Attorney-General of Victoria, he resisted attempts by some Protestants to ban a large procession through the streets of central Melbourne during a Eucharistic Congress.[7] In his first term as prime minister in 1939, he addressed a peace rally in Melbourne organised by the Australian National Secretariat for Catholic Action and stressed the shared faith of all present by drawing attention to his

---

[6] Frances McNicoll interview with Robert Menzies, 11 May 1972, Papers of Frances McNicoll, MS 9246, Series 6, Box 15, NLA, cited in Bramston, *Robert Menzies*, p 26.

[7] Robert Menzies, *Forgotten People*, p 22; Henderson, *Menzies' Child*, p 106.

William Morris (Billy) Hughes (1862-1952)
Archbishop Daniel Mannix (1864-1963)

Growing sectarianism marked Australian life for a hundred years from the mid-nineteenth century. In the referendum contests over conscription in 1916 and 1917, Prime Minister Billy Hughes, a nonconformist Protestant, and the Catholic Archbishop of Melbourne, Daniel Mannix, were major protagonists. Menzies' family was shocked when he appeared on a platform with Mannix, an "unthinkable offence", but throughout his public life Menzies sought to transcend and ameliorate Australia's sectarian divide.

presence as a Presbyterian on a Catholic platform.[8] Menzies, for his part, felt no compunction about associating publicly with churches of any Christian denomination, even at a time before a popular ecumenical movement had yet emerged.

As well as his broad Christianity, Menzies also saw sectarian attitudes as out of place in a liberal, pluralist democracy such as Australia. As an elected representative of the people, he believed that it behoved him to represent people of all faiths or, indeed, none, with no sectarian prejudice impairing that objective. When responding to the disapproval of his family over the opening of the Catholic primary school, Menzies defended his decision to attend on the basis that he represented people of all faiths in his constituency:

> Well, I understand what you feel but you are overlooking one thing. I am the Member for East Yarra – Presbyterians, Anglicans, Roman Catholics, Brahmins for all I know. Certainly a few Jews in this electorate. I think you have forgotten I am the Member for the lot – and consequently any of them who are of repute and respectable who want me to do something, I will do if I can.[9]

This was yet another point where his broad religious outlook intersected with his liberal principles. His acceptance of, and ease with, a diversity of Christian traditions accorded with his liberal instinct of religious toleration in civil society and each was anathema to the sectarianism of his youth. As David Kemp noted, Menzies' resolve to turn his back on old sectarian divisions, together with those of race and class, was part of his liberal mission to forge a new political culture based on mutual respect and understanding between citizens of all backgrounds.[10]

Menzies' fusion of Christian and liberal principles, which fostered

---

[8] Williams, *In God they Trust?*, pp 133-134.

[9] Frances McNicoll, interview with Robert Menzies, 11 May 1972. Papers of Frances McNicoll, MS 9246, Series 6, Box 15, NLA, cited in Bramston, *Robert Menzies*, p 26.

[10] David Kemp, "The Political Philosophy of Robert Menzies", *Menzies: Shaping of Modern Australia*, p 6.

this toleration of diversity within the communion of Christians, had historical roots in the early liberalism of modern Australia. Menzies stood very much in the tradition of Richard Bourke (1777-1855), the colonial governor of NSW and cousin of Edmund Burke. Like Menzies in his second term as prime minister, Bourke was forced to wrestle with sectarian tensions over education policy and funding during his governorship of NSW in the 1830s. A Whig liberal and a broad-church Anglican, Bourke had exercised a similarly even-handed approach to that of Menzies on the question of funding church-based institutions such as parishes and schools. Through the 1836 *Church Act*, Bourke established equitable funding for Catholic and Protestant churches and this helped to reduce tensions between the competing strands of Christianity in colonial NSW.

Like Menzies, Bourke was loyal to his denominational tradition yet favoured an inclusive and common Christianity as the basis for a moral society.[11] In common with the Whig liberal tradition, both men esteemed religious education, and Christian education, in particular, as critical to advancing faith, morality and human progress. Although both Bourke and Menzies were Protestant, their conception of Christianity was broad and each regarded Catholics as fellow Christians. In his relations with Catholics therefore, both within the Liberal Party and in the broader Australian community, Menzies was impelled by the conviction that Protestants and Catholics represented two different branches of a Christian tree that sprung from the common root of God in Jesus Christ.

The anti-sectarianism that Menzies brought to public office sprang from personal experience and deep-seated sensibilities, to be sure, but was also aided by broader changes in Australian society and public life. Even before the popular ecumenical movement came to the fore in the 1960s, there were a number of developments, on both the international and domestic fronts, that helped to improve

[11] David Stoneman, "Richard Bourke: For the Honour of God and the Good of Man", *Journal of Religious History*, Vol 38, No 3, September 2014, p 354.

relations between Protestants and Catholics in Australia, if only modestly. These developments forced each side to focus less on the historic differences that divided them and more on the social and moral principles they held in common.

The first, most obviously, was the Second World War that had generated different political and religious atmospherics in Australia to those of the Great War. With the timing of the First World War coinciding with the Irish struggle for Home Rule, it fuelled popular suspicions that Australia's Catholic community, of predominantly Irish origin, had divided loyalties. Added to this, the bitter debates over conscription served only to inflame sectarian animosity between Protestant British Empire loyalists and the more ambivalent Irish Catholics.[12] Australia's effort behind the Second World War, on the other hand, attracted far greater unanimity, at least along religious lines. The fight against Nazism, fascism and militarism in both Europe and the Pacific appeared to unite Australia's Catholics and Protestants against clearly common enemies. For both these branches of the Christian church, the existential threats to freedom posed by these enemies left little room for sectarian squabbles.[13] As Hogan recognised, the change of leadership in Australia's Catholic hierarchy from Archbishop Mannix to the more conciliatory posture of Cardinal Gilroy in the Second World War also helped to mobilise Catholic support for the war effort.[14]

Almost immediately after the Second World War, the spectre of Cold War communism emerged as yet another existential threat to the free world of the West, the preservation of which was a paramount concern for Protestants and Catholics alike. Christianity of most kinds deplored the ideology of communism as atheistic, materialistic and totalitarian. From Soviet Russia to Maoist China, communism was seen as the enemy of religion with the large-scale persecution of Christians, Jews and other religious minorities. In the

---

[12] Michael Hogan, *Catholic Campaign for State Aid*, p 5.

[13] Ibid.

[14] Ibid.

interests of preserving freedom, eschewing class conflict, upholding the dignity of the individual, defending the family, protecting private property and safeguarding the free exercise of religion, Protestants and Catholics maintained that Australia needed to be shielded from the perils of communism at all costs.

The concerns of Catholics about the advance of communism, and the much milder Australian tradition of socialism, were articulated by senior spokespeople of the Catholic church including Archbishop James Duhig of Brisbane, Dr Leslie Rumble of the Sydney Archdiocese and Brian Doyle of the *Catholic Weekly* who attacked the "socialist objective" of the ALP. With many Catholics questioning their traditional Labor loyalties, John Warhurst discerned that in NSW at least, "a realignment of major proportions" took place at the 1949 election.[15] With this shift, sizeable numbers of Catholics hitherto attached to the ALP joined their Protestant counterparts to help bring the new Liberal Party of Menzies to power. Thus, even before the state aid issue of the early 1960s brought many more Catholics into the Coalition fold, the anti-communist election pitch of Menzies succeeded in siphoning off some Catholic voters from the ALP to the Liberal Party. This arguably diversified the support base of what was then a heavily-Protestant dominated party and would strengthen Menzies' hand to make the Liberal Party more accommodating to Catholics and those of other faith traditions. The onset of communism thereby served as a catalyst for a co-belligerency, if not an ecumenism of sorts, between Protestants and Catholics within Menzies' own centre-right tradition of Australian politics.

The newfound common ground between Australian Catholics and Protestants in the Second World War and immediate post-war years found tangible expression in two major public statements that Menzies himself had occasion to allude to with approval. The first was a joint statement issued by the respective Anglican and Catholic

[15] John Warhurst, "Catholics, Communism and the Australian Party System: A Study of the Menzies Years", *Politics*, 14:2, November 1979, p 232.

Archbishops of Sydney, Dr Howard Mowll and Dr Norman Gilroy, on 28 June 1943. As the first joint statement of its kind by Anglican and Catholic prelates in Australia, it was published in the major newspapers including the *Sydney Morning Herald*.[16] Drafted in the midst of the Second World War just prior to the 1943 federal election, the statement presented a blueprint for a post-war political and social order undergirded by Christian moral principles affirming the dignity of the individual, the importance of the family, the freedom of worship, the right to private property, class harmony, and the value of a religious background to education. As would become evident in preparation of the Liberal Party platform, these principles were very familiar to Menzies and they resonated with his personal political philosophy. Accordingly, he welcomed this initiative as an "epoch-making statement" and commended the two archbishops for their denunciation of communism, fascism and Nazism on much the same grounds as he was seeking to do.[17]

In another show of unity, the 1951 *Call to the People of Australia* brought leaders of the Catholic and Protestant churches together publicly as they called for a mobilisation of moral strength to protect Australia's traditional values and freedoms from "dangers" at home and abroad. The "Call" was an initiative of Sir Edmund Herring, the Chief Justice of Victoria who was also an active Anglican and retired Lieutenant General.[18] Broadcast throughout the nation on Remembrance Day 1951, The Call challenged Australians to "advance moral standards" and reminded citizens that they were members of one another. Without mentioning communism by name, it warned that the "dangers" to the country "demand a restoration of the moral order from which alone true social order can derive". In language that resonated with Christians of all traditions, it concluded with the familiar New Testament exhortation to "Fear God, Honour the

---

[16] "Christianity's Role after War: Joint Statement by Sydney Archbishops", *Sydney Morning Herald*, Monday, 28 June 1943, p 4.

[17] Menzies, "The Communists", 2 July 1943.

[18] John Murphy, *Imagining the Fifties: Private Sentiment and Political Culture in Menzies' Australia*, UNSW Press, p 197.

King".[19] The "Call" expressed long-standing Christian beliefs that the health of the nation depended on its fidelity to God's moral laws.[20] For Prime Minister Menzies the initiative was "a notable challenge to us to restore our ancient faith, and to practice the ancient virtues upon which our greatness was founded".

Menzies' new Liberal Party and Catholics

Menzies' desire to build bridges with Australia's Catholic community was evident in his goal that the Liberal Party should be inclusive of Catholics and those of other faiths, notwithstanding the historical reality that the Protestant ascendency dominated the centre right of Australian politics. Owing to its primary pitch to the "forgotten people" of the middle class, Menzies' new Liberal Party, for historical and demographic reasons, similarly attracted a disproportionate number of Protestants to its rank and file. Like its immediate forerunner, the United Australia Party, the Liberal Party commanded the support of the majority of Australia's Protestants who were active in business and the professions. That said, however, the Liberal Party's predecessor had been far from devoid of a Catholic presence. It had been led for more than half its history by none other than Joseph Aloysius Lyons, a deeply pious Catholic who had served as Australia's second-longest serving prime minister during and after the depression. His Methodist-turned-Catholic wife, Enid Lyons, was also prominent in the UAP in her own right, having been one of the first two women elected to Federal Parliament in 1943 and later becoming the first woman to serve in Federal Cabinet in Menzies' new Coalition Government from 1949 to 1951. With this backdrop, Menzies appreciated the need for his new party to be open to Catholics even though roughly 10 percent, or two of seventeen ministers, of his 1949 cabinet were

---

[19] Based on 1 Peter 2:17.

[20] Hugh Chilton, *Evangelicals and the End of Christian Australia: Nation and Religion in the Public Square, 1959-1979*, PhD Thesis, University of Sydney, 2014, p 79.

Dame Enid Lyons (1897-1981)

Widow of Prime Minister Joseph Lyons, Methodist by birth and upbringing, Catholic by conversion, she was the first woman to be elected to the House of Representatives (in 1943), and, subsequently, the first to be a Cabinet minister (1949-51). (*Australian War Memorial*)

Catholic in a country where Catholics then made up around 20 percent of the population.[21]

In the Liberal Party's early years, the relatively low proportion of Catholics in senior ranks was more a product of history than of any personal reticence on Menzies' part to welcome Catholics into the Party. Reflecting on the small numbers of Catholics in the party, Gerard Henderson gave due credit to Menzies' absence of bigotry but concluded that "Menzies' attitude to Catholics had an air of noblesse oblige about it".[22] The historical evidence, however, would suggest that Menzies' overtures to Catholics sprang less from a mere sense of "duty" to "do the right thing" than from his deep-seated antipathy to sectarianism and religious discrimination combined with a pronounced reluctance to accept that Catholics would automatically support Labor. In May 1949, whilst still the Leader of the Opposition, Menzies received letters from a number of Catholic correspondents who were aggrieved that his Liberal Party was discriminating against Catholics. Citing a report from the *Catholic Weekly*, one correspondent expressed dismay that "the Liberal Party refuses to have as a member of our party, one of the Catholic faith".[23] Another lamented the "campaign conducted against the nomination of Catholics for the Liberal endorsement for the coming election".[24] Finally, a member of the Christian Brothers who said that he would vote for Menzies if he were in his electorate admitted that he would have great difficulty voting "for those so inimical to our views and interests".[25]

To allay the concerns of these correspondents, Menzies replied personally to all three. From the outset, Menzies made it clear that both he and his party would not entertain discrimination or

[21] Gerard Henderson, *Menzies' Child: The Liberal Party of Australia, 1944-1994*, Allen & Unwin, 1994, p 105.

[22] Ibid., p 106.

[23] Mrs O'Keefe to Robert Menzies, 5 May 1949, Robert Menzies Papers, NLA, MS 4936, Box 419, Folder 70.

[24] Kevin F McCarthy to Robert Menzies, 8 April 1949, Robert Menzies Papers, NLA, MS 4936, Box 419, Folder 70.

[25] Brother J P Harty to Robert Menzies, 21 April 1949, Robert Menzies Papers, NLA, MS 4936, Box 419, Folder 70.

sectarian bias against prospective Catholic members. Sceptical of the negative reports that his correspondents had cited about Party discrimination against Catholics, he assured them that "I have no reason to believe that the statements that are being made to the effect that discrimination against Roman Catholics is shown by the Liberal Party have any foundation in fact".[26] Menzies, to be sure, was speaking more from his own position of how he saw matters at the top of the Party than from the grassroots where the picture was less sanguine with sectarianism still flaring in some of the local branches. In the inner-west Sydney electorate of Lowe, for example, the preselection committee stipulated that their "perfect candidate" for the 1949 election had to be a "Protestant male".[27] For his part, however, Menzies affirmed that "I have myself been a consistent and open opponent of the introduction of any form of sectarianism into politics".[28] With the memory of his family's adverse reaction to his appearance at a Catholic school seared into his conscience, Menzies was not prepared to countenance sectarianism in any form, and he made this known.

As concrete evidence that the Liberal Party had accepted Catholics in its ranks, including at the parliamentary level, he drew attention to two of his colleagues in the House of Representatives, Dame Enid Lyons and Archie Cameron, as well as the Leader of the Liberal Party in the Senate, Senator Neil O'Sullivan, all of whom were members of the Catholic Church.[29] Educated at St Joseph's College Nudgee in Brisbane, O'Sullivan served from 1947 to 1962 as a Liberal Senator for Queensland. As well as leading the Party in the Senate from 1947

---

[26] Robert Menzies to Brother J. P. Harty, 19 May 1949; Robert Menzies to Jose O'Keeffe, 19 May 1949; and Robert Menzies to Kevin F McCarthy, 20 May 1949, Robert Menzies Papers, NLA, MS 4936, Box 419, Folder 70.

[27] Patrick Mullins, *Tiberius with a Telephone: The Life and Stories of William McMahon*, Melbourne: Scribe, 2018, p 65. William McMahon was eventually preselected as the candidate for Lowe at the 1949 election.

[28] Ibid.

[29] Robert Menzies to Kevin F. McCarthy, 20 May 1949; Robert Menzies to Jose O'Keeffe, 19 May 1949, Robert Menzies Papers, NLA, MS 4936, Box 419, Folder 70.

until 1958, O'Sullivan also served in Menzies' cabinet as Minister for Trade and Customs (1949-1956) and Attorney-General (1956-1958). In addition to these three sitting parliamentarians, Menzies also noted that he knew personally three Roman Catholic Liberal candidates, Councillor Cramer, Dr de Monchaux and Allen Fairhall, each of whom he regarded "as certain to win".[30] At the December 1949 election, Councillor John Cramer was subsequently elected to the House of Representatives as the Member for the Sydney seat of Bennelong and served in Menzies' government as Minister for the Army from 1956 to 1963. At the same election, Allen Fairhall was also elected as the Member for the NSW seat of Paterson and served as the Minister for Interior and Minister for Works (1956-1958) and Minister for Supply (1961-1966). From 1950 until 1956, Cameron was Speaker of the House of Representatives.

While embracing Catholics within the contemporary Liberal Party, Menzies conceded the historical reality that Catholics had been under-represented on his own side of politics. In the May 1949 letters, Menzies attributed this to demographic and socio-economic factors and not to any conscious, sectarian bias on the part of the Liberal Party's predecessors:

> It is probably historically quite true that the Labour Party at Canberra has always included a greater proportion of Roman Catholics than its political opponents. This is, however, not the result of some conscious selection but of the fact that people are, rightly or wrongly, affected in their political allegiance by their industrial associations.

To illustrate, Menzies explained that "a very substantial percentage of Irish-Australians, for example, had been industrial employees". As such, these largely Catholic employees were prominent in the trade union movement as members and thereby constituted much of the union support-base for the ALP.

---

[30] Robert Menzies to Kevin F McCarthy, 20 May 1949, Robert Menzies Papers, NLA, MS 4936, Box 419, Folder 70. At the 1949 election, Dr Charles de Monchaux was the only one of the three candidate not to get elected to parliament.

Notwithstanding this historical reality, Menzies concluded his letters with the assurance that "so far as my Parliamentary colleagues are concerned, we would not tolerate any idea of religious discrimination". On the contrary, "we welcome men and women of high character and deep religious principles to our ranks because we know that they can be relied upon to give disinterested public service".[31] Thus, far from viewing religious beliefs in negative terms as a justification for exercising favouritism or discrimination, Menzies held that people of deep faith could be relied upon to serve the country with impartiality. This was because the precepts of their religious world-view, whether Catholic, Protestant or Jewish, held that since every human being was created in the image of God, it behoved those in public office to honour all people and to seek the common good. While admitting that "every political party encounters occasionally some small group of people who are intolerant and bigoted", he did not "believe that in the long run they are a real factor or exercise any real influence".[32] In the Liberal Party, therefore, he would see to it that incidences of anti-Catholic prejudice at the local branch level, as witnessed by some of his correspondents, would not be reflected in the executive or parliamentary leadership of the Party.

Following the December 1949 election victory, Menzies continued to practise an inclusive approach to Catholics within the parliamentary party with Enid Lyons serving as Vice-President of the Executive Council, and O'Sullivan as Minister for Trade and Customs and Leader of the Government in the Senate. Fairhall and Cramer each later held ministerial portfolios. His relationship with Sir John Cramer, his one-time Minister for the Army, was particularly illustrative. Despite Menzies' own tolerant outlook, Cramer's path, as a Catholic, to political office in the Liberal Party of the late 1940s had been far from easy. Cramer recalled that the "sectarian bitterness" was "terrible" and that at his preselection meeting, he had even been

---

[31] Robert Menzies to Brother J. P. Harty, 19 May 1949, Robert Menzies Papers, NLA, MS 4936, Box 419, Folder 70.
[32] Ibid.

questioned as to whether he "owed his allegiance to the Pope or the King?"[33]

Serving as Minister for the Army in the Menzies Government from 1956, Cramer found Menzies very supportive of his efforts to rectify a remaining sectarian sore in the Australian Defence Force. The issue related to the ceremonial "Blessing of the Colours" at Army parades, where the chaplains of various churches would request God's blessing upon the regimental colours on parade. Since the chaplains, however, could not agree on a procedure suitable to all denominations, it was customary for the Catholic troops to retire from the parade while the ceremony took place. This exclusion aggrieved Catholics such as Cramer and so he sought, as Army Minister, to devise a new procedure that would include all denominations. After lengthy discussions with both the Catholic and Presbyterian chaplains, Cramer succeeded in getting all the chaplains to sign up to a new, inclusive ceremony. After reporting this agreement to Menzies, the prime minister reportedly leapt from his chair with delight, threw his papers into the air and exclaimed, "Thank God, John – this is great and lifts a load I have always felt off my shoulders".[34] At any such measure designed to salve sectarian wounds, the Prime Minister expressed his elation that the enmities of the past that had long dogged Australian public life were being finally remedied.

Redressing the "longest-standing political grievance"

As symbolically significant as the administrative tweak was to the "Blessing of the Colours", the single greatest measure taken by Menzies and his government to heal sectarian division was the granting of "state aid" to independent schools following the 1963 election, many

---

[33] John Cramer, *Pioneers, Politics and People: A Political Memoir*, Sydney: Allen & Unwin, p 101-102. Cramer did note, however, that Menzies would sometimes joke about his Catholic identity, pointing to the remark the Prime Minister would make when Cramer entered a ministers' room, saying to his colleagues, "Be careful boys, here comes the Papist". As sensitive as Cramer was to this jest, he accepted that it was done in "good humour" and did not reflect any anti-Catholic antagonism on Menzies' part.

[34] Ibid., p 167.

of which were Catholic. Judith Brett has described the absence of government support for Catholic schools as Australian Catholics' "longest-standing political grievance". Since the advent of free, compulsory and secular education in the latter nineteenth-century, parents of Catholic school pupils were required to pay taxes to fund government schools with no return benefit for their own schools, and this was in addition to fees already paid for the education of their own children. According to B. A. Santamaria, this injustice in education had been the subject of countless speeches at Catholic functions since the First World War. It was an injustice that neither side of politics seemed prepared to rectify until Menzies himself entertained the idea of state aid as early as the 1940s, with his government finally delivering on the policy after the 1963 election. Culminating in the Goulburn school strike of 1962,[35] the state aid issue had become more pressing during the post-war years as the baby boom, the influx of immigrants and the rapid growth of population centres all placed greater pressure on Catholic schools to make ends meet.[36] To satisfy the growing demand for places, Catholic schools required greater resources in terms of staff and infrastructure which an injection of government funding would help to provide.

Menzies' own understanding of the dire funding needs for Catholic and independent schools was evident long before the 1963 state aid decision of his government. As early as 1943, while neither prime minister nor party leader, Menzies had opined in a broadcast on "The Future of Education" that "it is unlikely that the church schools can in the post-war period efficiently survive unless there is some measure of state assistance to them". Foreshadowing the assistance

---

[35] The Goulburn school strike referred to the decision by families of students at six of Goulburn's Catholic schools to go on strike to protest at the lack of funding for essential amenities. By enrolling their children at local state schools instead, the protesters sent the message that Catholic schools such as St Brigid's needed government assistance to be able to operate. The strike in July 1962 lasted for a week, after which time, the Catholic schools reopened with the protesting families believing that their point had been made.

[36] Michael Hogan, *Sectarian Strand*, p 251.

package his government would eventually provide for such schools, Menzies concluded his broadcast with this appeal:

> My own belief is that the maintenance of Church schools of whatever denomination, is so important – because a religious background for education is so important – that we must all be prepared to come together in the post-war world to devise ways and means of ensuring that those who are content with a purely secular education should be able to get it while those whom such an education will never satisfy should be able to get the kind of training they want for their children without absolutely bankrupting themselves in the process.[37]

The point Menzies made was that, under existing arrangements, parents of private and Catholic school-educated children unfairly had to pay twice – once as taxpayers for the maintenance of the state schools, and again as parents for the maintenance of their children at church schools.[38] Accordingly, Menzies believed that some state aid for the Catholic and private sectors would relieve the financial burden for parents to pay high fees to send their children to independent schools. The fact that Menzies raised this issue in 1943 revealed that he had been committed to state aid as a matter of principle over decades. Contrary to popular belief, it was never a cause that he adopted merely out of political opportunism to curry electoral favour with Catholic voters.

Menzies' intimation of support for all church schools in 1943 raised the ire of some Protestant voices who feared that it was part of a calculated ploy by Menzies to chase the "Catholic vote" at the next election. Shortly after Menzies gave his "Future of Education" broadcast, the Rev W. D. McIlwraith, editor of the ultra-Protestant paper, *The Clarion*, excoriated Menzies, chiding him for "undoubtedly touting for Roman Catholic support for his Party at the approaching

---

[37] Robert Menzies, "The Future of Education", Broadcast, Melbourne, 19 February 1943, p 2.
[38] Menzies, "Future of Education", 1943. p 2.

elections". McIlwraith accused Menzies of "listening to the promises of Dr Mannix and others", suggesting that such Catholics had "his price".[39] In reply to the editor, Menzies denounced these charges as "untrue, defamatory, contemptible and un-Christian".[40] He regarded McIlwraith's sectarian views as completely contrary to the Christian teaching for fellow believers to love one another, whatever their differences in church background. Making it also known that his views on the need for more funding for all church schools were of his own accord, he told the editor that they were "in no sense inspired by pressure from the Roman Catholic Church".[41]

After founding the Liberal Party in 1944, Menzies again entertained the possibility of future state aid for all church schools if this meant that they would otherwise disappear. He took this position against the backdrop of a campaign waged by the United Protestant Association to oppose, outright, any state aid for church schools, fearing that such funds would end up going to Catholic schools.[42] Replying to a letter from the Association that had accused him of supporting Commonwealth aid for Catholic schools, Menzies poured scorn over the idea that it would be better to deny state aid to all church schools than to give anything to Catholic schools:

> I should consider my Christianity a poor, warped thing, full of hatred and quite inconsistent with the teachings of Christ, if I took the view that I would sooner see all Church schools disappear, and with them the last vestiges of religious educational background, than see one penny of public money, some of which is, after all, found by Roman Catholic

---

[39] Rev W D McIlwraith, *The Clarion*, 15 April 1943, Robert Menzies Papers, NLA, MS 4936, Box 419, Folder 70.

[40] Robert Menzies to Rev. W. D. McIlwraith, 8 May 1943, Robert Menzies Papers, NLA, MS 4936, Box 419, Folder 70.

[41] Ibid.

[42] Thomas Agst to Robert Menzies, 10 April 1946, Robert Menzies Papers, NLA, MS 4936, Box 419, Folder 70. Speaking for the United Protestant Association, Agst held that a policy of State aid for what he called "sectarian schools", be they Protestant or Roman Catholic, would "mean the death-knell of our democratic public education system".

taxpayers, make its way into Roman Catholic hands. As a loyal Presbyterian, I would find such intolerance and bigotry both unchristian and absurd.[43]

For Menzies, the value of supporting a broad religious education across multiple denominations far outweighed any peril of funding a system of church schools whose theology differed from that of his own church. Subsequently addressing a Presbyterian Church school in 1953, Menzies remarked that "I don't mind what branch of the Christian Church it is", so long as the Church schools of Australia could be supported.[44] This stemmed from his primary conviction that for all the theological differences separating Protestants and Catholics, these were far eclipsed by the gaping contrast between the morally bereft, godless paganism, characteristic of ideologies such as communism, and a common Christianity centred around the love of God and the teachings of Christ. As an antidote to a purely secular education, Menzies saw the cause of a faith-based education as best served by funding church schools of all denominations including the Catholic education system. Indeed, on the question of supporting Catholic schools, Menzies in 1946 could already sense the anomaly and injustice of Catholic families contributing taxes to public revenue without receiving any return benefit for their schools.

In Michael Hogan's view, Menzies' initial openness to supporting Catholic schools in the 1940s did not come necessarily from any external pressure by the Catholic Church and this was confirmed by Menzies himself. [45] As an alumnus of Melbourne's Wesley College, he identified more closely with the old church schools of the Protestant establishment than with Catholic education circles.[46] The eventual financial support that Menzies offered to Catholic schools, on the other hand, stemmed from his philosophically liberal impulses.

[43] Robert Menzies to Thomas Agst, 27 April 1946, Robert Menzies Papers, NLA, MS 4936, Box 419, Folder 70.
[44] Robert Menzies, "Speech Day", Scots College Sydney, 5 December 1953, Robert Menzies Papers, NLA, MS 4936, Box 259, Folder 56.
[45] Hogan, *Catholic Campaign for State Aid*, p 18.
[46] Ibid.

First, to accord benefits even-handedly to church schools across all denominations; and, second, to broaden the religious education base from which moral character could be forged. Whatever the church school's denomination, with the Roman Catholic tradition being no exception, Menzies believed that it made an invaluable contribution to the spiritual and moral fibre of the nation and thereby merited support. If Menzies held that a religious background to education was so essential, then it made eminent sense for government to lend support to as wide a range of church schools as possible. In this vein, Menzies envisaged the Catholic schools as having an invaluable stake in the moral formation of society. Again, this reflected his liberal philosophy of education as the cornerstone for building the moral character of the individual. As Hogan appreciated, this strand of Menzies' liberal thinking owed more to the conservative instincts of Edmund Burke than to the utilitarianism of either Jeremy Bentham or John Stuart Mill.

When Menzies led the Liberal Party into office, he remained true to the non-sectarian yet faith-affirming beliefs that informed his support for church schools. After returning to the prime ministership in December 1949, the first practical measure Menzies introduced to assist independent schools was an amendment in 1952 to income tax laws to allow a parent to claim up to £60 for school tuition fees as an allowable deduction. Given that parents of government school pupils paid little in school fees, the tax concession was of most benefit to private school parents.[47] A further concession Menzies made to the private school sector was a change to the tax laws in 1954 to enable donations made to schools for building purposes to be claimed as tax deductions. The prime minister held that this would give a considerable boost to the private school councils which could now more readily obtain gifts from individuals for school buildings.[48] In 1956, the Menzies Government gave the first direct aid to private schools in Canberra, whereby the Commonwealth undertook to reimburse the interest (up to 5 percent per annum) paid on loans

---

[47]   Bob Bessant, "Robert Gordon Menzies and Education in Australia", *Melbourne Studies in Education*, 2006, 47: 1-2, p 175.

[48]   Bessant, "Robert Gordon Menzies", p 175.

raised to finance new schools or extensions.[49] Indeed Menzies regarded this last decision as the precursor to what he would describe as "a quite revolutionary change in Government education policy" with the announcement of state aid in the November 1963 policy speech.[50]

Announcing an assistance package in his policy speech for the 1963 election, the Menzies Government pledged to fund science blocks for all schools to the tune of £5 million, and similar amounts of £5 million annually for state technical education.[51] In addition, the government launched a Commonwealth Scholarship scheme offering an annual grant of 10 000 scholarships to secondary school students. Like the funding for science and technical education, the two-year scholarships would be open to students of all secondary schools, both government and independent, without discrimination. The funding for science would accomplish the material goal of aiding technological progress and national development while the scholarships would advance Menzies' objective of raising an educated generation of future leaders to run the country. With 120 000 high school students attending Roman Catholic schools, the measures directly benefited a sizeable proportion (17.8 percent) of the 674 000 students enrolled in secondary school throughout Australia.

The efforts of the Menzies Government to deliver state aid could be attributed not only to the vision of Menzies himself, but also to the advocacy of John Carrick, the General Secretary of the NSW Division of the Liberal Party from 1948 to 1971. A key party strategist yet also a conviction politician, Carrick maintained that introducing state aid was essential to the Liberal Party's mission of broadening its base and presenting itself as a "truly national party".[52] According to his biographer, Graeme Starr, Carrick shared with Menzies and others a

[49] Ibid.
[50] Menzies, *Measure of the Years*, p 92.
[51] In real terms, £5 million pounds in 1963 would equate to approximately $147.9 million in 2020.
[52] Graeme Starr, *Carrick: Principles, Politics and Policy*, Ballan [Vic]: Connor Court Publishing, 2012, p 169.

concern that the Liberal Party was seen essentially as a "Protestant" Party.[53] For this reason, he believed that providing state aid to independent and Catholic schools would help dispel this image. To bring about this much needed policy, Carrick worked closely with Menzies and liaised with the Catholic Archbishop of Canberra/Goulburn, Eris O'Brien. Archbishop O'Brien, who also knew Menzies well, briefed Carrick on the need for the Government to act, especially for the poorer Catholic parochial schools which were facing a funding crisis.[54] As one of the lead voices within the Liberal Party for state aid, Carrick was strongly supported by a youthful John Howard who was then active in the NSW Young Liberals. Like Menzies and Carrick, Howard supported state aid as a matter of principle reinforced by practical political considerations.[55]

The state aid package that the Menzies Government had taken to the 1963 election paid dividends with the government increasing its overall majority, performing especially well in NSW where the state aid issue was most acute. The state aid funding measures were naturally welcomed by Australia's Catholic community that had been long aggrieved by the lack of financial help from governments.

In July 1964 Menzies was guest of honour at the Cardinal's Dinner.[56] Presided over by the Catholic Archbishop of Sydney, Cardinal Gilroy, the dinner was attended by 400 leading members of the Catholic community. The Auxiliary Bishop, Thomas W. Muldoon, thanked Menzies for granting financial assistance to Catholic schools. Bishop Muldoon observed that: "When the history of Australia is written, the name of Robert Gordon Menzies will surely be there as one of the greatest, and perhaps the greatest, Australians of all times".[57] Profoundly grateful for the Prime Minister's state aid initiative, he

---

[53] Ibid.

[54] Ibid., pp 169-170.

[55] Ibid., p 171.

[56] Robert Menzies, Speech by the Prime Minister, The Cardinal's Dinner, Sydney, 30 July 1964, pp 1-6.

[57] "Menzies gives Church Schools Assurance on Aid", Sydney Morning Herald, 31 July, p 4.

concluded that: "Among the monuments he will leave behind him there will be none greater than the monument of education".

Menzies himself joked that some "alleged Christian" would "say I'm cultivating your vote", to which he would reply, "Well, it's a little bit too late to do that".[58] Menzies was obviously referring here to the sectarian voices of dissent who would now have little ground for their objections, given that state aid had already been approved by the electorate at the 1963 election. Lamenting sectarian divisions, Menzies said that "although we are all the children of God and hope to serve his purposes in this world, there is an unbridgeable difference between those who do it this way and those who do it that way".[59] Essentially, he was affirming that different Christians, whether Catholic or Protestant, could still serve God in good faith, even if they did so differently, and thus deserved equal respect. Repudiation of sectarianism was so important to Menzies that he remarked that if he was forced to discriminate between Protestant and Catholic schools, he "wouldn't want to be in public life".

Finally, Menzies stressed the importance of a religious background to education and character formation, to which Catholic schools contributed richly, declaring that: "I am all for character. I am all for the man whose character is rooted in eternal beliefs because he is the man, she is the woman, who will assure the future of this country".[60]

The significance of an avowedly Protestant Prime Minister assuming centre-stage at a high-profile Catholic event was not lost on the press. Two days after the Cardinal's Dinner, *The Sydney Morning Herald* editorialised that: "It is doubtful whether a gathering of Roman Catholic dignitaries has ever looked upon a Presbyterian with such benevolence as Cardinal Gilroy and his bishops did upon Sir Robert Menzies on Thursday evening".[61] The *Herald* remarked that at the annual Cardinal's Dinner, which has

---

[58] Robert Menzies, Cardinal's Dinner, 30 July 1964.

[59] Ibid.

[60] Ibid.

[61] "A Blessing Upon Sir Robert", *Sydney Morning Herald*, 1 August 1964, p 2.

"become rightly celebrated for its atmosphere of goodwill", the Prime Minister "glowed with a matching spirit of tolerance and understanding". Applauding the government for its recent action on State aid, the *Herald* concluded:

> The Roman Catholic Church has good reason to be pleased with the Prime Minister. His decision on the eve of the last Federal election to pay £5m a year to State and independent secondary schools for science facilities produced ... the "break-through" of direct State aid for schools which the Church had so long and earnestly sought.[62]

Reflecting on this watershed policy some half-a-century later, John Howard similarly observed that the historic decision of Menzies on state aid not only rectified the injustice felt by Australia's Catholics for more than a century, but helped to reduce the sectarian divisions in Australian society still raw in the early 1960s.[63]

Together with Cardinal Gilroy and Bishop Muldoon of Sydney, Menzies enjoyed warm relations with other senior leaders of Australia's Catholic hierarchy. These included, especially, the Archbishop of Brisbane, Sir James Duhig, and the Archbishop of Canberra/Goulburn, the historian Eris O'Brien. Certainly in political terms, Archbishop Duhig was a fellow-traveller of Menzies in his affection for the British Crown and his anti-socialism. In the late 1940s, he spoke out against the Chifley Government's decision to nationalise the banks in 1947 and during the 1951 referendum campaign to dissolve the Communist Party, he openly advocated a "yes" vote.[64] In 1959, he also became the first Roman Catholic archbishop in Australia to accept a knighthood. Like Menzies, he was ecumenically-minded and sought to foster friendly relations with other Christian churches, even before ecumenism became a popular movement. Menzies credited his ministerial colleague, Queensland Senator Neil O'Sullivan, for introducing him to the Archbishop, and

---

[62] *Herald*, 1 August 1964, p 2.

[63] Howard, *The Menzies Era*, p 314.

[64] T. P. Boland, "Duhig, Sir James (1871-1965)", *ADB*, Vol 8, MUP, 1981.

Cardinal Norman Gilroy (1896-1977) with Robert Menzies, 1964, and (below) Archbishop Eris O'Brien (1895-1974)

Menzies found the sectarianism so prevalent in his youth objectionable. Among Catholics with whom he developed warm relations were Cardinal Gilroy, the Catholic Archbishop of Sydney, and Archbishop O'Brien of Canberra-Goulburn. Both were involved in decisions of the Menzies Government to provide financial support to private schools, including those run by churches. Underlining his hostility to sectarianism, Menzies declared that if forced to discriminate between Protestant and Catholic schools, he "wouldn't want to be in public life."

(*Sydney Morning Herald* and *Australian Catholic Historical Society*)

he remarked that they became "fast friends".[65] Joining Archbishop Duhig to open a new building at Brisbane's St Joseph's College, Nudgee, in 1967, the recently retired prime minister praised his friend as a "great ecclesiastical statesman" and credited him for beginning the ecumenical movement in Queensland "long before it became a matter of world interest".[66] Of Duhig, Menzies remarked that "he knew the lovely community and communion of Christians which so many destroy by hatreds which are foreign to the teachings of Christ". In the Irish-born prelate, Menzies evidently saw a kindred spirit in a church leader who envisioned a flourishing Christian community, marked by unity and fraternal affection.

Meanwhile, in the campaign for state aid, Menzies had also developed warm ties with Archbishop Eris O'Brien of the Canberra/ Goulburn diocese. Appointed archbishop of the diocese in 1953, he presided over a rapidly growing Catholic population in Canberra with the number of Catholic parishes in the ACT increasing from one to ten.[67] Eager to sustain the resources and personnel needed for his burgeoning diocese, O'Brien had welcomed the Menzies Government's offer in 1956 to subsidise interest on money borrowed to build or extend church secondary schools in the ACT.[68] Giving public support to the Goulburn school strike in 1962, the Archbishop became one of the Catholic Church's main points of contact for the Menzies Government as it agreed to state aid as the 1963 election approached. In March that year, Prime Minister Menzies shared a platform with O'Brien at the opening of his Church's Dominican Sisters Training College in the Canberra suburb of Watson. In his address, Menzies quipped: "what could be more ecumenical than to have a Presbyterian Prime Minister

---

[65] Robert Menzies, "Speech at St Joseph's College, Nudgee, Queensland, Opening of New Building", 21 May 1967, Robert Menzies Papers, NLA, MS 4936, Box 285, Folder 240.

[66] Ibid.

[67] Elizabeth Johnston, "O'Brien, Eris Michael (1895-1974)", ADB, Vol 15, MUP, 2000.

[68] Johnston, "O'Brien", ADB.

opening this Teachers' Training College".[69] Referring then to
Archbishop O'Brien and his efforts to develop his growing diocese,
he remarked that "the Archbishop who began life by being a scholar
has ended up by being a considerable builder". With Menzies
noting that they were "on the best of terms", he joked that once
the Archbishop left their meetings, he would find himself "almost
invariably conducting a violent altercation with the Treasury".[70]
This suggested that while Menzies was amenable and, indeed, full
of enthusiasm about meeting the Archbishop's request for funding
support, he would encounter frustration with the Treasury over
their presumed hesitancy to approve the expenditure.

The positive relations that Menzies cultivated with Australian
Catholics were no doubt aided by broader developments in society
that saw a thawing of tensions between Protestants and Catholics in
the post-war decades. These included not only emergence of a shared
spiritual and moral consensus in the face of Cold War communism,
as already noted, but also the upward mobility of Australian Catholics
into the middle class with larger numbers completing tertiary
education and entering the professions. This shift in demography
had palpable implications for the support-base of the Liberal Party
where upwardly mobile Catholics tended to migrate from the ALP to
the Democratic Labor Party and then eventually to the Liberal Party
where they joined Protestant counterparts. The trend that had begun
at the 1949 election, where anti-communism proved to be a major
drawcard for Catholics, only accelerated from the 1963 election when
the Menzies Government had pledged to provide state aid. Thus, by
the time Menzies retired in 1966, it could no longer be assumed that
the archetypal "Forgotten People" Liberal Party voter had a Protestant
identity, as was broadly so in the mid-1940s. The other development
was the rise of the popular ecumenical movement of which the
Roman Catholic Church's Second Vatican Council had been a major

[69] Robert Menzies, Speech at Opening of Dominican Sisters Training College,
Watson ACT, 24 March 1963, Robert Menzies Papers, NLA, MS 4936, Box 276,
Folder 179.
[70] Menzies, Opening of Dominican Sisters Training College, Canberra, 24 March
1963.

catalyst. Presided over by Pope John XXIII, Vatican II (1962-65) did much to foster the Catholic Church's friendly relations with other churches that helped to heal the centuries old Catholic-Protestant rift.[71] The ecumenical movement was unsurprisingly welcomed by Menzies himself as a step towards the greater "communion of Christians" he envisioned.[72]

Embracing Australia's Eastern Orthodox communities

In post-war Australia, this communion of Christians extended also to the small yet rapidly growing Eastern Orthodox community. Like most other faith traditions in Australia, Eastern Orthodoxy had been present in Australia since the nineteenth century, but it was the post-war immigration scheme that really boosted their numbers in the 1950s and '60s. During Menzies' post-war term as prime minister, Australia received thousands of new immigrants from war-torn Greece, together with new arrivals from Romania, Bulgaria and other Eastern Bloc countries, the majority of whom were Orthodox. The largest and most prominent Orthodox tradition in Australia was the Greek Orthodox Church, with parishes concentrated largely in Melbourne and Sydney. As prime minister, Menzies reached out to these communities and celebrated not only their spiritual and social contribution, but also the "Christian heritage" they shared with Australians at large.

On two occasions as prime minister, Menzies sent official greetings to the Greek Orthodox community. The first was to the Greek Orthodox Community in Wollongong at the opening of their church on 30 August 1962. After commending the community for "catering to the spiritual and social needs of the adherents of the Greek Orthodox Church", Menzies remarked that "Australia and Greece have many common bonds, not least of which is their

---

[71] Judith Brett, *The Australian Liberals and the Moral Middle Class: From Alfred Deakin to John Howard*, New York: Cambridge University Press, 2003, p 130.
[72] Menzies, St Joseph's College, 21 May 1967.

common Christian heritage".[73] The following year, Menzies sent greetings to the Greek Orthodox Community in the Melbourne suburb of Frankston, where he similarly affirmed the common Christian heritage of Greece and Australia. Commending them for the opening of their new Church of the Epiphany, he expressed his hope that "the first services of this house of worship will serve to strengthen our bonds".[74] As Australia's growing Eastern Orthodox community opened new churches, Menzies welcomed this as adding to the vitality and catholicity of Australia's Christian life.

---

[73] Robert Menzies, "Greek Orthodox Church Opening, Wollongong", Canberra, 30 August 1962. Accessed from https://pmtranscripts.pmc.gov.au/sites/default/files/original/00000599.pdf

[74] Robert Menzies, "Greek Orthodox Community, Frankston", Canberra, 20 August 1963. Accessed from https://pmtranscripts.pmc.gov.au/sites/default/files/original/00000786.pdf

6

MENZIES, JUDAISM AND THE JEWISH COMMUNITY IN AUSTRALIA

There is a long history in Australia of distinguished service to our country by Jewish citizens. The Jews in Australia are good Australians.[1]

In the 1994 ABC documentary series, *The Liberals*, Sir Robert Menzies' daughter, Heather Henderson, remarked that 'sectarianism was alive and well in the 1950s and that her 'father fought against that always'. Appreciating that her father was at the helm of what was then a heavily Protestant-based party, she added that the Liberal Party founder 'went to great pains to consult and talk to the Jews, the Catholics and everybody he could'.[2] Whilst some of the existing scholarship on Menzies' religious views has touched on his formative Presbyterianism, his espousal of middle class Protestant values and even his contribution to healing Australia's sectarian divide, the important relationship he cultivated with Australia's small yet significant Jewish community remains largely unexplored. Accordingly, this dimension to Menzies' prime ministership has escaped the attention of most scholarship. None of the studies on Menzies, including the authoritative two-volume biography by A. W. Martin, makes any mention of the prime minister's connections with Australian Jewry. Meanwhile, the major narratives on the history

[1] Robert Menzies, "Anti-Semitism in Australia", Canberra, 26 January 1960.
[2] Tim Clarke, Bruce Belsham and Pru Goward, *The Liberals: Fifty Years of the Federal Party* [videorecording], Sydney: ABC Video Enterprises, 1994.

of the Jews in Australia by Rutland and Rubinstein among others make only very occasional references to Menzies, but do not probe his relationship with Australian Jewry in any great depth. What then was Menzies' relationship with the Jewish community? How had it been forged and in what ways did it manifest itself in the post-war Australia he led as prime minister?

As well as helping to salve the long-running sectarian wounds between Australia's Protestants and Catholics, Menzies enjoyed an excellent rapport with Australia's Jewish community. As Josh Frydenberg and David Kemp have acknowledged, "Sir Robert Menzies exhibited a marked degree of respect and admiration for the Jewish people" throughout his life.[3] As a friend of Israel, he deeply respected the Jewish legacy for its profound contribution to Western civilisation and admired the Jewish people for their cultural traditions of scholarship, civic-mindedness and enduring sense of kinship. Frequently invited to speak at ceremonies organised by the Jewish community, Menzies praised the Jewish people for their contribution to Australia. Remarking that he felt "completely at home" in the company of the Jewish community, Menzies enjoyed friendships with its leaders and rabbis including Sir Israel Brodie, Baron Snider, Maurice Ashkanasy and Herman Sanger. Together with exploring these relationships, this chapter will consider formative influences that contributed to Menzies' high esteem of the Jews, his avowed support for Israel, his stand against anti-Semitism and his affirmation of the Jewish community's place in the broader fabric of the nation.

For a Protestant prime minister who led what was then a majority Christian nation, of which the Jewish community comprised around 0.5 percent of the general population, what were the factors that accounted for his warm affinity with Australian Jewry? The first was arguably his own Presbyterian background where its theological tradition of Scottish Calvinism had generally fostered a "high esteem" for the Jewish people. Second, the young Menzies had moved in university, legal and

---

[3] Josh Frydenberg and David Kemp, "Menzies: An Enemy of Tyranny and Friend of Freedom", *The Australian Jewish News*, 24 January 2013.

political circles where he would have had personal encounters with the growing number of Jews active in public life in Victoria, coming to appreciate their sense of public duty. Third, the ethnic character of Australian and Melbourne Judaism during Menzies' early life was still largely anglophone which he found eminently congenial to his own cultural sensibilities. Finally, he appreciated that many in the Jewish community championed the values of faith, family, and community so integral to his creed of liberalism.

The Presbyterian tradition into which Menzies was born was not only critical to shaping his Christian beliefs but also relevant to informing his outlook on Judaism and the Jewish people. From the outset, this was a religious tradition that also influenced the attitudes of Australian society at large towards the Jews. Whilst Jews in Australia had historically faced discrimination and other legal disabilities, especially in the earlier colonial years, incidences of anti-Semitism and community antipathy towards Jews were relatively low, particularly when compared to some other nations in Europe. The Australian Jewish historian, Serge Liberman, attributed this to his observation that "Australia's Gentiles have, to a large extent, been heirs to a Calvinist-derived religious tradition which has shown considerable philo-Semitism and admiration for the Jews".[4] Liberman here was referring to Australia's Protestant ascendency, comprised chiefly of Anglicans, Presbyterians and some Nonconformists, whose attitudes to Jews, whilst far from perfect, were fairly enlightened and accommodating for their time, giving scope for Jews to contribute richly to Australian civic life. An exemplar of this approach was the co-founder of Port Phillip, John Pascoe Fawkner, who submitted the case for Jews on the basis of Christianity's Jewish ancestry. Praising Christ, the Apostles and King David for their Jewish lineage, the Melbourne pioneer called for no exertions to be spared "in order that Victoria might be the first of the British colonies to extend to the Jews their full rights as British citizens".[5]

[4] Serge Liberman, "Gentile Champions of Jews in Australia", W. D. Rubenstein (ed.), *Jews in the Sixth Continent*, Sydney: Allen & Unwin, 1987, p 77.
[5] Ibid., p 68.

From Fawkner to Menzies, Australia's Protestant ascendency was the inheritor of the British Calvinist (or puritan) tradition that promulgated what the historian and theologian, Donald M. Lewis, described as a "Teaching of Esteem" towards the Jews.[6] In their sermons, tracts and popular publications, these Protestants had portrayed the Jews not as 'Christ killers', as medieval theologians had typically done for centuries, but as "beloved for the father's sake".[7]

In contrast to other Protestants such as the Anabaptists, the disciples of the Reformation leader, John Calvin, affirmed both the Old and New Testaments of the Bible as equally inspired and authoritative. Together, they were revelations of the same unchangeable God. Accordingly, such Calvinists appreciated the indebtedness of their Christianity to the Hebrew Scriptures of the Old Testament, authored by the Jews and cherished by their descendants down the centuries. To Calvinist scholars, the Jews were esteemed not only for being God's original covenant people, but for their linguistic and philological skills. In Menzies' own Scots Presbyterian tradition, this appreciation was particularly evident. The Scots Confession of 1560, considered to be the foundational document of the Church of Scotland, celebrated the Jews as the "depositories of the Old Testament, and of Hebrew scholarship".[8]

On a number of public occasions, Menzies exhibited this characteristically Presbyterian appreciation of the Hebrew Scriptures, most notably when he welcomed establishment of Israel as a Jewish State in 1948. Hailing this milestone as one of "world significance" and "delivery from bondage" for the Jewish people, Menzies quoted a passage of verse that was, in part, a paraphrase of Exodus 20:2: "When Israel, of the Lord beloved, out of the land of

---

[6] Donald M Lewis, *The Origins of Christian Zionism: Lord Shaftesbury and Evangelical Support for a Jewish Homeland*, Cambridge: Cambridge University Press, 2014, p 12.

[7] In the words of the King James Version of Romans 11:28.

[8] Lewis, *Origins of Christian Zionism*, p 65.

bondage came, Her father's God before her moved an awful guide in smoke and flame".[9] Menzies took this line directly from the Scottish historical novelist, playwright and poet, Sir Walter Scott (1771-1832), who was likewise steeped in the Scots Presbyterian tradition. This passage, that celebrated God's deliverance of the Israelites from slavery in Egypt, appeared in a Presbyterian hymn composed by Scott in 1817, and again in his 1819 novel, *Ivanhoe*.[10] Having lived through the years of Nazi tyranny, Menzies evidently saw establishment of modern Israel and the deliverance it would usher in for the Jewish people as redolent of the great biblical drama of Exodus. In so thinking, he had invoked the Scottish hymn writer and his iteration of Hebrew verse for inspiration.

His esteem for the Hebrew Scriptures was also tied to the importance he ascribed to the Old Testament in moulding human character. In a speech in 1940 to mark the centenary of the British and Foreign Bible Society, Menzies paid tribute to the influence of the Bible on English-speaking peoples and drew particular attention to the contribution of the Hebrews. He acknowledged that while the Greeks had valued the importance of "knowledge" and clarity of thought, it was the Hebrews who had bequeathed to modern civilisation the importance of personal character and "quality of conduct". To illustrate, he retold the familiar story of David and Goliath, in which the future King of Israel demonstrated great courage and faith in triumphing over his Philistine adversary (1 Samuel 17:40-46). Twenty years later, in his second term as prime minister, Menzies reiterated similar themes when officiating at the opening of an extension to Mount Scopus Memorial College. Praising the role of Melbourne's leading Jewish school in forming the moral character in its pupils, Menzies again compared the Hebrew legacy to that of the Hellenistic, lauding the Hebrew tradition for the premium it placed on the 'quality of conduct' and the "enormous

---

[9] Robert Menzies, Speech on the Establishment of Israel as an Independent State, 1948, cited in David Furse-Roberts (ed.), *Menzies: The Forgotten Speeches*, Redland Bay [Qld]: Jeparit Press, 2017, p 234.
[10] The title of the hymn was, "When Israel, of the Lord beloved".

contribution" this made to the world.[11] To his Jewish audience, he acknowledged that he was in the presence of those who understood the Hebrew tradition "much better" than he did.

Tellingly, Menzies was not the only twentieth century statesman to exhibit this Calvinist-derived affection for the Jews. With the Calvinist interpretation of Scripture and its "teaching of esteem" exerting a wide impact on the attitudes of English-speaking Protestants towards the Jews, other public figures were similarly affected. Arthur Balfour, architect in 1917 of the Balfour Declaration that pledged support for establishment of a national home for the Jewish people in Palestine, was raised in a strongly evangelical Scottish Presbyterian home that no doubt informed his outlook. Like Balfour, David Lloyd George also had a Calvinistic background. Speaking to the Jewish Historical Society of England in 1925, the former prime minister of Britain highlighted how his Welsh Baptist upbringing, schooling and Sunday School had inculcated in him a "natural sympathy" toward the Jews and Zionism.[12]

In addition to his Presbyterian background, Menzies' high esteem for the Jews could be attributed to personal encounters he would have had with individual Jews in the educational, professional and political spheres he inhabited in Melbourne during the early decades of the twentieth century. Studies by Hilary L. Rubinstein reveal that from the gold rush era, Victoria's Jewish community became more established in public life with fifteen Jews serving in the Victorian Parliament between 1860 and 1901.[13] As well as politics, Victorian Jews were active in the legal profession. In Melbourne, these included the respected barrister, Samuel Leon, the legal scholar Louis Horwitz, who compiled the nine volume *Victorian Statutes* and, of course, Isaac Isaacs (1855-1948), whom Menzies would eventually meet. Called

---

[11] Robert Menzies, Opening of Senior School Building, Mount Scopus Memorial College, 18 September 1960, p 13. Robert Menzies Papers, NLA, MS4936, Box 210, Folder 131.

[12] Lewis, Christian Zionism, p 3.

[13] Rubinstein, Hilary L., *The Jews in Victoria 1835-1985*, Boston: Allen & Unwin, 1986, p 49.

Maurice Ashkanasy (1901-1971)

A leading figure in the Melbourne Jewish community, Ashkanasy was at various times President of the Executive Council of Australian Jewry, and also foundation President of the Jewish Board of Deputies in Victoria. Prior to admission to the Bar he read with Menzies and the two formed a life-long friendship. On one occasion in 1960 they shared a platform at the opening ceremony for a new building at Mount Scopus Memorial College. Menzies genially informed those present that Ashkanasy had been a pupil of his: "He read in my chambers when he went to the Bar and, of course, whatever success he has had since can be traced back just as the oak tree can to the acorn."

to the Bar in 1882, Isaacs served as Attorney-General of Victoria in the 1890s, a role Menzies himself would later fill from 1932 to 1934. In the 1890s, Isaacs was also a member of the Conventions on the Federation. Switching to Federal politics in 1901, Isaacs represented the Victorian seat of Indi before his appointment in 1906 as a Justice of the High Court. In 1930, he was appointed Chief Justice of the High Court and, within a year, Governor-General of Australia, the first Jew and Australian-born figure to hold that office.

The Victoria of Menzies' birth and early life was therefore one in which its Jewish community had already assumed a very active role in its professional and public life. By the time Menzies commenced his schooling at Wesley College in the years leading up to the Great War, a sizeable number of Jewish families were sending their children to Melbourne's leading private schools including Wesley, Scotch, Melbourne Grammar and Presbyterian Ladies College.[14] Owing to its fairly close proximity to St Kilda, Wesley College proved a popular choice for Jewish families. Along with Menzies, a number of these Jewish pupils eventually matriculated to the University of Melbourne into degrees such as law and medicine where the student composition would have again been comparable.

Entering Melbourne's legal circles after his admission to the Bar in 1918, Menzies joined a profession where Jews constituted a considerably higher percentage than that of the general population. As such, he would have had frequent contact with Jews as solicitors, barristers and members of the judiciary. The most eminent of these was Isaac Isaacs, who served as a judge on the bench of the High Court for the entire period Menzies was active at the Melbourne Bar. Isaacs was the author of the Court's main decision in the Engineers case (1920), in which Menzies appeared as counsel for the appellant.[15] Menzies had known Isaacs personally and offered this mixed assessment of the High Court judge and Governor-General:

[14] Ibid., p 80.
[15] *The Amalgamated Society of Engineers v The Adelaide Steamship Company Limited and Ors* (1920) 28 CLR 129. Menzies acted for the appellant, the Amalgamated Society of Engineers.

Issacs was a considerable scholar and a prodigious worker, deficient in humour and addicted to the writing of voluminous dissenting judgments; this addiction arose partly from vanity – he liked as many goods as possible in the shop window – and partly from a quite real difference of approach to the problems of constitutional interpretation.[16]

Despite some of these criticisms, Menzies admired Issacs as one of Australian Jewry's greatest sons. In his speech on the establishment of Israel as a state in 1948, Menzies singled out Issacs and Sir John Monash as "enduring and honoured names" of the Jewish community whom he praised as "great Australians".[17] For Menzies, a distinguished leader such as Issacs epitomised the positive contribution Jewish Australians had made to professional and public life.

The Jewish figure with whom Menzies had closest association, however, was the Melbourne barrister and Jewish community leader, Maurice Ashkanasy (1901-1971). Born in London, Ashkanasy was educated at Melbourne High School and the University of Melbourne where he graduated with a Master of Laws. Admitted to the Bar in 1924, he had read with Menzies for his Bar examinations and the two men forged a lifelong friendship. In conjunction with his legal career, Ashkanasy emerged as a leader of Melbourne's Jewish community, serving as President of the Executive Council of Australian Jewry and the foundation President of the Victorian Jewish Board of Deputies.[18] At special Jewish Community events, Prime Minister Menzies crossed paths with his old friend from the Bar. At a 1960 ceremony to open a new building at Mount Scopus Memorial College, Menzies and Ashkanasy shared the same platform. In his own speech, Menzies alluded to his protégé with some pride: 'He was a pupil of mine. He read in my chambers when he went to the Bar, and of course, whatever success he has had since can be traced back just as the oak tree can to the acorn'. Not least admiring

---

[16] Menzies, quoted in Ibid., p 176.

[17] Menzies, "Establishment of Israel", 1948.

[18] Zelman Cowen, "Ashkanasy, Maurice (1901-1971)", *ADB*, Volume 13, Melbourne University Press, 1993.

Ashkanasy's leadership role in the Jewish community, Menzies paid tribute to "the immense amount of work that he has contributed to this community". Invited by Ashkanasy in August 1963 to lay the foundation stone at the Kew Jewish Centre, Menzies again referred to his former pupil and remarked that even though they were on opposite sides of politics, with Ashkanasy active in the Labor Party, they were "always delighted to see each other".[19] For Menzies, it was enormously gratifying to see Ashkanasy making his mark not only in the law but in his leadership of the Victorian Jewish community.

Beyond the legal fraternity, freemasonry is the other sphere in which Menzies interacted closely with middle class, professional men of Jewish background. Menzies was a member of Melbourne's Austral Temple Lodge (No 110), where he was initiated on 10 March 1920 whilst working as a young barrister. With Roman Catholics prohibited by their Church from joining the lodge, and more devout evangelical Protestants shunning freemasonry for theological reasons, the majority of men who joined the masonic lodge in Australia early in the twentieth century tended to be either mainstream Protestants, predominantly Anglicans and Presbyterians such as Menzies or, indeed, Jews. According to Rubinstein, a considerable number of middle class Jews in Victoria, as in the rest of Australia, were active in freemasonry. Given that the fraternity specified only "belief in a Supreme Being" and "good character" as criteria for admission, it gave Jewish men "complete social equality" in the lodge.[20] For Menzies, freemasonry represented yet another domain in which he found common cause with Jews in the fraternity's commitment to fostering good character and serving the community.

As well as these formative spheres of influence, Menzies' positive disposition towards the Jewish community was also aided by the fact that Australian Jewry in the early decades of the twentieth century was still largely anglophone in character and outlook. These British

---

[19] Robert Menzies, Kew Jewish Centre Laying of Foundation Stone, Melbourne, 25 August 1963, p 1, Robert Menzies Papers, NLA, MS 4936, Box 276, Folder 185.

[20] Rubinstein, *Jews in Victoria*, p 81.

origins could be traced back to 1788 when a dozen Jewish convicts from London arrived with the First Fleet and were subsequently joined by successive numbers of English Jews, both convicts and free settlers.[21] Like Menzies, Jews in Australia cherished Australia's British colonial heritage, were loyal to the Crown and affirmed Australia's place in the British Empire. Prior to the larger numbers of Eastern European Jews that arrived in the waves of immigration before, and especially after, the Second World War, Australia's Jews were predominantly of British stock and this was evident in both their cultural characteristics and attitudes which, in many respects, aligned with those of Australia's Protestants.

Suzanne Rutland observed that the Jewish community sought to "conform to middle class English standards" and, as a result, became "more British than the British".[22] Liberman went so far as to describe the typical early Australian Jew as displaying an "intense Anglophilia".[23] Architecturally, the early synagogues of Melbourne and Sydney resembled English-style cathedrals. In Jewish religious life, the chief rabbis developed an Anglo-Jewish form of modern orthodoxy culturally conditioned by British and Anglo-Australian influences.[24] In political outlook as well, the Jewish community displayed pro-British sentiments that contrasted with those of Australia's Irish Catholics. For the safe, democratic haven that Australia had afforded them, Jews felt a strong sense of obligation to their new homeland and loyalty to the British Empire of which it was part. This was evident with the outbreak of the Great War when Australia's Jews rallied to support the war effort. Rabbi Francis Lyon Cohen of Sydney's Great Synagogue, and Rabbi Jacob Dangalow of the St Kilda Hebrew Congregation in Melbourne, encouraged their congregants to contribute by either enlisting or serving on the home front. With public debate raging over the two

---

[21] Suzanne D. Rutland, *The Jews in Australia*, Melbourne: Cambridge University Press, 2005, p 11.

[22] Ibid., p 9.

[23] Liberman, "Gentile Champions", p 77.

[24] Rutland, *Jews in Australia*, p 9.

conscription referenda called by Billy Hughes, in 1916 and 1917, Australian Jewry joined most Protestants to side with the "Yes" case.[25] Menzies did not make any secret of his own Anglophilia and affection for the Crown, and the kindred sentiments of Australian Jews during this period did much to endear that community to him. It was undoubtedly one of the reasons why he valued the Jewish community as not just being *in* Australia but *of* Australia.[26]

It was not, however, simply the traditional pro-British disposition of Australian Jewry that impressed Menzies. It was also the innate characteristics of the Jewish religion itself for which Menzies accorded high praise. Chief amongst these was its emphasis on faith, family and community, nourished through thousands of years of war, peace and persecution. Opening the Jewish War Memorial Hall in the Sydney suburb of Waverley in February 1960, Menzies pointed to three attributes that distinguished the Jewish community. Beginning with their tenacious adherence to their "faith", Menzies remarked:

> You've been persecuted for it in the course of the centuries; you've been attacked for it; you've almost been ordered to abandon it from time to time and you have adhered to it through thick and thin until it has been hammered into true steel. Now that's a wonderful thing – your deep, loyal and abiding religious faith.[27]

Describing himself as an "unblushing Presbyterian", Menzies deeply respected the faith of the world's oldest monotheistic religion. Through the sacred writings of the *Torah* and the *Talmud*, he recognised that it had gifted Christianity and, indeed, the wider world, with the belief in a sovereign, just and loving God as the creator and ruler of the universe, the concept that all human beings bore the image of God, the decalogue of Moses, the lively oracles of the Old Testament prophets and the hope in the resurrection of

[25] Ibid., p 46.
[26] Robert Menzies, Menzies Forest Inauguration Gala Concert, Canberra, 23 October 1965, p 2, Robert Menzies Papers, NLA, MS 4936, Box 283, Folder 228.
[27] Menzies, Jewish War Memorial Hall, 7 February 1960.

the dead. Presiding as prime minister over the post-war immigration of thousands of displaced Jews from Germany, Austria, Poland, Russia, Hungary and other parts of war-torn Europe, Menzies was acutely aware of the persecution they had suffered. With the Nazis attempting to extinguish every vestige of their faith and cultural identity, he marvelled at the resilience of Australia's Jews in being able to rekindle their religious beliefs in a free country.

Menzies' appreciation of the Jewish faith tradition again came to the fore when he issued a press release in 1962 to mark the Jewish New Year, known as *Rosh Hashanah*. Sending his "cordial greetings to members of the Australian Jewish community", the Prime Minister reflected that "on this most important holiday in the Jewish Calendar, it is appropriate to look over the past year and to look forward, to renew friendships, to cancel disputes, to eschew enmity, and to seek atonement in its real sense". On *Rosh Hashanah*, Jews believe that God reviews the state of His creation and examines the deeds of men and women.[28] To mark the day, a ram's horn (*shophar*) is blown in the synagogue and Jewish families partake in a feast of apples dipped in honey to wish others a "good and sweet new year".[29] With Menzies making mention of 'atonement' in his New Year greetings, he would have also had in mind the 'Day of Atonement', or *Yom Kippur*, falling just ten days after *Rosh Hashanah*. This day is typically characterised by fasting, prayer and public confession of sin where atonement is sought through personal repentance. *Yom Kippur* is seen to offer believers a fresh start where they consider themselves to have been spiritually reborn.[30] As a Presbyterian familiar with Christianity's own theme of atonement through the blood of Christ, Menzies appreciated the profound significance of restitution, fresh beginnings and spiritual rebirth for Australia's Jews. He accordingly praised the restorative impulses of the Jewish festivals as "admirable aims".

---

[28] Apple, Raymond, *The Jewish Way: Jews and Judaism in Australia*, Sydney: The Great Synagogue, 2002, p 53.

[29] Pat Alexander, *The World's Religions* (Lion Handbooks), Oxford: Lion Publishing, 1996, p 274.

[30] Ibid.

The second virtue of the Jewish community that Menzies drew attention to was its "remarkable sense of family". For Menzies, the Jews were the great exemplars of "family values" in Australia. Praising them for their filial piety, he observed:

> I have never known a Jewish family in which the welfare of the family wasn't the constant task of the lot. Now that's a marvellous thing because the family – a good family, a healthy family, a proud family, a family generous in itself – this is of the very essence of community life. There can be no great nations without great family feeling and I admire your community immensely because all through my life I have observed this extraordinary, devoted sense of family pride and family responsibility.[31]

This devotion to family that Menzies so admired sprang from the centrality of family life to Jewish belief and practice. Rabbi Raymond Apple noted that "home and family life have always held supreme importance for Jews". The family home is the sphere in which parents not only raise their children but inculcate them with the values of their Jewish heritage by teaching the Scriptures and observing the festivals. So much of Jewish life is centred upon the home and, together with the synagogue, the mini-community of the household provides a relaxed, natural environment to experience Jewish life. In the Jewish home, the ideal is *Shalom bayit* – family harmony. Jewish tradition teaches that members of a family love and respect each other. Children are commanded to honour father and mother, and parents, in turn, are called to "make people out of children", or "*machen menschen fon kinder*" (in Yiddish). During times of persecution, the Jewish home represented a sanctuary of comfort and refuge.[32]

With community representing the family writ large, Jewish emphasis on community service and civic obligation also excited the admiration of Menzies. In what he termed "friendliness", he praised Australia's Jewish community for its desire to contribute its "great

---

[31] Menzies, Jewish War Memorial Hall, 7 February 1960.

[32] Apple, *Jewish Way*, pp 51-52.

talents and immense industry" to the life of the nation. In the Victoria of his youth, Menzies had witnessed Melbourne Jewry's considerable contributions to the legal profession and politics, and now, as prime minister, in the post-war years, he admired the ways in which a fresh wave of Jewish immigrants and refugees from Eastern Europe were enriching the business, professional, community and public life of Australia. As with family, this Jewish commitment to community and nation was deeply rooted in faith. Their contribution to Australia was inspired consciously, or otherwise, by the exhortation of the Old Testament prophet Jeremiah to "seek the peace and welfare of the place in which one dwells".[33]

For Jews, this was made all the more possible by Australia's values of equality and religious freedom. Affirming this reality, Menzies told his Jewish audience that for "those who have come into Australia, particularly since the war, out of the horrors of Europe, in particular, I know that you've breathed more freely since you came here and that you are in a free land". For Menzies, Australia would be all the richer as a country if the Jewish community's championing of faith, family and "civic friendliness" could be given as much of a free rein as possible. These very values had formed the bedrock of Menzies' Liberal philosophy that he saw as key to Australia's flourishing beyond the Second World War. In the *Forgotten People* speech of May 1942, Menzies had spoken about the importance of humanity's dependence upon God, the "home" as representing the foundation of "sanity and sobriety", and the "great question" that needed to be asked of "How can I qualify my son to help society?". With Menzies seeing Australia's recent Jewish arrivals as epitomising these very attributes in their religious and cultural customs, he esteemed the Jewish community for its contribution to realizing his vision for a socially thriving, post-war Australia.

Support for Israel

Recognising the pre-eminent spiritual significance of Israel to Jewish history and identity, Menzies emerged in the post-war years as a

---

[33] Ibid., p 20.

Sir Israel Brodie (1895-1979)

A contemporary of Menzies, Brodie was a close ally of the Prime Minister in his support for Israel. Serving as rabbi to the Melbourne Hebrew Congregation, Brodie co-founded the Zionist Federation of Australia in 1927 and became the chief rabbi to the British Commonwealth in 1948.

warm friend of Israel, applauding its creation as a modern state in 1948. By the time Menzies welcomed the creation of modern Israel, Australian Jewish opinion was more or less of similar mind, but this had certainly not always been the case. The modern Zionist movement to create a Jewish state on the ancient soil of Israel had emerged in the latter part of the nineteenth century in much of the English-speaking world.[34] The Zionist cause in Australia was championed largely by Jews and some evangelical Protestants, but even within the Jewish community, support for establishing a modern Israel was far from unanimous during the first half of the twentieth century. The factors that mitigated against the Zionist cause during this time included Australia's geographical remoteness, the relatively small size of the Jewish community (especially pre-1930s) and, perhaps most significantly, the concern that support for and allegiance to a future state of Israel would detract from the existing loyalty of Australian Jews to the British Crown.[35]

Together with the *Australian Jewish Standard*, a Perth-based community newspaper, the most vocal and powerful voice for this anti-Zionist sentiment was Sir Isaac Isaacs. The reasons for his objection to the creation of a Jewish state were complex. In addition to seeing it as compromising the strong devotion of Australian Jews to the British Crown, he believed that a Jewish state in Palestine would encourage Australian Jews to think that instead of being proud citizens of Australia, they were simply sojourners in exile divorced from their true homeland of the Middle East.[36] Furthermore, he feared that creation of such a state could make Australian Jews the target of anti-Semitism where their demands for Jewish statehood could be viewed with suspicion and contempt by the wider public.[37] This contrasted with the views of both Menzies and the majority of the Jewish community who would see no such tension between supporting Israel and maintaining their long-held allegiance to Australia and the Crown.

---

[34] Rutland, *Jews in Australia*, p 80.
[35] Ibid., p 82.
[36] Rubinstein, *Jews in Victoria*, p 174.
[37] Ibid.

The lead apologist for this majority pro-Zionist view was the highly respected engineer and military hero, General Sir John Monash. Together with Rabbi Israel Brodie, with whom Menzies enjoyed a close association, Monash co-founded the Zionist Federation of Australia in 1927. According to Alan Crown, these two figures were a major factor in helping to mobilise Anglo-Jewish support for the Zionist cause. With Monash's brilliant war service, it was difficult for anti-Zionist Jews to accuse Monash of any disloyalty to the Crown.[38] As well as the inspired leadership of Monash, other developments that swayed the bulk of Australian Jewry to support Zionism from the 1930s onwards were the rise of Nazism and the influx of European Jewish immigrants to Australia between 1938 and 1961. Fleeing from violent anti-Semitism and then the ravages of war, these refugees felt acutely the need for a Jewish homeland to provide a sanctuary from persecution.[39]

As well as mobilisation of popular Jewish support for Zionism, the actions of the immediate post-war Labor government had helped pave the way for Menzies to harness Australian goodwill towards Israel. Led by Ben Chifley, prime minister from 1945 to 1949, the Australian Government played a key role in the establishment of the State of Israel in 1948.[40] The Minister for External Affairs, Dr H. V. Evatt, not only contributed to the founding of the United Nations but chaired the UN Ad Hoc Committee on Palestine that voted in favour of Resolution 181 to bring the new State of Israel into being. Evatt was serving as President of the UN General Assembly when Israel was admitted as a member on 11 May 1949.[41] Initially, Evatt had been sympathetic to the anti-Zionist position of his friend, Issacs, but was persuaded by two eminent Jewish legal scholars, Professor Julius Stone and Louis D. Brandeis, to support the Zionist cause.[42]

[38] Alan D. Crown, "Demography, Politics and Love of Zion": The Australian Jewish Community and the Yishuv, 1850-1948", Rubinstein, *Sixth Continent*, p 234.
[39] Rutland, *Jews in Australia*, p 85.
[40] Ibid., p 86.
[41] Ibid., p 87.
[42] Crown, "Demography, Politics and Love of Zion", pp 244-245.

For his contribution to the establishment of Israel, Evatt was feted by the Australian Jewish community at a dinner held in his honour by the Zionist Federation.

In spite of the many policy differences Menzies had with his immediate Labor predecessors, Australian foreign policy on Israel was emphatically bipartisan and Menzies applauded the creation of the modern State of Israel as both a milestone for Israel's Jews and a significant moment for Australia's Jewish community. In a short yet powerful speech to commemorate the establishment of Israel in 1948, Menzies declared that "the civilised world saw in the establishment of Israel not only the providing of an independent home to many Jewish people but also a shining symbol of delivery from bondage". Reflecting upon the oppression and discrimination that the Jewish people around the world had suffered through the ages, from the medieval pogroms to the horrors of the holocaust, Menzies welcomed the establishment of Israel as a new beginning for the world's Jews to thrive and prosper once again. Familiar with the Old Testament, Menzies drew on the perennial themes of "deliverance" and "redemption" that originated in the Exodus of the Israelites from slavery in Egypt under Pharaoh.

With the much more immediate historical backdrop of Nazism, Menzies drew on another biblical theme to welcome the establishment of Israel as a symbol of "world repentance". With even the best efforts of the Allies in the Second Word War failing to avert the extermination of six million Jews in central Europe, Menzies saw the support of Australia and the free world for the establishment of Israel as a gesture to provide the global Jewish community with at least some recompense for the incalculable losses it had suffered at the hands of the Nazi regime. In this spirit of world contrition, Menzies was joined by the remarkable leader of post-war Germany, Konrad Adenauer, who felt a particular weight of responsibility for the past deeds of his own country. Like Menzies, Chancellor Adenauer was a statesman of the centre-right who presided over a long period of his country's economic growth and prosperity. One of Adenauer's signature foreign policies was the *Luxemburger Abkommen,* a

reparations scheme by which West Germany agreed to pay Israel for
resettlement of Jewish refugees, and to compensate individual Jews
for losses resulting from Nazi persecution.

In the domestic realm, Menzies' firm support for Israel reflected
the leadership of the Australian Jewish community that was more
unequivocally Zionist than at any previous time. His protégé, Maurice
Ashkanasy, welcomed establishment of Israel as "Zionist aspiration
translated into reality" and remained active in the Executive Council
of Australian Jewry.[43] He was joined by Rabbis Israel Brodie, who
became the chief rabbi of the British Commonwealth in 1948,
and Herman Sanger of Melbourne. As co-founder of the Zionist
Federation of Australia in 1927, Brodie had been a longstanding
supporter of the cause. He believed that Zionism was not only just in
itself, but a necessary corollary of Judaism and a stimulus to Jewish
consciousness.[44] Likewise Sanger, whom Menzies declared to be
"Australia's greatest orator", was one of the few outspoken Zionists
before the Second World War and was responsible for enlisting many
of Melbourne's European Jewish refugees to the cause.[45]

Menzies and his government continued to provide strong support
to Israel after coming to office in December 1949. With the Suez
Crisis of 1956 bringing Israel, France and Britain into conflict with
Egypt over control of the international shipping waterway, Menzies
not only sided with Britain and France but spoke in support of
Israel's interests. In a speech in the House of Representatives about
Australia's position on the Suez crisis, Menzies affirmed that "the
people of Israel have a perfect right to know that their national
integrity will be respected".[46] With the Suez crisis representing yet
another flashpoint in the long history of conflict between Israel

---

[43] Cowen, "Ashkanasy", *ADB*.
[44] Hilary I. Rubinstein, "Brodie, Sir Israel (1895-1979)", *ADB*, Volume 13, Melbourne University Press, 1993.
[45] J. S. Levi, "Sanger, Herman Max (1909-1980)", *ADB*, Volume 16, Melbourne University Press, 2002.
[46] Robert Menzies, *Commonwealth Parliamentary Debates*, House of Representatives, 8 November 1956.

and its Arab neighbours, Menzies was eager to see the territorial integrity of the Jewish State respected. Towards the end of his long prime ministership, Menzies reaffirmed his affection for Israel at an Israel Gala Concert in Canberra on 23 October 1965. Once again invoking the biblical story of Exodus, Menzies saw the modern State of Israel as providing for the Jews, at a second great time in history, a sanctuary for an oppressed people delivered from the "house of bondage". At the concert, the Jewish community presented the prime minister and his wife with an olivewood-bound testimonial deed prepared in Jerusalem acknowledging the planting and naming of a forest in his honour in the Hills of Samaria in the Galilee region of the Holy Land. Accepting the deed, Menzies said Australia's 70 000 Jews were making a wonderful contribution to the Commonwealth. The affection was reciprocated, with Baron Snider of the Victorian Parliament remarking that Australian Jews had funded the memorial forest "to honour Australia's greatest citizen".[47]

Stance against anti-Semitism

With the gruesome legacy of Nazism still fresh in public consciousness, Menzies as prime minister was instinctively at one with the Jewish community in his stand against anti-Semitism, both in Australia and internationally. According to Rubinstein, it was reasonable to conclude that the public exposé of the extermination camps and other Nazi atrocities "did more than anything else to discredit old fashioned right wing and racist anti-Semitism".[48] In Australia, the other factor that contributed to the decline of anti-Jewish prejudices was the admission and settlement of substantial numbers of Central and Eastern European Jews since 1947 that helped to broaden public attitudes towards different races and cultures. A report in 1957 on Australia in *The American Jewish Year Book* observed that "Australian Jewry enjoyed the same civic and political status as all

---

[47] "Israel Honours the Menzies", *Canberra Times*, 25 October 1965, p 1.
[48] Rubinstein, *Jews in Victoria*, p 179.

other Australians [where] anti-Semitism was at a minimum.'[49] That said, Menzies was aware that pockets of prejudice against Jews still existed in post-war Australia and this was something he needed to take a lead in opposing as a matter of principle.

Where anti-Semitism did surface, it emanated mostly from what Menzies himself called the "lunatic fringe". This was inhabited largely by extreme right-wing groups such as the Australian League of Rights. Founded by Eric Butler in 1946, the League exuded a veneer of conservative respectability with its motto of "loyalty to God, King and Country", yet this disguised a dark, anti-Semitic underbelly. The League frequently published anti-Semitic materials and promoted the notorious *Protocols of the Elders of Zion*, a fabricated anti-Semitic text purporting to expose a Jewish plot for world domination. Entering the House of Representatives in 1955 as a young MP, Malcolm Fraser recalled that Menzies told him to have nothing do with Butler or his organisation. Anti-Semitism manifested itself in other forms such as offensive graffiti scrawled in public places, threatening letters, insulting phone calls and even carefully considered commercial advertisements.[50] Discrimination against Jews also appeared to persist in some organisations such as exclusive gentlemen's clubs and the Melbourne Stock Exchange which did not elect its first Jewish member until 1960.[51]

On at least two occasions, Menzies went public to denounce these incidents of community anti-Semitism. On Australia Day 1960, he issued a statement on "Anti-Semitism in Australia", prompted by evidence of what he called "the painting up of slogans on walls and other malicious or foolish activities".[52] Noting how "many of our Jewish fellow citizens are genuinely distressed at these recent events", Menzies declared that "there is absolutely no room in Australia

---

[49] Billie Einfeld, "Australia", *The Australian Jewish Yearbook*, Volume 58, 1957, p 370.

[50] Rubinstein, *Jews in Victoria*, p 202.

[51] Ibid.

[52] Robert Menzies, Statement on Anti-Semitism in Australia, Canberra, 26 January 1960, Robert Menzies Papers, NLA, MS 4936, Box 269, Folder 124.

for anti-Semitism, no justification for it, and that I believe there is no real substance in it".[53] With the legacy of the holocaust serving emphatically to discredit anti-Semitism, Menzies honestly could not see any moral or intellectual rationale for the prejudice. Accordingly, he concluded that "any attempt to create an anti-Jewish feeling in Australia is doomed to failure".[54] Confident, however, in the decent, tolerant outlook of mainstream Australians, Menzies suspected that such incidents were "those of irresponsible people on the lunatic fringe". Reiterating similar sentiments in a speech to open the Jewish War Memorial Hall the following month, Menzies assured his Jewish audience that such anti-Semitic activity did not "represent anybody of intelligent, decent Australian opinion and it never will".[55]

Menzies' stance against anti-Semitism extended to the international front where Australia became the first country to debate the matter of Soviet Jewry in the Commonwealth Parliament and then raise the issue at the United Nations in the early 1960s.[56] In the post-war Soviet Union, most notably under the dictatorship of Joseph Stalin, Jews in Soviet Russia had been the victims of state-sponsored anti-Semitism, and after 1958, the situation only deteriorated further with synagogues closed, the baking of Passover bread forbidden and a high proportion of Jews sentenced to death for economic crimes. Following requests from members of Australia's Jewish community, most notably from Isi Leibler of the Victorian Jewish Board of Deputies, the Minister for External Affairs, Sir Garfield Barwick, agreed to bring ill-treatment of Soviet Jews to the attention of the UN in November 1962. Overruling the concerns of some officials in the Department of External Affairs, Barwick directed Australian diplomats to criticise Soviet policies towards their Jewish citizens in the UN Third Committee, proposing that the Soviet Union either change their treatment or,

---

[53] Ibid.
[54] Ibid.
[55] Menzies, Jewish War Memorial Hall, 7 February 1960.
[56] Suzanne D. Rutland, 'Australia and the Struggle for Soviet Jewry: 1961-1972', *Australian Journal of Politics and History*, Vol 60, No 2, 2014, p 197.

alternatively, permit emigration.[57] Australia's statement to the UN predictably incurred the ire of the Soviet Union but attracted warm praise from the Israeli Government. Subsequently, in the House of Representatives, Menzies himself alluded to the Soviet Jewry issue when he denounced anti-Semitic Soviet propaganda such as *Judaism without Embellishment* (1963) as that "wretched publication". He assured his parliamentary colleagues in April 1964 that Australia would express its opposition both to racial and religious intolerance at the nineteenth session of the UN General Assembly later that year.[58]

Australian Jewry: integrated yet distinctive

In repudiating anti-Semitism, Menzies affirmed the special place of the Jewish community in Australia. In his 1960 anti-Semitism statement, Menzies noted that "There is a long history in Australia of distinguished service to our country of Jewish citizens. The Jews in Australia are good Australians".[59] From his own careers in law and politics, Menzies had firsthand awareness of the manifold contributions Jews had made to Australian professional and public life. From his own formative years in the Victoria of the early twentieth century, the Jews were never a people "in exile" nor a ghettoised community that kept to themselves. They were an integrated, active and, on the whole, esteemed strand within the broad community tapestry.

With Jewish figures such as Isaacs fearful that support for the establishment of Israel as a Jewish state could foster segregationist impulses both from within and outside the Jewish community, Menzies made the point that whilst the founding of Israel provided a special homeland for the Jewish people, it did not in any way imply that Australia's Jews should be considered a separate people from the rest of Australia. In 1948, Menzies had stressed that the 70 000 Jews in Australia were "not only *in* Australia but *of* Australia":

For here, you are not, and should not be, a race apart. In

[57] Ibid., p 212.
[58] Robert Menzies, *Commonwealth Parliamentary Debates*, House of Representatives, 15 April 1964.
[59] Menzies, Anti-Semitism in Australia, 26 January 1960.

this free country, all are free; all are equal before the law; religious or sectional prejudices tend to "fade into the light of common day" … The great Jewish contribution to Australia is not sectional or sectarian but a community contribution, neither discriminating nor being discriminated against.[60]

He articulated similar sentiments in 1962 when officiating at the opening of a Jewish aged care facility. The Prime Minister told his audience of Jews that: "I marvel more and more at what your community has been able to do and when I say your community, no-one knows better than I do that it has not made itself something apart in Australia, it has infused its influence throughout Australia".[61] Speaking from the historical standpoint of observing more than fifteen years of post-war immigration to Australia, Menzies was able to appreciate how Jewish immigrants and refugees, often arriving with so few possessions, were able to bring new industrial skills to Australian industries, start new businesses, excel in the arts and contribute to the professions, thereby helping to give shape to modern Australia.[62]

At the same time as affirming the full embrace of Australia's Jews within the national fabric, Menzies was also sensitive to their desire to conserve their own heritage, character and identity forged over thousands of years. In a speech to open a Jewish college in Melbourne, it was evident he saw no tension between these two imperatives:

> I don't know of any group in the community which preserves its character, its family character, its intimate association, its own pride and its own faith, while at the same time, being so integrally bound up with the community as a whole.[63]

Whilst Menzies is frequently viewed by historians as a champion of assimilation, whereby immigrants of different cultural and religious backgrounds were compelled to relinquish their old ways to conform

---

[60] Menzies, Establishment of Israel, 1948.

[61] Menzies, Montefiore Jewish Home Opening, 19 August 1962.

[62] Rutland, Jews in Australia, pp 120-121.

[63] Menzies, Mount Scopus Memorial College, 18 September 1960.

to existing Australian customs and beliefs, the reality with Menzies was more nuanced. To be sure, he was no modern multiculturalist in the mould of an Al Grassby or a Malcolm Fraser, as he still held to a hegemonic British cultural paradigm, yet his ambition for modern Australia was not necessarily one of bland cultural conformity.

Menzies, for his part, envisioned a British-derived Australian society enriched by "the lively imaginations of thousands of people whose cultural background is remote from our own".[64] Accordingly, when it came to Australian Jewry, he embraced them as part of the broader Australian community with their own religious and cultural identity intact.

---

[64] Robert Menzies, Opening of the Citizenship Convention in Canberra, 22 January 1958.

7

Christianity, Liberalism
and Anti-communism

*In a civilised community, not one of us can
live to himself. In the immortal phrase of St
Paul, "we are members one of another". My
freedom must be limited if I am to live at
peace with my neighbour and his freedom.*[1]

Together with a predecessor, Alfred Deakin, and a successor, John
Howard, Robert Menzies was one of the three great exponents of
Australian Liberalism. Born in the late Victorian age and educated in
the early decades of the twentieth century, Menzies represented the
Australian liberal tradition of Deakin as well as the earlier British Whig
liberalism of Edmund Burke, T. B. Macaulay and W. E. Gladstone. The
Liberal Party founded by Menzies in the 1940s affirmed the values of
individual freedom and dignity, private property rights, free enterprise,
class harmony, cooperation between employer and employee as
well as the freedoms of speech, religion and association. As in other
Western nations, these principles were informed by both the British
Lockean Enlightenment and the Judeo-Christian tradition. As both
Larry Siedentop and Tom Holland acknowledge, Christianity played a
foundational role in shaping the liberal precepts of human dignity and
equality which helped to define modern societies in the West.[2]

---

[1] Robert Menzies, William Queale Memorial Lecture, 22 October 1954.
[2] Siedentop, *Inventing the Individual*, 2014; Tom Holland, *Dominion: The
Making of the Western Mind*, London: Abacus, 2020.

Australia was no exception as the Liberal creed expounded by
Menzies sprang likewise from this spiritual well. Menzies' Liberal
philosophy was not explicitly Christian in a confessional sense,
as befits a secular polity such as Australia's, but this chapter will
demonstrate that it drew considerably from the Protestant tradition
of cultural puritanism and aligned closely with much Catholic social
teaching. This infusion of Christian thought became evident in the
platforms of the new Liberal Party. With this spiritual complexion,
Menzies' Liberalism affirmed that Judeo-Christian precepts of human
dignity and freedom, the natural law, private property, the family
and neighbourly love were fundamental both to the character of civil
society and the survival of freedom. As such, Menzies regarded the
spectre of Cold War communism as a perilous threat. This chapter
will reveal that his opposition to the ideology was not only economic
and geopolitical, but innately moral and spiritual.

A Christian-inspired Australian Liberalism

As the antidote to the "soulless materialism" propagated by the
menace of either Soviet communism or Nazism/fascism, Menzies
espoused a Liberalism for post-war Australia infused with Christian
ideals. At least in its understanding of the divine origins of human
dignity and freedom, it was not philosophically dissimilar to either the
British Whig liberalism of Burke and Gladstone, the US Republican
tradition of Lincoln or, more contemporaneously, the Christian
democracy of post-war Europe, most notably in West Germany.
Like democratic traditions in both Europe and the United States,
Menzies' own philosophy of liberalism was based on a conception
of democracy that viewed all individuals as possessing equal dignity
and worth in the sight of God. Speaking in October 1942 on the
"Nature of Democracy", Menzies pronounced:

> Democracy is more than a machine, it is a spirit. It is based
> upon the Christian conception that there is in every human
> soul a spark of the divine; that, with all their inequalities of
> mind and body, the souls of men stand equal in the sight
> of God.

For Menzies, this foundation of liberal democracy was basic and broad enough to appeal to Protestants, Catholics, Jews and other Australians of faith, particularly when counterposed with the common enemy of "godless communism".

The Christian ideals of the Australian Liberalism that Menzies revived in the 1940s were evident in its applause for humane social reforms, affirmation of a selfless individualism, pursuit of a "good neighbour" foreign policy, commitment to a civilised capitalism, and appeal to the "natural law". Much of this character to the Liberalism of Menzies could be attributed to the historical reality that he represented an heir to the Federation Liberal tradition of Alfred Deakin. Menzies made little secret of his admiration for his fellow-Victorian predecessor, lauding him as "one of the greatest men we ever had in Australia".[3] In the tradition of Deakin, Menzies held to a Liberal vision for constitutional liberty under the Crown, responsible citizenship, industrial justice, high living standards and a regulated free enterprise that eschewed the extremes of *laissez-faire* capitalism and socialism. Deeply influenced by the idealist social liberalism of the British philosopher, T. H. Green, Deakin held to a non-utilitarian form of social liberalism that affirmed the primacy of the common good, the moral duties of the individual citizen within society, and the place for ameliorative social reform. In this vein, Deakin had supported factory legislation and minimum wages to ensure that "wealth would be prevented from taking unfair advantage of the needy" and that "all should have what was their due".[4]

Such social reform measures had deep Christian roots, both in the Evangelical social activism of figures such as Wilberforce and Shaftesbury, and in the Catholic social teaching of Pope Leo XIII. Menzies, likewise, had identified with these social reform impulses of liberalism, welcoming "abolition of slavery, "abolition

---

[3] Robert Menzies, "Commercial Travellers Association (CTA) Smoke Social", Melbourne, 9 August 1958, Robert Menzies Papers, NLA, MS 4936, Box 265, Folder 102.

[4] Alfred Deakin, "What is Liberalism?" (1895), cited in Marian Sawer, *The Ethical State: Social Liberalism in Australia*, Melbourne University Press, 2003, p 36.

of child labour" and "the compulsory fixing of wages and industrial conditions on a civilised basis" as some of the great achievements of liberal democracy.[5] In his own record as prime minister, he had also presided over the humane reform to aged care through the *Aged Persons Homes Act 1954* (Cth).

With individualism characteristically representing one of the defining traits of liberalism, Menzies' own particular emphasis on a *selfless individualism* gave his Liberal creed a decidedly Christian inflexion. By "selfless individualism", Menzies meant that whilst the state fulfilled an important ameliorative role, it fell primarily to the compassionate spirit and self-sacrifice of individuals to succour the needy and further the common good. In short, it was the moral character and agency of individual men and women who determined the well-being of society. For Menzies, the ethic of selfless individualism could be summed up in the biblical concept of being "my brother's keeper",[6] whereby individuals took responsibility for the welfare of their neighbours. Hailing it as the "noblest embodiment of the Christian philosophy",[7] this ethic was so foundational to Menzies that he once observed that the "oldest expression of democracy" was inherent in the question, "Am I my brother's keeper?"[8] When he founded the Liberal Party late in 1944, he invoked the biblical phrase when emphasising the selfless nature of the new Party's individualistic focus:

> If we stand for anything as Liberals we stand for the inescapable responsibility of the individual, his dignity, his significance, his responsibility for every other individual. In that sense we are an individualist movement, not in the

---

[5] Robert Menzies, "The Achievements of Democracy", *Forgotten People*, pp 182-183.

[6] In Genesis 4:9., Cain asked "Am I my brother's keeper?" when the Lord asked him, "Where is Abel thy brother?"

[7] Robert Menzies, "Freedom in Modern Society", 1935.

[8] Robert Menzies, Wesley Church PSA, "Democracy and Sir Alan Newton", Melbourne, 4 September 1949, Robert Menzies Papers, NLA, MS 4936, Box 254, Folder 21.

bad sense of saying, "Each for himself and the devil take the hindmost", but in the good sense of saying that every man is his brother's keeper.[9]

From its inception, the individualist ethos of the Liberal Party perceived individual men and women as beings existing and flourishing within the rich social tapestries of family, friends, community and nation. In its appeal to individual unselfishness, it channelled Frederic Eggleston's principle of "the good neighbour", that the Australian liberal philosopher saw as integral to what he called "the Christian ethic".[10] Drawing upon his Methodist heritage, Eggleston warned that "enlightened selfishness" was "not enough" and that "the separate pursuit of material good" would result "in chaos" and "wreck the social structure".[11] On the other hand, the "Christian ethic" of "individual social responsibility" that Eggleston regarded as the "essence of moral character", made it possible for individuals to co-operate in all circumstances. It was a principle to which Menzies held fast. As he told an audience of Young Liberals in 1963, if Liberalism stood for anything, it was "civic unselfishness"; "a passion to contribute to the nation, to be free but to be contributors".[12] As such, it was a vision for individuals that went far beyond Mill's minimalist ethic of "no harm" to others.

The Christian ideals of Menzies' Liberalism also came to the fore in its outlook on foreign policy. As well as promoting a selfless ethic amongst individual citizens, the Liberal creed of Menzies applied a similar principle to nation states such as Australia. In what could be characterised as a selfless patriotism or a benevolent internationalism, the Liberal philosophy of Menzies held that a prosperous nation

[9] Robert Menzies, Speech at Conclusion of Albury Conference (to Inaugurate the Liberal Party), 16 December 1944, Robert Menzies Papers, NLA, MS 4936, Box 253, Folder 14.

[10] Frederic Eggleston, *Search for a Social Philosophy*, Melbourne University Press, 1941, p 320.

[11] Ibid., p 325.

[12] Robert Menzies, "Speech to Young Liberal Movement Convention", Sydney, 27 July 1962, Robert Menzies Papers, NLA, MS 4936, Box 274, Folder 167.

like Australia not only had loyalties to its traditional North Atlantic allies, but special obligations to help its poorer neighbours in the Asia Pacific region.

In practical policy terms, Menzies called this Australia's "good neighbour" policy. Initially announced in his 1949 Election Speech, this policy with Australia's Asia-Pacific neighbours would entail friendly trade and commerce, humanitarian aid and technical assistance, cultural cooperation and bilateral defence partnerships. In employing the phrase, "good neighbour", this critical limb of Menzies' foreign policy took its cue from Christ's parable of the "Good Samaritan". Australia's "good neighbour" policy in the Asia-Pacific found its most tangible expression in the Colombo Plan of 1950, which facilitated educational and cultural exchange between Australia and its regional neighbours, followed by the SEATO defence pact of 1954, that brought Australia into military partnership with nations such as Pakistan, Thailand and the Philippines. In particular, the good neighbour policy of Menzies had Australia's northern neighbour, Indonesia, in its sights. During a period of confrontation over Malaysia, Menzies told an audience in New York in 1964 that "We have one ambition as far as Indonesia is concerned, and that is that we should be good neighbours and friendly neighbours and live in peace and occasionally make some contribution to the much-needed economic improvement of that country".[13]

To place it in its due historical context, Menzies' good neighbour policy was a part of the benign liberal internationalism that emerged in the aftermath of the Second World War, whereby Western nations were awakened of their international responsibilities to provide foreign aid to areas of need.[14] This new consciousness was best exemplified by the 1948 Marshall Plan that the United States

---

[13] Robert Menzies, "Speech by the Prime Minister to the American Australian Association", New York, USA, 20 June 1964, p 2.

[14] Michael G. Thompson, *For God and Globe: Christian Internationalism in the United States between the Great War and the Cold War*, Ithaca: Cornell University Press, 2016. Thompson explained how this movement had deep Christian roots.

delivered to war-torn Europe. Menzies himself welcomed this positive development in international relations as "one of the great, good things of this century".[15] Moreover, the good neighbour policy was arguably part of Menzies' Cold War geopolitical strategy to contain communism in the region, particularly when it came to developing defence partnerships. Menzies conceded that helping Australia's neighbours would equip them with the strength and wherewithal "to resist the onset of the strange, mad doctrines of communism".[16]

Important as these considerations were, it was also evident that this key aspect of Menzies' foreign policy was informed by religious faith. As prime minister, Menzies consistently defended his government's good neighbour approach on the basis of Christian moral principles. Invoking biblical language, he asserted that Australian aid to its Asia-Pacific neighbours should be motivated primarily by "love for one's neighbour" and must also be "the expression of a true understanding of what is involved in being your brother's keeper".[17] Reminding fellow citizens that they belonged to a prosperous nation of the free world, Menzies said that Australia "must turn aside from time to time and have a look at our neighbour, though the neighbour may be five thousand miles away, and say: What about him? Is he coming along too?" As was the case with human individuals in society, he emphatically rejected the attitude of "each [nation] for itself and the devil take the hindmost".[18]

Menzies' approach to foreign aid was arguably informed by the Christianity of his SCU years at Melbourne University, where the liberal Protestant movement had impressed the importance of rendering practical Christian service at home and abroad. As Renate Howe acknowledged, the SCU movement influenced Australia's relationship with the Asia-Pacific region, especially

[15] Robert Menzies, PSA Address, Wesley Church, Melbourne, 4 September 1960, p 2, Robert Menzies Papers, NLA, MS 4936, Box 270, Folder 132.

[16] Robert Menzies, Speech at the Opening of Legacy Week, 5 September 1960, Robert Menzies Papers, NLA, MS 4936, Box 270, Folder 132.

[17] Menzies, Pleasant Sunday Afternoon Address, 4 September 1960, pp 3-4.

[18] Menzies, Opening of Legacy Week, 5 September 1960.

through aid organisations such as Community Aid Abroad and Australian Volunteers Abroad.[19] Thus, in many respects, Menzies' good neighbour policy represented an expression of his practical Christianity.

In the domestic realm, Menzies' Liberal creed also affirmed the need for a "civilised capitalism". He did not accept that the only choice for post-war Australia was between *laissez-faire* capitalism and socialism. As well as being an avowed opponent of state socialism, he was also critical of an unbridled capitalism, an "economic law of the jungle", where the strong would trample over the weak. In "Has Capitalism Failed?", Menzies strongly defended the free enterprise impulses behind capitalism, and credited it as a major driving force for employment growth, economic prosperity and material progress. At the same time, he emphasised that it also had social obligations to protect employees and serve the common good. He thus concluded:

> ... the choice is not between an unrestricted capitalism and a universal socialism. We shall do much better if we keep the best elements of the capitalist system, while at the same time imposing upon capital the most stringent obligations to discharge its social and industrial duty.[20]

In the following year he outlined some of these social obligations for capital:

> So we must say to capitalism, to private interests, to the employers of Australia – "You are a vital element in this new world, but you must be prepared as a condition to meet your obligations, to pay the highest wages that your industry can bear, to provide civilised working conditions for your people, and to provide constant employment for as many people as possible ..." All these burdens must be placed on industry. They are fair burdens in a social world.[21]

Having witnessed the trauma of the Great Depression leave so

[19] Howe, *A Century of Influence*, p 18.
[20] Robert Menzies, "Has Capitalism Failed?", *Forgotten People*, p 114.
[21] Robert Menzies, "The Individual in the New Order", Brisbane, 21 January 1943.

many workers bereft, there could be no going back to what he called the "old and selfish notions of *laissez-faire*" with the "government merely keeping the ring in which the competitors will fight".[22] Menzies would have regarded a return to the old industrial capitalism of the Victorian-era factory system and sweatshops as reactionary, inhumane and unchristian. What he envisioned was an enlightened and humane capitalism that was rewarding of individual enterprise and affirming of profit, yet eminently conducive to the best interest of labour.

Menzies' Liberal creed was anchored in the Christian tradition of natural law. According to Christian thought, the "natural law" refers to the universal law inscribed upon the hearts of all people, to which all of humankind is bound and by which all civil laws are judged.[23] Whilst it is widely regarded as a Christian concept, natural law theory had classical roots where it was recognised and expounded by the philosophers of Ancient Greece, including Plato, Aristotle and the Stoics. Aristotle, in particular, was credited with recognising the distinction between conduct which corresponded with nature, and was thus deemed morally good, and that which was merely legal, because it abided by positive human law.[24] In the Christian tradition, the Bible was seen as bearing witness to the existence of the natural law with the Apostle Paul testifying to the concept when he referred to the law as written in the hearts of people.[25] Drawing on Scripture and the doctrines of the Church Fathers such as Augustine, natural law theory was developed by the Catholic Church, most notably in the thought of Thomas Aquinas. Meanwhile, in the Presbyterian tradition

---

[22] Robert Menzies, "The Forgotten People", *Forgotten People*, 22 May 1942, p 10.

[23] Jonathan Stonebreaker and Sarah Irving, 'Natural Law and Protestantism: A Historical Reassessment and its Contemporary Significance', *Oxford Journal of Law and Religion*, 2015, 4, p 433.

[24] "The Natural Law", Pastoral Statement on the Basis of Social Justice by the Catholic Bishops of Australia, Social Justice Sunday, 6 September 1959, cited in Michael Hogan (ed.), *Justice Now! Social Justice Statements of the Australian Catholic Bishops, First Series: 1940-1966*, Department of Government and Public Administration, University of Sydney, 1990, p 208.

[25] Romans 2:15.

of Menzies, the Calvinists taught that the Ten Commandments were "the best summary of the natural law and conscience and the clearest source of principles of how to love God, neighbour and self".[26] Natural law, notwithstanding, is not exclusively religious, with Christians, rationalists and others alike accepting it as the basis of morality and human rights.

Menzies appealed to the natural law when he reflected in 1954 that: "The most important thing in the world, may I say for myself, is man's relation to his maker: his relation to the divine and spiritual law".[27] He did not venture to explain in detail what this "divine and spiritual law" was, but given his own background and familiarity with Scripture, it can be deduced that he was alluding to the moral precepts of God articulated in passages of the Bible such as the Ten Commandments and the Sermon on the Mount, as he understood them. For Menzies, however, the natural law was not only essential to his personal relationship with God, but provided the essential moral foundation to the good ordering of society for all people. In his own conception of a democratic society, he believed it was based on a divine order that equated to the natural law. Speaking of Australian democracy in the middle of the twentieth century, he observed: "Democracy is neither accidental nor inevitable. It is the product of generations of self-sacrifice, of conscious struggle, of belief in the vital significance of individual men and women, of a sense of a Divine order in a distracted human world".[28] Given the imperfection of human society and its susceptibility to descend into chaos or tyranny, as the Nazi and Soviet regimes had demonstrated to devasting effect, it was deemed necessary for democracies such as Australia to be based on a divine natural law that would bring ordered liberty and social cohesion.

In this vein of thinking, Menzies differed sharply from the

---

[26] Stonebreaker and Irving, "Natural Law", pp 433-434.
[27] Robert Menzies, "Education and its Application", 17 March 1954.
[28] Robert Menzies, Broadcast on the Occasion of Australia's Jubilee Celebrations, 9 May 1951.

Benthamite tradition of utilitarianism that rejected natural law as "nonsense on stilts". Unlike John Stuart Mill, Menzies was no utilitarian and he stood very much in the Whig tradition of Burke who similarly appealed to the natural law. When pursuing the prosecution of Warren Hastings in 1788 for alleged abuses of British rule in India, Burke held that rulers and ruled alike were subject to a higher law: "We are all born in subjection – all born equally, high and low, governors and governed, in subjection to one great, immutable, pre-existent law".[29] Believing similarly in both the natural law and the rule of law, Menzies' quoted Burke approvingly in a 1954 lecture where one of his main points was that freedom depended upon the pre-existence of both order and virtue:

> As Edmund Burke said at Bristol in 1774, "The only liberty I mean, is a liberty connected with order; that not only exists along with order and virtue, but which cannot exist at all without them". We see therefore, that sensible discipline cheerfully accepted and public laws scrupulously obeyed are not the enemies of freedom, but its essential friends.[30]

By defending the necessity of obeying public laws, Menzies comprehended that there was an essential need for positive human law to supplement the natural law by applying it specifically to the practicalities of daily life. As a lawyer, Menzies' understanding of positive law was no more evident than in his reverence for the English common law, developed over centuries by the courts of England and then Australia. In his familiarity with the common law as a King's Counsel, he could see the genesis of so many of the basic individual rights and freedoms that formed the bedrock of his Liberal philosophy. Such rights to life, liberty, private property and natural justice were also natural law precepts that the common law enshrined. Incorporating these natural law precepts into the platform of the Liberal Party, Menzies' 1954 draft of the Party's statement *We*

---

[29] Edmund Burke, quoted by Stonebreaker and Irving, "Natural Law", p 436.
[30] Robert Menzies, "The First William Queale Memorial Lecture", Australian Institute of Management, Adelaide, 22 October 1954, pp 5-6.

Believe affirmed the rule of law; honest administration of the law; the freedoms to worship, think, speak and choose; protection of the weak; and preservation of family life.[31]

The blueprint of Menzies' Liberal creed: The "Forgotten People"

In what has come to be regarded as one of the touchstones of Liberal Party philosophy, Menzies delivered the "Forgotten People" address on 22 May 1942, less than a year after relinquishing the prime ministership (August 1941) and the party leadership (October 1941). Identifying a largely middle class constituency whom Menzies regarded as the "forgotten people", sandwiched between the rich and powerful and the mass of unionised employees, this speech appealed to many of the spiritual sensibilities held by the Australian middle class. Representing the opening address to a series of 27 radio broadcasts, modelled on President Roosevelt's homely "Fireside Chats", his address was part of a pitch to re-engage the electorate at a time of political ferment with the disintegration of the UAP and subsequent foundation of the Liberal Party. In this context, the aim of the "Forgotten People" speech was to define the constituency he was addressing, and to appeal to the values and aspirations of this middle class stratum of "salary-earners, shopkeepers, skilled artisans, professional men and women, farmers, and so on". Eschewing the doctrine of class war, he was eager to project a national ideal that would embrace citizens of all classes and creeds. On this occasion, he felt that it was appropriate to say something about the "middle class", whose interests, in his mind, had been overlooked and forgotten.

Menzies had four reasons for his concern for the middle class. Firstly, they had a "stake in the country", particularly in terms of home ownership; second, they provided "the intelligent ambition which is the motive power of human progress", by which he meant the drive to contribute to society; third, "the middle class" provided "the intellectual life which marks us off from the beast", particularly in literature, art, science, medicine and the law; and, finally, the "middle

---

[31] Liberal Party of Australia, *We Believe*, 3 November 1954.

class maintains and fills the higher schools and universities, and so feeds the lamp of learning". He contrasted these aspirations with the "cult of false values" preoccupied with money, fame and applause, and also with what he lamented as a "dependence on the state", robbing individuals of their dignity and independence. In short, Menzies extolled the virtues of family and domestic life, frugality and thrift, industriousness, learning, public and community service, and sturdy independence, all within the spiritual framework of dependence upon God.

These virtues that Menzies esteemed spoke to the Protestant sensibilities of many from the middle class and resonated with his own traditions of Presbyterianism and Methodism. Aside, however, from observing that "human nature is at its greatest when it combines dependence upon God with independence of man", his "Forgotten People" speech was silent on the doctrinal specifics of Protestantism. In keeping with his own form of Christianity, his speech was less concerned with creed and dogma than with conduct and instinct.[32] That said, the cultural values he appealed to had perceptible roots in the Calvinist strand of Protestantism that emerged in both the Scottish Presbyterian and English Puritan traditions. This cultural puritanism that Menzies channelled, according to Raphael Samuel, did not so much mean "prudishness" as the positive attributes of "independence, adherence to conscience, tolerance, high seriousness and hard work".[33] Menzies had absorbed these not only through his Presbyterian upbringing but also through the English literature of the period. Such literature impressed the importance of individuality, self-reliance and striving, accompanied by a disciplined, world-embracing sense of duty to improve society.[34] Whilst having a foundation in cultural puritanism, these values were also intrinsic to

---

[32] Chavura and Melleuish, *Forgotten Menzies*, p 59.

[33] R. Samuel, "The Discovery of Puritanism, 1820–1914: A Preliminary Sketch," in *Revival and Religion since 1700: Essays for John Walsh*, ed. J. Garnett and C. Matthew (London: Hambledon Press, 1993), pp 201–47. Cited in Chavura & Melleiush, "The Forgotten Menzies", *JRH*, p 358.

[34] Ibid., p 359.

Ernest Burgmann (1885-1967), Bishop of Canberra-Goulburn, 1934-60

Notwithstanding Menzies' regard for churches and their contribution to the community in education and welfare, there were occasions when he took issue with their interventions in public debate. His definitive address on "The Forgotten People" was, indeed, provoked by a prelate, Bishop Ernest Burgmann, who had written to a "great daily newspaper [about] the importance of doing justice to the workers...He sought to divide the people of Australia into classes. He was obviously suffering from what has for years seemed to me to be our greatest political disease – the disease of thinking that the community is divided into the rich and relatively idle, and the laborious poor... In a country like Australia the class war must always be a false war."

(*Portrait by Judy Cassab*)

liberalism, particularly the Whig tradition which balanced personal rights with duties, and held that the personal moral character of individuals was essential for freedom to take root and flourish.

It is evident in the text of the "Forgotten People" itself that his ideal of the good society, informed by cultural puritanism, was also different from that of Christians of other traditions. In the opening sentence, he referred to a "bishop" who had written "a letter to a great daily newspaper" on the importance of doing justice to the workers.[35] For Menzies, the problem with the bishop's letter was that he had afforded only a narrow definition to workers, as those who laboured with their hands, and was therefore seeking to "divide the people of Australia into classes".

Menzies was referring to Bishop Ernest Burgmann (1885-1967), Anglican bishop of Canberra-Goulburn. He had written to the *Sydney Morning Herald* calling for a "sense of justice for the workers".[36] Burgmann hailed from the theologically and socially progressive broad-church wing of Anglicanism and saw his main mission in public life as rousing his flock to ally themselves with the working class in a peaceful effort to transform the capitalist system.[37] In common with the broad social gospel movement, Burgmann believed that the pathway to effecting positive change was transforming what he saw as the unjust structures of society. In his eyes, the capitalist system was responsible for oppression of the workers. This contrasted with the outlook of Menzies, and other cultural puritans, who held that the key to such change lay in the moral reformation of individuals, whereby the transformation of men and women into more independent, upright, responsible and selfless citizens provided the fundamental driving force to shaping a better world.

Elsewhere in the speech, the backdrop of cultural puritanism was

---

[35] Robert Menzies, "The Forgotten People", 22 May 1942, *Forgotten People*, p 1.
[36] E. H. Burgmann, "Unity and Workers", *Sydney Morning Herald*, Tuesday 21 April 1942, p 3.
[37] Peter Hempenstall, "Burgmann, Ernest Henry (1885-1967)", *ADB*, Vol 13, 1993.

evident, particularly in his appeal to the virtue of independence. Such "independence", however, meant more than simply an individual's ability to stand on one's own feet and look after themselves. It also referred to an individual's wherewithal to serve others and contribute selflessly to the common good, to be "lifters not leaners". After Menzies condemned the idea of citizens all living on the state as the "quintessence of madness", he made it clear that the end goal for citizens in a democracy should be about getting themselves onto the list of contributors and removing themselves from the list of beneficiaries.[38] For Menzies, therefore, "independence" was much more than a mere private virtue, but a quality that had a direct bearing on an individual's relationship with fellow citizens in a democracy.[39] As such, it was not the independence of radical individualism, implying "each for himself and the devil take the hindmost", but an independence pregnant with social obligations towards one's neighbour.

The virtue of family and domestic life was yet another feature of cultural puritanism that Menzies articulated in the *Forgotten People* address. For Menzies, the family home was "the foundation of sanity and sobriety". It was "the indispensable condition of continuity" and its health determined the health of society as a whole. Implying much more than just bricks and mortar, the family home was not simply a physical dwelling but a human and spiritual abode. This spiritual dimension of homelife was epitomised nowhere more strikingly than in the "The Cotter's Saturday Night", a ballad composed by Robert Burns and one frequently read to the young Menzies and his siblings by their father.[40] By appealing to this poem of his boyhood,[41] Menzies was seeking to evoke Burns' homely scene of a Scottish labouring family gathered together for their supper of porridge and worship

---

[38] Menzies, "Forgotten People", p 6.
[39] Menzies, "Democracy and Sir Alan Newton", 4 September 1949.
[40] Judith Brett, *Robert Menzies' Forgotten People*, Melbourne: Melbourne University Press, 2007, p 62.
[41] Menzies, "Forgotten People", p 5.

around the family Bible. In his poem, Burns had captured the family piety characteristic of so many Presbyterian households throughout his native Scotland. Like Burns, Menzies believed that this domestic custom that the Scots had learnt from Puritan divines was a source of moral strength and national greatness. Burns wrote: "From scenes like these, old Scotia's grandeur springs that makes her lov'd at home, rever'd abroad".[42] Whilst appreciating that not all Australian households in the 1940s would necessarily conform to the pattern of piety celebrated by Burns in eighteenth-century Scotland, Menzies similarly held that a family household steeped in spiritual beliefs and practices formed a mainstay of national character.

Menzies' appeals to thrift and frugality throughout the *Forgotten People* address also channelled culturally puritan ideals. As Judith Brett correctly observed, "Calvinism", from which cultural puritanism sprung, "was carried on most fully in Presbyterianism" and Menzies exhibited this thinking in his praise for citizens who exercised prudence and restraint in the management of their finances.[43] Thrift and frugality for Menzies, however, implied not a miserable stinginess or parsimony, but the responsible stewardship of personal wealth to enable an individual to provide for oneself and one's family and to help others in need.

This was essentially based on the Calvinist teaching that all riches were a blessing and provision from God, to be stewarded wisely by men and women for their own well-being and that of their neighbours. As well as aligning with his own Presbyterian sensibilities, Menzies regarded thrift and frugality as an essential antidote to future dependency on the state, whereby a citizen's personal savings would enable them to live an independent and dignified life. Accordingly, he questioned whether "most of our policy [is] designed to discourage or penalise thrift, to encourage dependence on the State".[44] He added that in his fourteen years in politics, he could not "readily recall many

---

[42] Robert Burns, "The Cotter's Saturday Night", 1786.

[43] Brett, *Robert Menzies' Forgotten People*, p 64.

[44] Menzies, *The Forgotten People*, p 7.

occasions upon which any policy was pursued which was designed to help the thrifty, to encourage independence, to recognise the divine and vanuable variations of men's minds". In the context of the early 1940s, Menzies therefore held that if thrift and frugality were to be fostered, the pressing policy priority for governments was to curb excessive taxation of income from savings. He praised "frugal people", who sought to save money for themselves and others, as "the whole foundation of a really active and developing national life".[45] As Chavura and Melleuish argue, the themes that Menzies enunciated in the *Forgotten People* speech were "an expression of the cultural puritanism that animated much of British culture", something Menzies cherished as part of Australia's great inheritance.

The spiritual inspiration behind the Liberal Party platform

Following his signature broadcast of May 1942, the appeal to Christian moral principles was similarly evident when Menzies established the Liberal Party of Australia late in 1944.

Whilst the Liberal Party was commonly perceived of as a "Protestant Party",[46] deriving from a perception of the predominant faith of its "forgotten people" constituency, the Liberal Party, in reality, was never founded as an avowedly "Christian Party" like some of the Christian Democratic parties in post-war Europe where "Christian democracy" prevailed as the philosophy on the political centre-right. In contrast to the Christian Democratic Union of West Germany led by Menzies' contemporary, Chancellor Konrad Adenauer from 1946 to 1966, the Liberal Party did not have confessional Christian foundations.

Menzies had no desire for the party to become the political wing of any church and completely rejected the idea of a denominational "church party". In an address in 1958 to a large Methodist church in Sydney, he remarked that "I can't imagine anything worse than for me to be leading a Presbyterian party and somebody else the

---

[45] Ibid., p 8.
[46] See, for example, Gerard Henderson, *Menzies' Child*, p 67.

Methodist party and somebody else some other party".[47] Pledging to govern for all Australians in the broad national interest, the Liberal Party would be a non-sectional and non-sectarian party open to people of all faiths and none. Even so, Menzies and the philosophical platform of the new party still embodied broadly Christian ideals that resonated with both Australia's Protestant and Catholic traditions. Its guiding ethos spoke to the Protestant social ethics of selfless individualism, industry, thrift and frugality, whilst its vision for a civilised capitalism, preference for subsidiarity and defence of private property and the family aligned with much of Catholic social teaching.

The Protestant values of cultural puritanism that Menzies espoused in the *Forgotten People* broadcast were reiterated in the conference speeches to, and policy platform of, the new Liberal Party of Australia. Addressing the opening of the Canberra Conference on 13 October 1944, Menzies again extolled the virtues of thrift and independence, telling conference delegates that "without thrift there can be no independence and without independent citizens there can be no independent nation".[48] Crucially for Menzies and the new party, these values had practical policy implications, especially for taxation, social services and monetary policy:

> Thrift and independence must therefore be positively encouraged by our political policies. This involves a complete overhaul of our taxation system in order to help people with family responsibilities. It involves the conversion and extension of our social services on a contributory insurance basis and it involves the use of the Central Bank and of Government economic policies not to create short-term political advantages but to produce stability not only of employment but of currencies.[49]

The end goal of thrift, therefore, was not simply about encouraging

---

[47] Menzies, Farewell to Dr Rayward, 30 March 1958, p 4.

[48] R G Menzies, Opening Speech, 13 October 1944, cited in *Forming the Liberal Party of Australia*, p 10.

[49] Ibid., p 11.

individuals to save for themselves but to enable citizens to fulfil their family responsibilities and social obligations. In the policy platform of the new party, the principle of individuals funding superannuation, sickness, unemployment and widowhood on a "contributory basis" was enshrined.[50] With Menzies applying these cultural puritan values of thrift, independence and responsibility to party policy, Brett observed that Protestantism was still at work in the "Liberal imagination" personified by Menzies and this gave "weight to Liberalism's promotion of the political, social and economic virtues of independent individualism and responsible citizenship".[51]

The historical contribution of the similarly influential Catholic tradition to the philosophical formation of the Australian Labor Party has been widely recognised,[52] but its relation to the guiding ethics of the Liberal Party was also far from insignificant. For all of the Catholic Church's differences with Protestants over various points of theology, Catholic social teaching intersected with much of Menzies' Protestant cultural puritanism when it came to the Liberal Party's conception of a flourishing society, and this became evident in the founding principles of the new Party. This was not to suggest that the social vision of the two traditions were strictly identical, for Catholic social teaching was arguably less enthusiastic about liberal capitalism and not so individualistic in its focus as traditional Protestant thought.

Nevertheless, the commonalities were apparent. Firstly, Catholic social teaching and cultural puritanism emphasised the essential spiritual element of humanity and humanity's dependence upon God, with each of these rooted in the thought of Thomas Aquinas and John Calvin. In addition, both traditions staunchly defended the family, the right to private property, the inherent dignity of human

[50] Name and Objectives, *Forming the Liberal Party of Australia*, pp 14-15.
[51] Judith Brett, *Australian Liberals*, p 57.
[52] Adrian Pabst, *Story of our Country: Labor's Vision for Australia*, The Kapunda Press, 2019, pp 4, 9-12.

labour, class cooperation and subsidiarity. In political terms, Catholic social teaching and cultural puritanism also shared common ground in rejecting both state socialism and *laissez-faire* individualism as incompatible with a Christian social order deemed necessary for human flourishing.[53]

In the 1940s, the two primary sources of Catholic social teaching were the papal encyclicals, *Rerum Novarum* (1891) and *Quadragesimo Anno* (1931). Whilst there is no evidence to suggest that Menzies himself was necessarily conversant with these texts, many of the principles they enunciated were reflected in the founding platform of the Liberal Party. Formulated at a time when the Church was coming to terms with the social upheavals wrought by the Industrial Revolution, *Rerum Novarum* derived primarily from biblical principles and the natural law precepts of Aquinas to set forth a Christian social vision. The encyclical affirmed the natural right to private property, the dignity of labour, class cooperation, promoting the interests of the poor, well-regulated family life, respect for religion and justice, the moderate and fair imposition of public taxes, and the abundant yield of the land as integral to "making the citizens better and happier".[54] Rejecting the class warfare of socialism, *Rerum Novarum* emphasised the complementarity of capital and labour, holding that: "in a State it is ordained by nature that these two classes should dwell in harmony and agreement, so as to maintain the balance of the body politic. Each needs the other; capital cannot do without labour, nor labour without capital".[55] Building on the teachings of *Rerum Novarum*, the subsequent social encyclical, *Quadragesimo Anno* articulated the important principle of subsidiarity, teaching that "The supreme authority of the State ought, therefore, to let subordinate groups handle matters of and concerns of lesser importance".[56]

In the Australian context, Catholic social teaching found its

[53] Chavura and Melleuish, *Forgotten Menzies*, p 57.
[54] *Rerum Novarum* (1891), para 32.
[55] Ibid., para 19.
[56] *Quadragesimo Anno* (1931), para 80.

primary expression in the series of annual "Social Justice Statements" issued by the Australian Catholic Bishops between 1940 and 1966. Amid the crisis of war, the Australian bishops believed that it was timely for the Church to reaffirm and apply the Catholic social teaching of the encyclicals to the Australian setting.[57] Like Menzies himself, the bishops were focussed on articulating their vision for the world that would emerge from the years of depression and war. While the social justice statements were attributed to the bishops of the Australian Catholic Church, it was the secretariat of Catholic Action that was commissioned with preparing drafts. Within the secretariat, B. A. Santamaria was primarily responsible for preparing all the annual drafts from 1941 to 1955.[58] In common with Menzies, these statements denounced the menace of both fascism and communism, whilst also drawing distance from the old *laissez-faire* capitalism that had its shortcomings exposed by the crisis of the Great Depression. Michael Hogan discerned the similarity in outlook between the bishops and Menzies. He noted that whilst Australian Catholic social thought shared the concerns of both sides of politics, it aligned with Menzies and the new Liberal Party in its wariness of state controls over individuals and sections of the economy as well as in its emphasis on the natural rights and freedoms of the individual.[59]

The platform of the nascent Liberal Party, drafted at the Canberra Conference in October 1944, set forth a number of clear objectives that corresponded closely with Catholic social teaching. To accord with the subsidiarity principle, objective 5 encouraged "decentralisation of industries" in rural communities. Affirming class harmony and cooperation, objective 7 provided that "We will strive to have a country in which employer and employee have a sense of common interest and duty, and share as co-operators in all advances of prosperity". Lastly, in recognising the importance of supporting

[57] Michael Hogan, *Australian Catholics: The Social Justice Tradition*, p 57.
[58] Ibid.
[59] Ibid.

family life, the final tenth objective provided that "We shall strive to have a country in which family life is recognised as fundamental to the wellbeing of society, in which every family is enabled to live in a comfortable home at reasonable cost, and with adequate community amenities".

During Menzies' time as prime minister and Liberal leader, these founding objectives of the Party were sustained, mirroring, to a large degree, both the Protestant legacy of cultural puritanism and the social justice tradition of the Catholic Church. In a revised platform for the Party, *We Believe*, co-drafted by Menzies and Sir William Anderson in November 1954, the fourteenth of seventeen enumerated points stated that: "We believe in social justice; in encouraging the strong and protecting the weak; in widening opportunities for education; in the preservation of family life; in good homes owned by those who live in them".[60] In a noteworthy addition to the original 1944 platform, the 1954 platform also made explicit reference to God in its final point, stating that: "We believe that, under the blessing of Divine Providence, and given goodwill, mutual tolerance and understanding, energy, and an individual sense of purpose, there is no task which Australia cannot perform, and no difficulty which she cannot overcome". Given, however, that Menzies' philosophy of Christian-inspired Liberalism remained non-confessional on the specifics of Christian doctrine, it could be accepted by citizens of all faiths in Australia who affirmed its essential values of human freedom and dignity, private ownership, free enterprise, family life and social justice as critical to the common good.

Christianity and anti-communism

The religious faith of Menzies evidently informed his opposition to communism which he regarded as a "godless", "anti-Christian" and "materialistic" philosophy, denying both the existence of God and the basic spiritual nature of the human individual. Menzies' anti-communism has been typically assumed to be on chiefly political

---

[60] Menzies to Anderson, *We Believe*, 3 November 1954, p 2.

and economic grounds. This is perfectly understandable given that Menzies himself denounced communism as being inimical to the liberal and capitalist ideals of individual freedom, parliamentary democracy, the rule of law, private property, national security and defence, free enterprise and competition, industrial harmony, freedom of speech, freedom of association and, indeed, freedom of religion.

What is less widely appreciated is that Menzies' opposition to communism was every bit as impelled by deep moral and spiritual sensibilities. Writing for a Presbyterian Youth Magazine in 1947, Menzies stated: "I have many grounds of objection to the Communists, the greatest of which is that they have based their ideas upon pure materialism and therefore deny the importance and value of religion, and indeed the human spirit generally".[61] As his own reading and pronouncements on the ideology revealed, Menzies was cognisant of the anti-religious thrust of communism, originating from Karl Marx's dictum of 1843 that "religion is the opiate of the people". With the Russian Revolution sweeping the Bolsheviks to power in 1917, the large-scale persecution of Jews, Christians, Muslims and other religious minorities in the Soviet Union more than confirmed Menzies' worst fears about communist resolve to annihilate religion.

The presence of communist activity on Australia's domestic front naturally gave Menzies angst as he regarded its anti-democratic totalitarianism and atheism as completely alien to Australia's robust democratic tradition and Judeo-Christian inheritance. To be sure, the communist movement in Australia had always inhabited the political fringes. With the exception of one candidate elected to the Queensland Parliament in 1944, the Communist Party of Australia (CPA) had failed to win parliamentary representation since its founding in 1920 in the aftermath of the Russian Revolution. Following the Great Depression, however, the CPA experienced some growth in the

---

[61] Robert Menzies, "The Way to Industrial Peace", draft article for the Presbyterian Youth Magazine, the *Front Line,* May 1947.

1930s and, by the outbreak of the Second World War, its presence within the Australian trade union movement was felt. Attracting a membership of 20 000, the Party began to win positions in trade unions such as the Miners' Federation and the Waterside Workers' Federation of Australia. With its activity in the union movement of organising strikes and impeding war production, the Party sought to sabotage Australia's war effort against Nazi Germany until Hitler's invasion of the USSR forced the Soviet-led communists to join the allied cause. For this reason, Menzies deplored the communist movement as not only anti-democratic and anti-Christian, but also as subversive and disloyal to Australia.[62]

Alarmed at the traction communism was gaining in the trade union movement during the Second World War, Menzies, speaking on radio in July 1943, alerted his listeners to what he saw as the perils of communism and explained why Marxist ideology should be condemned. Menzies explained his reasons for his "own detestation of the Communist policy and viewpoint". After denouncing communism as "the enemy of Australian democracy" and reminding his audience of its efforts to undermine Australia's war effort, Menzies turned to its spiritual dimension to declare that "communism is and must be anti-Christian".[63] As evidence, he pointed to the founders of Russian communism who had denounced religion as "the opium of the people" and sought to "drive many churches out of existence". Recognising that it was impossible, however, for communism to extinguish the spiritual impulses of the human heart, Menzies drew attention to the propaganda techniques used by the communists to otherwise persuade people that religion was "a lot of irrational nonsense". He concluded by declaring communism to be "illiberal, pagan, violent, and essentially dictatorial".

In another address after the war had ended, Menzies delved into further detail as to why he saw communism as hostile and

---

[62] Robert Menzies, "Communist Party Dissolution Bill 1950", Second Reading Speech, *CPD*, Thursday, 27 April 1950.
[63] Robert Menzies, "The Communists", Broadcast, 2 July 1943.

incompatible with Christianity. Entitled "Communism and Christianity", he essentially juxtaposed the two world-views to draw attention to what he saw as their innate incongruity. His purpose in outlining their incompatibility was to dispel the perception that communism and Christianity could exist as happy bedfellows. According to Menzies, this perception was perpetuated by the success of Australian communists in wooing the support of active Christians, including some of the clergy.[64]

One such clergyman that would have to sprung to Menzies' mind would have been the Anglican Bishop, Ernest Burgmann, the "Bishop" whom Menzies had referred to in the opening sentence of the *Forgotten People* speech. Dubbed Australia's "Red Bishop", Burgmann had entertained a positive view of the Bolshevik revolution and supported a wartime alliance with the Soviet Union.[65] Essentially, his reason for supporting the Soviet Union was that he saw its Marxist-Leninist ideals of equity and justice as noble and essentially Christian. Indeed, he regarded these as more Christian than what he deplored as the "debauched values" which Western capitalist civilisation thrust upon the world.[66]

In a national broadcast in November 1942, at the height of the war, Burgmann had painted the Soviet Union as closer to the ideals of the Gospels than the Christian West. He asserted that communism was at the very heart of the Christian religion.[67] These sanguine views of communism no doubt emanated from his progressive, broad-church tradition of Anglican theology that focused more on remedying structural injustices of society than on redeeming the individual human soul. Infused with the early twentieth century social gospel movement, it affirmed that the key to social and moral renewal lay primarily in making changes to society and the state more so than in the transformation of the human heart. Transformative programs

---

[64] Robert Menzies, "Communism and Christianity", 1946.
[65] Peter Hempenstall, *The Meddlesome Priest: A Life of Ernest Burgmann*, p ix.
[66] Hempenstall, *Meddlesome Priest*, p 225.
[67] Ibid., p 226.

such as socialism and communism thus appeared to offer great promise for progressive-minded clergy like himself.

In Menzies' "Christianity and Communism" broadcast, the contrast could not have been starker between his outlook on communism and that of Burgmann. Admitting that he was not a theologian, it nevertheless appeared "crystal clear" to him that there was a "great gulf" between Christianity and communism. In his characteristically broad and ecumenical approach, Menzies cut through doctrinal differences between churches to appeal to a "common Christianity", and used that as the basis of his critique. For Menzies, the Christian and communist conceptions of the human individual and of life were "as far apart as the poles".[68] First and most obviously, it was because they had completely different theological outlooks. Communism emphatically denied the existence of any God, whereas Christianity affirmed its belief in an all-powerful, creator God who revealed himself in the person of Jesus Christ.

Secondly, the two world-views had radically different conceptions of the human person. In its world-view of dialectical materialism, communism regarded the human person as merely a machine in the great struggle between capital and labour. Christianity, by contrast, cherished men and women as innately spiritual beings created in the image of God. Communism, moreover, was founded upon a theory of class warfare between the "bourgeois" and the "proletariat", where the end goal was overthrow of the capitalist system and establishment of the communist state by armed force and bloodshed if necessary.

For Menzies, Christianity was a radically different creed that preached the obligations of mutual understanding and love. Pointing to the commandment of Christ to "love your enemies, bless them that curse you; and pray for them which despitefully use you", he concluded that Christianity "rejects hatred of human beings as an instrument of true human progress".[69] Like communism, Christianity envisioned justice and equality, but it did not see the realisation of these ideals as

---

[68] Menzies, "Christianity and Communism", 1946.
[69] Ibid.

something achieved by class war and the violent clash of economic interests. On the contrary, Christianity subordinated the purely material factors of life to the spiritual, exemplified by the life and teachings of Jesus Christ.[70] Stressing the high value that Christianity accorded to marriage and family life, Menzies also denounced communism for its manifesto of favouring "the abolition of the family; [and] the abolition of what is called 'bourgeois marriage'."[71]

In his public critique of communism, Menzies was curious about the spiritual and philosophical impulses behind this enormously consequential world-view. As such, he consulted, "for convenience and accuracy," not only the *Communist Manifesto* (1848) by Marx and Engels, but also *The ABC of Communism* (1919) by N. Bukharin and E. Preobrazhensky.[72] Written for the simple purpose of explaining the newly adopted program of the Russian Communist Party, *The ABC of Communism* came to be widely regarded as the "manifesto" of latter-day Marxism embodied in the Bolshevik Party, the Soviet state and the Communist International. According to Sidney Heitman, this made it "one of the most widely read and best-known political documents of the twentieth century".[73] To prove that the anti-religious thrust of communism was not simply a perception held by anti-communists but a reality espoused by communists themselves, Menzies quoted directly from Bukharin's blueprint to expose the ideology. He underlined Bukahrin's stated objective of the communist party:

> ... to impress firmly upon the minds of the workers, even
> upon the most backward, that religion has been in the past
> and still is today one of the most powerful means at the
> disposal of the oppressors for the maintenance of inequality,
> exploitation, and slavish obedience on the part of the toilers.[74]

---

[70] Menzies, The Communists, 2 July 1943.

[71] Menzies, "Communism and Christianity", 1946.

[72] Ibid.

[73] Sidney Heitman, "Introduction", in N Bukharin and E. Preobrazhensky, *The ABC of Communism: A Popular Explanation of the Program of the Communist Party of Russia*, University of Michigan Press, 1919, p i.

[74] Bukharin and Preobrazhensky, *ABC of Communism*, p 247 quoted by Menzies, "Communism and Christianity", 1946.

Elsewhere, *The ABC of Communism* stated that, "in practice, no less than in theory, communism is incompatible with religious faith". Attacking religious education in particular, the blueprint railed against what it called "the teaching of ecclesiastical obscurantism in the schools".

From his own reading of *The ABC of Communism*, Menzies would have been cognisant of the antipathy of communism towards religious education and this is likely to have contributed to his staunch advocacy for church and other religious schools. *The ABC of Communism* held that "the decree whereby the school is separated from the church must be rigidly enforced". It called for such schools "to assume the offensive against religious propaganda in the home".[75] The blueprint desired that "from the very outset the children's minds shall be rendered immune to all those religious fairy tales which many grown-ups continue to regard as truth".[76] Whilst there is no evidence suggesting that Menzies ever saw Australia's public schools as beholden to communist agendas of that kind, his conception of religion's place in education was diametrically opposed to that of communism. For Menzies, religious faith was critical to education, not only in the teaching of Scripture and religious precepts, but in a broader sense of moulding the character of the pupil, whether the form of religious instruction was Protestant, Catholic or Jewish. As such, Menzies turned to church and Jewish schools as the great standard-bearers for his vision of education informed by religion.

When Menzies returned to office in the post-war years, his opposition to communism on religious grounds remained essentially unchanged. In the policy speech for the 1949 election, he denounced communists as "the most unscrupulous opponents of religion, of civilised government, of law and order, of national security".[77] These remarks were made in the context of his keynote pledge to outlaw communism and dissolve the Communist Party,

---

[75] Bukharin and Preobrazhensky, *ABC of Communism*, p 252.

[76] Ibid., p 253.

[77] Robert Menzies, Election (Policy) Speech, Melbourne, 10 November 1949.

after previously opposing such a policy. Delivering on his promise to ban the Communist Party, the prime minister, just four months after taking office, introduced the Communist Party Dissolution Bill into the House of Representatives on 27 April 1950. With the bill to "outlaw and dissolve the Australian Communist Party" framed primarily as a national security measure, Menzies appealed largely to familiar political grounds for dissolving the party, citing its agenda to cause economic chaos, social disorder and weakening of democratic institutions as a prerequisite to its goal of seizing state power by revolutionary force.[78]

At the election the next year, he returned to the anti-religious essence of the ideology. In the policy speech for the 1951 election, he referred to the damage that communism did to industry and production but warned that "the real disease of Communism is deeper and more deadly". Reiterating the themes of his anti-communist speeches of the 1940s, Menzies said:

> Communism is a materialistic doctrine, void of spiritual content. It is not only anti-Christian, but is opposed to all those nobler aspirations which spring from the religious faith of decent people. True, Communism itself has been called, by some, a religion. But it is a religion of hatred; it derives from the darkest recesses of the human mind; it has nothing in common with the Christian gospel of love and brotherhood. If it had, it could not preach the class war or use envy and malice as its characteristic weapons.[79]

Menzies, resolved to root out communists from key positions, such as those in the trade unions, made it clear that his crusade was not about an attack on "individuals as such" but upon "a set of evil ideas which are quite foreign to our civilisation, our traditions, and our faith".[80] Like the message of the Apostle Paul in the Epistle to the Ephesians, Menzies saw his battle with communism not so much as a

---

[78] Robert Menzies, "Communist Party Dissolution Bill 1950", Second Reading Speech, *CPD*, Thursday, 27 April 1950.

[79] Robert Menzies, Election (Policy) Speech, Canterbury (Vic), 28 March 1951, Robert Menzies Papers, NLA, MS 4936, Box 255, Folder 47.

[80] Ibid.

"wrestle" against "flesh and blood", but "against principalities, against powers, against the rulers of the darkness of this world".[81]

Whilst Menzies proved ultimately unsuccessful in banning the Communist Party, having lost the 22 September 1951 referendum to amend the Constitution that would have enabled him to do so, his opposition remained unflagging. With the spectre of Cold War communism continuing to haunt Australia and the world throughout his prime ministership, Menzies was awake to what he saw as its grave spiritual dangers. He interpreted the Cold War not simply as a geopolitical contest between the US-led Western alliance and the Eastern Soviet bloc, but as a spiritual battle for the soul of the human race in which the very essence of freedom was at stake. In a Pleasant Sunday Afternoon at Melbourne's Wesley Church in 1961, the year in which the inauguration of President John F. Kennedy had emboldened America and the free world, he spoke of the challenge confronting free nations such as Australia:

> Don't let us succumb to the idea that the great conflict in the world is a conflict between the power of the United States, for example, and the power of the Soviet Union. This is a false picture. The conflict in the world is a conflict between basic principles, profoundly important ideals, differences of outlook on the spirit of man, and the significance of man; a conflict, as we would wish to believe, between what, from our point of view, is the Christian conception of the freedom of the human mind and of the human spirit, and the dictated, dominated, unfree human spirit that exists under totalitarian government in the Communist regime.[82]

For Menzies, this was what the struggle between the free world of the West and the communism of the Soviet Union was about. Like the celebrated Russian intellectual and Soviet dissident, Aleksandr Solzhenitsyn, Menzies recognised that the gravest threats to freedom came not only in the physical form of arrest or imprisonment but

---

[81] See Ephesians 6:12.

[82] Robert Menzies, Pleasant Sunday Afternoon Address, Wesley Church, Melbourne, 3 September 1961.

also in the spiritual form of suppressing one's faith and conscience. As such, people who were otherwise free to enjoy comfortable beds or full stomachs could be enslaved if their freedoms of belief and conscience were denied.[83] In short, Menzies held that "while physical slavery is a terrible thing, spiritual slavery is much worse", and this was the real danger of communism with its suppression of faith and persecution of religious believers.[84]

This conception of the Cold War as a spiritual struggle was evident in Menzies' pronouncements behind two major defence and foreign policy decisions of his government, namely, involvement in the Korean War and, in the 1960s, support for the South Vietnamese government against the Communist North.

When communist North Korea invaded South Korea on 25 June 1950, Menzies announced that Australia would support the United States, Britain and other allies in the UN-led mission to defend the free state of South Korea.[85] Justifying the decision to send Australian troops to Korea, Menzies declared that Australia is: "with all our imperfections, a Christian nation, believing in man's brotherhood, anxious to live at peace with our neighbour, willing to go the second mile to help him if he is less fortunate than we are".[86] Resorting characteristically to biblical turns-of-phrase, Menzies was essentially making the point that, since we were our "brother's keeper", the communist assault on the free people of South Korea was an attack on free people everywhere, including Australians. As such, it behoved a nation with Christian sensibilities, such as Australia, to come to the defence of the South Korean people whose freedoms to think, act, believe and worship would be trampled underfoot by

---

[83] In an earlier speech that Menzies gave entitled "Bond or Free", at Wesley Church, Melbourne, on 7 September 1947, he remarked that "If freedom means only full stomachs and comfortable beds, then there are millions of slaves who enjoy freedom".

[84] Menzies, Pleasant Sunday Afternoon Address, 3 September 1961.

[85] Troy Bramston, *Robert Menzies*, p 214.

[86] Robert Menzies, 6 July 1950, quoted in Manning Clark, *A Short History of Australia*, revised edition, London: William Heinemann Ltd, 1969, p 252.

the North Korean communists dedicated to the extirpation of all religion.

In what became the acrimonious public debate over Australia's involvement in the Vietnam War in the 1960s, the Menzies Government decision to join the American war effort in South Vietnam similarly owed much to his antipathy to communism on spiritual grounds. From 1962, Australia had provided intelligence and economic aid to South Vietnam. On 29 April 1965, the Menzies Government announced it would send a combat battalion to South Vietnam.[87] In the House of Representatives, Menzies justified Australia's intervention in the Vietnam War primarily on defence and geostrategic grounds, holding that defence of South Vietnam was necessary to halt the downward thrust of communist China through South-East Asia. This reflected the "domino theory", prominent in the 1960s, that the successive fall of South-East Asian nations to communism would lead eventually to Australia succumbing to the same fate. Menzies saw it as directly in Australia's interests to support the War.

Although defence and security interests were at the forefront of public debate over the Vietnam War, religious concerns about the dominance of communism in Vietnam were far from absent in Menzies' mind. As with other sections of the Australian community, the Vietnam War deeply polarised opinion within Australia's churches. Some church leaders, such as Alan Walker, Superintendent of the Central Methodist Mission in Sydney, vehemently opposed the war on social conscience or pacifist grounds. Others defended the war, such as Archbishop Hugh Gough, Primate of the Anglican Church, as a principled Christian stand for religious freedom against godless communism. With Menzies himself falling into the latter category, his lead of Australia's involvement provoked the ire of left-leaning clergy strongly encouraged by Sydney journalist, Francis James, who, in the previous decade, had been prominent in opposing the

---

[87] Bramston, *Robert Menzies*, p 236.

The Rev Sir Alan Walker (1911-2003)

In public controversy about the national service scheme introduced in 1965, and the later commitment of Australian troops to Vietnam, few people outside mainstream politics were more prominent in criticism of the Government than the Reverend Alan Walker, Superintendent of the Central Methodist Mission in Sydney, 1958-78. Not least through his Sunday afternoon TV show, *I challenge the minister*, Walker condemned the Government's policies on pacifist and social conscience grounds. (*Lifeline Australia National Archives*)

attempt to ban the communist party.[88]   One of the most outspoken clerics was John Moyes, the Anglican Bishop of Armidale (NSW). Hailing from a similarly broad-church Anglican tradition to that of his contemporary, Bishop Burgmann, Moyes joined several other Anglican bishops in March 1965 to voice concern at the Government's commitment to send Australian forces to Vietnam. Writing to the Prime Minister on 12 March, the bishops called the Government to take "positive steps, with others, towards an honourable and peaceful settlement of the fighting in Vietnam".[89]

In his reply on 24 March, Menzies agreed with the bishops that the war was "costing many lives and damaging Vietnam", but took issue with their claim "that we are not concerned here to canvass the merits of the respective attitudes of the North and South Vietnamese Governments, or of the Governments of the United States and China". Appreciating the radically different world-views between the anti-communist South of Vietnam, supported by the US-led coalition of allies, including Australia, and the North of Vietnam, supported by its communist allies, Menzies regarded the bishops' observation as a case of indifference at best and moral equivalence at worst. Addressing them rhetorically, he asked:

> Are there no merits here to be considered by church leaders? There can be no true comparison between atheistic and materialistic Communism and countries with deep religious beliefs. True, there can be, given good faith on both sides, peaceful coexistence and mutual tolerance. But these cannot continue if aggression continues and grows and is unchecked except by fine words.[90]

Believing earnestly that the Catholics, Buddhists and other faith

---

[88] Francis James managed the Church of England publication, *The Anglican*, through which, in the 1960s, he voiced his opposition to the Vietnam War.

[89] Bishops' Letter, 12 March 1965, in Exchange of Letters between the Prime Minister, the Rt Hon. Sir Robert Menzies, KT, CH, QC, MP and The Rt Rev J S Moyes, CMP, and certain Archbishops and Bishops, Prime Minister's Department, Canberra, 20 April 1965.

[90] Ibid.

John Stoward Moyes (1884-1972), Bishop of Armidale, 1929-64

Another bishop to engage Menzies in public was Bishop Moyes of Armidale (NSW). Moyes led a group of churchmen who contested the decision to commit Australian troops to Vietnam in 1965, calling on the Government to take "positive steps, with others, towards an honourable and peaceful settlement of the fighting in Vietnam". Menzies countered, inter alia, that the Catholics, Buddhists and other faith communities of Vietnam deserved to have their freedoms of belief and worship safeguarded from communist interference. He affirmed that America's policies in relation to South Vietnam "were right" and "should be supported" because they derived "from a courageous and generous acceptance of responsibilities for the protection of human freedom." (*Anglican Diocese of Armidale*)

communities of Vietnam deserved to have their freedoms of belief and worship safeguarded from communist interference, Menzies affirmed that America's policies in relation to South Vietnam "were right" and "should be supported" because they derived "from a courageous and generous acceptance of responsibilities for the protection of human freedom". In September 1957, the President of South Vietnam, Ngo Dinh Diem, had visited Australia where he addressed a joint sitting of parliament. Menzies applauded the President's message that the "moral and spiritual rearmament" and "moral unity" of the people were key factors in fighting the spread of communism.[91]

For Menzies, the moral imperative to uphold religious freedom in the face of communist aggression was undoubtedly one of the great rationales for supporting the American war effort in South Vietnam. The Vietnam War again highlighted the fact that his stance on communism was informed by a world-view that regarded Christianity and the Marxist ideology as antithetical. For Menzies, light could not have fellowship with darkness. In contrast to clerical figures from more leftish streams of Christianity, his thinking aligned with that of both evangelical Protestantism and Roman Catholicism which regarded communism as anathema. In his own words: "there could be no compromise between Christ and the anti-Christ, between the cynical and merciless doctrines and practices of imperialist Communism and the old, yet new, evangel of the Sermon on the Mount".[92]

---

[91] "Spiritual Rearmament Needed in Asia's Fight", *The Age*, 4 September 1957, p 5. Diem was the first foreign head of state to visit Australia. In addition to addressing the Parliament, he was created an honorary Knight Grand Cross of the Order of St Michael and St George (GCMG).

[92] Robert Menzies, "Defence", General Elections 1955, Broadcast by the Prime Minister over National Stations, 17 November 1955, p 7, Robert Menzies Papers, NLA, MS 4936, Box 261, Folder 73.

8

RELIGION AND MENZIES' PHILOSOPHY
OF EDUCATION

*And the function of this school is to produce
character, not a lot of clever men with destructive
minds, with no conception of their obligations to
their fellow men, and no conception of their duty
to God, but people of character, of high morality,
trained with a background of religion.*[1]

Presiding over the expansion of Australian universities and the
provision of state aid to Catholic and independent schools,
Menzies regarded education as one of his signature policy
achievements. He esteemed education not simply as a vocational
training business but as a discipline that moulded the mind, soul
and spirit of the individual, with faith assuming a pre-eminent place.
Officiating at the opening in February 1965 of Whitley College, a
new Baptist College at the University of Melbourne, Menzies paid
tribute to its educational vision and explained why he saw a religious
backdrop to education as so important:

> I believe that education reaches its highest point when it
> is conducted against a background of religion, and yet it is
> a background which constantly reminds the student that
> however clever he may be, he is not his own maker, however
> self-confident he may think he is, he is living in a world not
> created by him, that he has responsibilities, that he has great
> inheritances, that he is responsible in his own proper fashion

---

[1] Robert Menzies, Opening of Westminster School, Adelaide, 13 February 1961.

for the people who come after him, and this spirit is one which has never developed so completely in the institution which doesn't have a background in religion, a background of faith, a background of humility because that, after all, must be the inevitable product of religious belief.[2]

There were multiple factors that accounted for the importance Menzies attached to education being underpinned by a religious background. Firstly, there was his Scots Presbyterian heritage through which he learnt the importance of broad-based, liberal arts education for all. Added to this was his belief that religious values represented an antidote to the secularism and destructive materialism of the twentieth century; his philosophy of liberalism that focused on the spiritual as well as the material; the recognition that the spiritual dimension to human beings was essential to a holistic conception of humanity; and the conviction that religion represented the biggest contributor to the formation of personal moral character.

In each of these aspects of his philosophy of education, Menzies was profoundly influenced by the thought of the Anglo-Irish classical scholar and university administrator, Sir Richard Livingstone (1880-1960), whose works he quoted approvingly in speeches on education. With Livingstone's emphases on education in the spiritual as well as the scientific, the value of the liberal arts, and the supreme importance of education to building human character, he was critical to informing Menzies' own outlook on education. Born in the English city of Liverpool, Livingstone studied and tutored at the University of Oxford before appointment in 1924 as vice-chancellor of the Queen's University, Belfast. An avid scholar of both classical Greek civilisation and early Christianity, he once observed that "Christianity and Hellenism are the spiritual bases of our civilisation".[3] He accordingly likened Western culture

---

[2] Robert Menzies, Whitley College Opening, University of Melbourne, 27 February 1965, Robert Menzies Papers, NLA, MS 4936, Box 282, Folder 219

[3] Richard Livingstone, *On Education: The Future in Education and Education for a World Adrift*, Cambridge: Cambridge University Press, 1954, p 95

to "a lake fed by the streams of Hellenism, Christianity, science and democracy".[4] Identifying as a liberal, broad-church Anglican, Livingstone valued the importance of Christianity and religion immensely. As a sign of the importance he ascribed to education being informed by religion, he established a faculty of theology at Queen's University. Two of his keynote publications on education included the two-volume *The Future of Education* and *Education for a World Adrift* (1954), followed by *The Rainbow Bridge* (1959). In each of these books Livingstone made the case for a more liberal, humanities-based education embracing both philosophy and religion. Menzies is on record as quoting from each, and prophesying that Livingstone's books would "have a profound effect upon educational reform all over the English-speaking world".[5]

The Scots Presbyterian inheritance

For Menzies, the importance of education was imparted from an early age. His parents, James and Kate Menzies, had received little formal education, but both were "great readers" and said to have spoken "educated English". In his boyhood, Menzies grew up on what he described as a "fascinating melange of books" that included Henry Drummond for evangelistic theology, Jerome K. Jerome[6] for humour; and *The Scottish Chiefs*[7] for historical fervour. Through periodic stays with his devoutly Presbyterian grandmother in Ballarat, his schooling in literary classics was crowned by a thorough education in the Bible. This diet of reading no doubt furnished the young Menzies with a lifelong interest in English literature, history and humour

---

[4]   Richard Livingstone, *The Rainbow Bridge and other Essays on Education*, London, Pall Mall, 1959 , p 27.

[5]   Robert Menzies, Debate on Education, *CPD*, House of Representatives, 26 July 1945.

[6]   Jerome K. Jerome (1859-1927) was an English writer and humourist, known for his works including *Idle Thoughts of an Idle Fellow* (1886) and *Three Men in a Boat* (1889).

[7]   *The Scottish Chiefs* (1810) was a historical novel about William Wallace the thirteenth-century Scottish knight, authored by the Scottish historical novelist, Jane Porter (1776-1850).

which frequently coloured many speeches he gave during his long public career. In addition to instilling their son with a penchant for reading and learning, James and Kate firmly believed in the value of formal education and were resolved to provide young Robert with opportunities they had not enjoyed themselves.[8] Accordingly, they looked further afield from their small district of Jeparit to the regional city of Ballarat to enrol Robert in the Humffray Street State School, an institution noted for academic excellence.[9] At Humffray, followed by Wesley College and the University of Melbourne, Menzies thrived academically in his own right.

Menzies took immense pride in this Scottish Presbyterian legacy of education. In *The Forgotten People*, he marvelled at Scotland's contribution to education:

> If Scotland has made a great contribution to the theory and practice of education, it is because of the tradition of Scottish homes. The Scottish ploughman, walking behind his team, cons ways and means of making his son a farmer, and so he sends him to the village school. The Scottish farmer ponders upon the future of his son, and sees it most assured not by the inheritance of money but by the acquisition of that knowledge which will give him power; and so the sons of many Scottish farmers find their way to Edinburgh and a university degree.[10]

Praising the aspirational spirit of Scottish families to see the next generation better educated than the one before, he believed this was something Australia could emulate on its path to greater education and progress after the Second World War. It no doubt influenced his government's decision in 1951 to introduce the Commonwealth Scholarship scheme as a means to expand the reach of higher education. By giving high-achieving students access to university education that money alone may not have afforded, the Scholarship

---

[8] Menzies, *Afternoon Light*, p 10.
[9] Martin, *Robert Menzies*, p 12.
[10] Menzies, *The Forgotten People*, p 4.

scheme drew from the same educational aspiration that Menzies so admired in Scottish homes.

It was not only Scotland's contribution to the development of formal education, but a natural penchant for learning for learning's sake, that excited the admiration of Menzies. In a speech to Melbourne Scots that he gave in his retirement, he waxed lyrical about his ancestral homeland and singled out "the traditional Scottish desire for learning and for making a contribution to learning". To illustrate what he regarded as signs of a Scottish exceptionalism when it came to learning, he provided examples of a Station Master and Porter who respectively read Greek and Latin for pleasure as well as a cowherder who discussed philosophical and metaphysical questions. He took great delight in reiterating the memorable phrase of the Scottish novelist and playwright, J. M. Barrie, who referred to the "poor proud homes of Scotland". If many Scottish homes were materially poor, especially those humble dwellings of the crofters and farmers, they could take great pride in the contribution they made to the national pursuit of learning and education, in both a formal and informal sense.

The Scottish esteem for education that Menzies embodied and championed had many sources, not least the early scholastic legacy of the Ancient Universities and, in more modern times, the Scottish Enlightenment of the eighteenth century. It would not, however, have had the form, substance and extent of influence that it did without the seminal contribution of John Knox to the Scottish education system. With his pioneering vision for a universal, broad-based national education, combining biblical instruction with the liberal arts, its reach extended far and wide as Scottish Presbyterians emigrated to Australia and elsewhere in large numbers during the nineteenth century.

Antidote to materialist excesses

Drawing from this rich Scottish tradition of education that affirmed the value of both the divine and the human, Menzies believed that

inculcation of such values would serve as the necessary antidote to
the excesses of scientific materialism in the twentieth century. While
praising the twentieth century as an age of tremendous material,
scientific and technological progress, he saw it as having been
grievously disfigured by the barbarism of two diabolical world wars.
Speaking to a Catholic residential college at the University of Sydney,
he gave his unflattering diagnosis of the age:

> In common I think with most thoughtful people I feel that
> this hasn't been a noble century. It has been a clever one, a
> brilliant one, it has pushed back the boundaries of knowledge,
> particularly in science, to an extent never dreamed of before,
> but it has been disfigured as no other century has for a long
> time by war, and worse than wars, by bitter inhumanity,
> by barbarism, by an inadequate sense of responsibility for
> others, by greed, by pressure. And there is only one correction
> for this and that is that education should never lose sight
> of its ethical responsibilities. We are not to produce clever
> barbarians. We are to produce educated Christian people as
> much as we can.[11]

He attributed this disfigurement and mass destruction to absence
of both human and spiritual values, of which it was the urgent task
of education to recover and revive. The twentieth century, on the one
hand, had brought remarkable breakthroughs with motor vehicle
travel, air travel and even space travel, together with a whole gamut
of new inventions and innovations, but, on the other a corresponding
decline in spiritual and humanist values.

This diagnosis of the twentieth century was shared by the
educationalist, Sir Richard Livingstone, who, like Menzies, viewed
revival of the liberal arts as holding the key to the recovery of
Western civilisation. In *Education for a World Adrift*, he similarly
regarded the twentieth century as "an age of demolition". On the
positive side, the twentieth century had seen "great undertakings"

---

[11] Robert Menzies, St John's College, University of Sydney, Opening of Menzies
Wing, 14 May 1961, Robert Menzies Papers, NLA, MS 4936, Box 272, Folder
149

in commerce, industry and science, but in the realm of morals and religion, it was "a wasteland of shaken beliefs and shattered standards".[12] According to Livingstone, the depletion of traditional spiritual values left a vacuum that was filled by Nazism, communism and fascism, leading to the conflagration of the Second World War.[13] With respect to Germany itself, Livingstone made the sobering observation that the spiritual roots of that country had been cut off, leaving rootless values "precarious" which partially explained the plausibility of the holocaust in a nation widely thought of as decent, highly educated and civilised. What was needed, therefore, was not only vocational and social education, but spiritual education in disciplines such as philosophy and theology to equip people with what he called a "knowledge of good and evil" and a "definite philosophy of life".[14]

Menzies similarly identified materialism and the loss of religious faith, or what he called "paganism", as root causes for the barbarism of the twentieth century. Employing deliberately biblical language, he decried the modern vice of materialism:

> If ever man has set up a golden calf to worship, it is in the last forty-years or so, when he has been worshipping at the shrine of his own diabolical cleverness, and because he has become so great a worshipper of the material, the world has been rocked into such ruinous disaster.[15]

Menzies made these remarks in the midst of the Second World War, a global conflagration he saw as ultimately wrought by the relentless pursuit of scientific materialism. This materialistic impulse, however, was apparent to Menzies even before outbreak of the Second World War when, on the eve of the conflict, he lamented: "We have commercialised most things; we have fallen down and worshipped idols of gold and silver and brass, and most of them with feet of

---

[12] Livingstone, *On Education*, p 130.
[13] Ibid., p 131.
[14] Ibid., pp 131, 133.
[15] Menzies, "Christian Citizen in a New Era", 27 February 1944.

clay".[16] So when outlining in 1939 what he believed a "university was for", his major point was that in the midst of a materialist age, a university should be directed not so much by commercial objectives as the pursuit of "pure learning" in the humanities. The value of the humanities, for Menzies, lay in their ability to "develop the humane and imperishable elements in man", and against the backdrop of modern materialism, they could point to "the moral that the mere mechanics of life can never be the sole vocation of the human spirit".

He deplored the loss of religious belief in the Western world during the twentieth century, denouncing it publicly as "the bitter wretched paganism that has beset the world in the last 50 years".[17] Like Livingstone, he appreciated that loss of genuine religious belief could only lead to disaster and ruin as it had palpably done in the first half of the century with destructive ideologies filling the vacuum. Addressing the House of Representatives on the future of education, Menzies warned his parliamentary colleagues about the danger of a school education bereft of religious sensibilities:

> Nobody can suppose that we are educating our children, except for disaster, by turning them out of purely secular establishments at the age of fourteen, fifteen or sixteen, merely educated to a point at which they think that there is nothing for them to learn, aggressively conscious of what they suppose to be their rights, and oblivious of that penetrating feeling of moral obligations to others, which alone can make a community of men successful. [18]

Viewing the separation of state education from religion as detrimental, Menzies would have agreed with Livingstone's assessment that "the more men have become separated from the spiritual heritage which binds them together, the more education has

[16] Robert Menzies, "The Place of a University in the Modern Community", Address delivered at the Annual Commencement of the Canberra University College, 1939, p 10, Robert Menzies Papers, NLA, MS 4936, Box 251, Folder 5.
[17] Robert Menzies, Opening of New Wing, Newington College, Sydney, 29 April 1961, Robert Menzies Papers, NLA, MS 4936, Box 272, Folder 148.
[18] Menzies, "Motion on Education", CPD, p 4616.

become egoist, careerist, specialist and asocial". As Menzies turned his sights to the kind of society he wanted Australia to be after the War, he held that an education grounded in religious faith would give children the selfless impulses needed to build a successful, flourishing community of honourable citizens. As a counterpoint to the materialistic and selfish paganism that had led the world to war, such a society would resemble the green shoots of a new civilisation emerging from the ashes of war. Inspired by the English Education Act of 1944, Menzies had no doubt looked to the example of Churchill who reintroduced religion into normal class hours. With Britain still under siege from Nazi Germany, it was a period of revival for the notion of "Christian civilisation".

As well as viewing an education informed by religion as a necessary corrective to the destructive materialism of the twentieth century, Menzies regarded it as essential to a holistic understanding of humanity. In stark contrast to world-views such as communism that conceived human beings in materialistic terms as economic units, Menzies appreciated the spiritual dimension. Indeed, he once observed: "Every man above all is a spirit. Man is a spiritual animal".[19] In his anthropology, he reflected a long tradition of Christian thought by such theologians as St Augustine of Hippo, St Thomas Aquinas and John Calvin who each affirmed that since men and women bore the image and likeness of God, they were intrinsically spiritual beings. With a broad Christian consensus existing on this conception of humanity, it was a theme Menzies could emphasise to both Protestant and Catholic audiences, whether it was at a Methodist institution such as Lincoln College at the University of Adelaide or the Christian Brothers College, Waverley, in Sydney.

Menzies saw nourishment of the spirit and development of the mind of the individual as inextricable:

I have never believed that we ought to regard the cultivation

---

[19] Robert Menzies, "Freedom and the Call to Action", Lecture to Junior Chamber of Commerce, 4 August 1947, Robert Menzies Papers, NLA, MS 4936, Box 253, Folder 17.

of the mind as something entirely detached from the cultivation of the spirit. It is, in my opinion, a disaster when education in any country comes to be almost rigidly separated from religious faith or religious teaching or religious background, because it becomes a one-sided thing.

Menzies respected the historical reality that Australia's public education system, as envisaged by its late nineteenth century pioneers, was "free, secular and compulsory". Owing to the religious plurality of Australian society, he accepted that public education needed to be *secular* in the interests of avoiding sectarian rancour. In this context, "secular" implied that public education needed to be neutral when it came to different Christian denominations and faith traditions. For Menzies, however, this did not mean divorcing education from religion. Like the 1960 Ramsay Report into Victorian Education, Menzies would have held that the secular clause entailed the absence of *dogmatic* religion, but never the exclusion of *general* Christianity from state schools.[20] In this vein, a secular approach to education in Australia would still allow public schools to offer religious instruction in addition to providing for the establishment of faith-based schools and colleges. As he saw it, an education with no religious background at all would be disastrous, stunting the spiritual growth of the individual deemed so essential to personal moral character and human flourishing.

A liberal philosophy affirming of the spiritual

Menzies' philosophy and approach to education was an outworking of his Liberal philosophy that expressly "aimed at the highest standards of life, both material and spiritual".[21] With the spiritual purpose always in focus, he believed in education as one of the great intellectual forces

---

[20] *Report of the Commission on State Education in Victoria [Ramsay Report]*, 1960, p. 32, cited in Stephen Chavura, John Gascoigne, and Ian Tregenza, *Reason, Religion, and the Australian Polity: A Secular State?*, New York: Routledge, 2019, p 117.

[21] Robert Menzies, The Foundations of Australian Liberalism, Perth, 12 May 1970, Robert Menzies Papers, NLA, MS 4936, Box 576, Folder 38.

of modern civilisation. In an early speech, he explained how education and learning could act as a catalyst for greater human freedom: "No society can confer the benefit of mental or spiritual freedom upon its members unless at the same time it encourages the search for truth and the fearless facing of the problems of the intellect."[22] Appraising the progress of human civilisation over the previous century, Menzies welcomed the tremendous advances in science, technology and nutrition "directed towards the attainment of a higher degree of bodily wellbeing". At the same time, he warned that the modern "conception of a liberated body inhabited by a stunted mind and a poor spirit is not a noble one".[23] Accordingly, Menzies believed future investment in education was essential if human civilisation was to flourish both intellectually and spiritually.

For Menzies and other liberals, the power of education lay in its capacity to improve individuals, thereby allowing them to bring a better world into being. Liberals saw education as having the potential to furnish individuals with the great faculties of reasoning, wisdom, sound judgment, moral character and religious faith which would equip them to become eminently better citizens. Menzies extolled the merits, especially, of a humanities-based education which provided the indispensable intellectual foundation for the liberal ideal of human freedom to flourish. His was a Christian-inspired humanism that emphasised the relationship of people to each other as well as their relationship to their God. Menzies articulated his humanist philosophy when addressing the Australian College of Education:

> I have stressed the point of ethics because I believe that the most important thing to consider and learn in this world is the nature of man, his duties and rights, his place in society, his relationship to his Creator.[24]

According to Menzies, the sciences served an invaluable purpose in helping people to understand and know more of God's creation

---

[22] Robert Menzies, *Freedom in Modern Society*, 1935, p 4.

[23] Ibid.

[24] Menzies, "Challenge to Education", 19 May 1961, p 5.

by learning about biology, geology, physics, and chemistry, but these were not enough for knowing about God:

> The humanists must learn more about science and, if I may say so, the scientists must learn more about the humanities, otherwise we may get to the stage, of course, of becoming so scientific, so knowledgeable on God's creation, that we begin to think we all know about God. This is a cardinal error.[25]

Religion, education and moral character

As somebody steeped in Methodism who believed that Christianity made people better men and women, Menzies held that religion in education was the greatest contributor to the building of moral character. For this reason, he held a special affection for what he called "church schools". Historically, most private schools in Australia were founded by the churches of Christian denominations; most notably, Catholic, Anglican, Presbyterian and Methodist, together with a small number of schools founded in the Jewish tradition. Officiating at the opening of Westminster, a new Methodist school in Adelaide, Menzies explained how formation of moral character represented the main objective of schools such as Westminster:

> Now this is a Church School. This is one of those schools standing vividly and enduringly for that most important conception of education over the whole field – a belief that we should not only have humane letters as well as science, but that we should have character as well as knowledge. And the function of this school is to produce character, not a lot of clever men with destructive minds, with no conception of their obligations to their fellow men, and no conception of their duty to God, but people of character, of a high morality, trained with a background of religion.[26]

Having witnessed the barbarism of two world wars in the first half of the twentieth century, coupled with what he perceived to be

---

[25] Ibid.

[26] Robert Menzies, "Westminster School Opening", Adelaide, 13 February 1961, Robert Menzies Papers, NLA, MS 4936, Box 272, Folder 145.

a decline of traditional moral standards in the second half, Menzies turned to the religiously-informed education of the private schools as the great hope for reviving personal moral character.[27]

Aside from instilling pupils with a sense of obligation to their neighbours and duty to God, what were the roots of this personal "moral character" and what form did it actually take in practice? With religion providing the obvious backdrop, its roots, in the Australian educational context of Menzies' time could be found in the Judeo-Christian tradition. In both Catholic and Protestant church schools, the person and teaching of Jesus Christ represented the guiding light for personal ethics and character. Menzies, himself, regarded Christ's Sermon on the Mount, recorded in the Gospel of Matthew, as a "counsel of perfection" which spoke of the "meek", the "merciful", the "pure in heart", the "peace-makers", and those "which do hunger and thirst after righteousness".[28] For Christians, Jesus was indeed, the perfect image of God and the "the Word made flesh". It was by accepting his gospel of new life and living by his teachings that pupils could cultivate moral character. As well as the Christ of the four gospels, Christians also had the New Testament apostolic Epistles as sources of character building. In particular, the exhortations of the Apostle Paul to "Let all bitterness, and wrath, and anger, and clamour, and evil speaking, be put away from you, with all malice", and instead, "be ye kind one to another, tender-hearted, forgiving one another, even as God for Christ's sake hath forgiven you".[29] With pupils striving to put these teachings into practice, they would develop the moral character to make human relationships good.

Jewish schools also provided essential training in moral character. In common with Christianity, Judaism drew from the ethical teachings of the Hebrew Scriptures and its own schools sought to impart these virtues to their pupils. Menzies recognised this

---

[27] Menzies, *Measure of the Years*, p 93.

[28] Menzies, Christianity and Law, 15 December 1946; Menzies, "Communism and Christianity", 1946.

[29] Ephesians 4:31-32.

when invited by Melbourne's leading Jewish school, Mount Scopus Memorial College, to open its new "Korman Wing". He praised the Hebrew tradition of the College for its emphasis not simply on the "clarity of thought" but on the "quality of conduct" which went to the essence of human character. Of the Jewish school's contribution to formation of personal character, he remarked:

> I am a tremendous believer in schools which have the background of religion; I think it is a marvellous thing that the boys and girls who are at this school, and who will be at it in future, should be able to grow up adhering to their faith, knowing the foundations of their faith, and keeping in contact with the great literary and religious tradition which serves to decorate that faith. This is a marvellous thing because, in the long run, we may have clever citizens, ingenious citizens, even brave citizens, but unless they are citizens whose character has been enriched by the background of religious training, they will not be the best citizens for Australia.

In later life, Menzies looked back upon church and independent schools as great standard-bearers of what he called the "ancient virtues": In *The Measure of the Years*, he reflected:

> In my declining years, witnessing a world in which moral values are treated with such complete contempt in some intellectual circles, or more accurately, pseudo-intellectual circles, and in which the powerful influence of the Press seems to be, all too frequently, hostile to received standards of social behaviour, I retain my belief in the ancient virtues, and value the service which the church schools and colleges render to them.[30]

The "ancient virtues" for Menzies referred to traits of personal character bequeathed from ancient civilisations including not only the Judeo-Christian but also the Classical. The Bible was not simply a "repository of faith" but also of "virtue" where sources of moral goodness were to be found in the precepts of the Hebrew

---

[30] Menzies, *Measure of the Years*, p 93.

Scriptures, together with the life and teachings of Jesus and the pastoral letters of the Apostles that taught such virtues as love, joy, peace, longsuffering, gentleness, goodness, faith, meekness and temperance.[31] Appreciating that supreme patterns of goodness could also be found outside the Bible, the Classical Greek tradition had furnished Western civilisation with Plato's cardinal virtues of wisdom, courage, temperance and justice, together with Aristotle's of intelligence, moral insight, liberality, munificence, high-mindedness, right ambition, good temper, friendliness, truth, just resentment and modesty. In the rapidly secularising age of the late 1960s, in which Menzies saw the cult of "self" as eroding traditional values, Menzies esteemed the church schools for the education and character-training they offered in the received virtues of Western civilisation.

Support for higher education

For Menzies, the educational objective of developing moral character also extended to universities with their long tradition of cultivating civilised minds. In the *Forgotten People* speech, widely interpreted as the text for Liberal revival, Menzies asked:

> Are the universities mere technical schools, or have they as one of their functions the preservation of pure learning, bringing in its train not merely riches for the imagination but a comparative sense for the mind, and leading to what we need so badly – the recognition of values which are other than pecuniary? [32]

Far from functioning only as utilitarian "degree factories" to churn out the greatest volume of graduates, Menzies saw universities as great incubators of civilisation. Together with the British institutions of parliament and the courts, the universities of Oxford and Cambridge represented the highest form of British civilisation to Menzies. As Bob Bessant observed, "the university was the ultimate expression

---

[31] See Galatians 5:22-23.

[32] Menzies, *The Forgotten People*, 1942, p 7.

of Menzies' faith in education as a civilising agent".[33] In addition
to merely equipping undergraduates with essential training and
vocational skills, the university would serve to cultivate the character
of their students and encourage them to seek truth and beauty in
their chosen discipline. Instead of standing aloof from the world,
the university would bridge the gulf between the "academician" and
the "good practical man". In so doing, it would be in a position to
contribute to the common good by producing an educated generation
who understood the practicalities, values and aspirations of ordinary
citizens.

Menzies was committed to advancing both the stature and scope
of Australia's universities. In the post-war world, he envisaged these
institutions as playing an ever-important role in raising educated
individuals to become the future leaders of Australian democracy.
To facilitate the greater participation of Australian citizens in higher
education, Menzies took steps towards Commonwealth funding of
universities beginning with a scheme of undergraduate university
scholarships inaugurated from the early 1950s. This initiative was
followed by the establishment in 1956 of the Prime Minister's
Committee on Australian Universities chaired by Sir Keith Murray,
Chairman of the University Grants Committee in the UK. The
Chifley Labor Government in 1949 had set up an investigation
into the funding of universities and the need for a permanent and
comprehensive scholarship scheme. The Menzies Government, on
taking office, modified its terms of reference, leading eventually to
establishment of the Murray Committee.[34] A long-serving Rector
of Lincoln College, Oxford, Murray's philosophy of university
education was essentially traditional, broad and non-utilitarian.
He saw universities as guardians of received intellectual standards
and intellectual integrity of the community, intent on discovery of
new knowledge and training of future professionals who were to
have "a wide general education as a background to their professional

---

[33] Bessant, "Robert Gordon Menzies", p 166.
[34] Harman, "Development of Higher Education", p 243.

knowledge".[35] The need for education in the humanities was as great, if not greater, than ever before.

As well as being repositories of received intellectual traditions, Menzies maintained that universities, like schools, served an essential moral purpose. Addressing an audience at St Joseph's College, Nudgee, after his retirement from the prime ministership, Menzies reflected:

> I would even like to strike a blow for the moral responsibilities of Universities. For, in spite of what we now call the "permissive society", meaning by that the "licentious" society, there are great moral issues in life, a moral quality in the highest statesmanship, a great moral element in the assessment of national power, and a basic morality in a good community life, which no University can either reject or ignore. Universities exist to produce good and capable citizens, who have learned, not merely to serve their own purposes with knowledge and ability, but to serve the community which has made their studies possible.[36]

Even with all of the social and moral changes in society wrought by the 1960s cultural revolution, he maintained that Australia's universities had a responsibility to nourish the moral character of the community and nation at large beginning with education of each individual student. For universities to discharge this mission, they needed to hold true to one of its great purposes as being the "home of pure learning" in the "ancient virtues" inherited from the Jewish, Classical and Christian traditions.

At both school and university level, Menzies consistently advocated the merits of an education informed by a religious background. His thinking, however, was not simply a reaction or a moral corrective to what he perceived to be the spiritual deficiencies of the twentieth century – with two barbarous world wars in the first half and moral

---

[35]   Sir Keith Murray, "Guest of Honour talk", Australian Broadcasting Commission, 2FC, Sydney, 22 September 1957, quoted in Bessant, "Robert Gordon Menzies", p 179.

[36]   Robert Menzies, Address to St Joseph's College, Nudgee, 21 May 1967.

decline in the latter half. It stemmed from deep-seated convictions that men and women created in the image of God were endowed with an innately spiritual disposition, and intended to be in a relationship with God and their fellow human beings.

For Menzies, it was the great task of education to draw out these truths and make them effective in the lives of young men and women. This was best done through religious instruction and other liberal arts disciplines such as philosophy, history and literature which provided essential insight into the human condition. The spiritual quality and moral character of pupils were then shaped in more practical ways by the social environment, leadership opportunities and extra-curricular activities afforded by the school or college. Whether institutions were informed by a Protestant, Catholic or Jewish background, the objective of education for Menzies was always to nourish the spiritual as well as the intellectual, and to cultivate personal character. The flourishing and, indeed, the survival of liberal democracy was contingent upon a citizenry, both educated and virtuous, schooled in the faith that furnished them with a "sensitive understanding of their obligations".

NOURISHED BY THINGS BEYOND
THE MATERIAL

*It is not enough to be a rich country, it is not
enough to be a prosperous country, it is not
enough to have a superb system of industrial justice, it is not enough to have security, because not
one of these things will distinguish us from the
brute. It is what exists in the minds of men, in
the spirit of men, that matters in a new world.*[1]

As Sir Robert Menzies entered his ninth decade in 1974, he spoke
about what he saw as the drift of the contemporary Liberal
Party from its founding principles. Speaking to a different world
from that of the 1940s, Menzies realised that changing circumstances
had necessitated changes to the Party's approach and policies, but
affirmed that it was the principles that gave the movement its essential
timelessness and continuity:

> When we commenced the Liberal Party, we had principles…
> In the whole of my political life, I have never arrived at
> something that I thought to be a matter of principles lightly
> or casually. They have represented deep beliefs on my part;
> and I am old-fashioned enough to believe that principles
> adopted after much thought and much consideration do not
> change. The circumstances to which they are to be applied,
> of course, will change with the change of circumstances, but
> the principles remain.[2]

The principles to which he was referring were enshrined in

---

[1] Robert Menzies, St Columba's Presbyterian Church, Woollahra, NSW, 27
February 1944.
[2] Robert Menzies, "Looking Around at Eighty", Recorded Speech, Melbourne,
12 December 1974, Robert Menzies Papers, NLA, MS 4936, Box 576, Folder 39.

the founding platform of the Liberal Party he had established three decades earlier. Australia had changed much since 1944, but Menzies still regarded the principles that spoke of personal freedom, human dignity, home and family life, social justice, free enterprise, responsible citizenship and reliance upon God as remaining integral to the Party's essence and its vision for a flourishing society. They remained not only relevant to specific fields of policy such as health, education and economic management, but could be applied to broader matters of citizenship and personal moral character. In short, they went to the heart of who we are, and who we ought to be, both as individuals and as a people.

Addressing the United States House of Representatives on 1 August 1950, Menzies appealed to the Almighty for the protection of America and Australia's most cherished values: "May all that you stand for and that we stand for be preserved under the providence of God for the happiness of mankind". This ringing exhortation was given with the outbreak of hostilities in Korea and the onset of the Cold War as Western democracies such as the United States and Australia feared that communism represented an existential threat to the survival of human freedom. For Menzies, survival of freedom and democracy rested on the preservation and championing of Judeo-Christian principles that affirmed the innate dignity and worth of every human being.

Democracy was a "spirit", "based on the Christian conception" that in every human soul there was a "spark of the divine" where every person "stood equal in the sight of God".[3] Menzies' Christian conception of democracy extended to civil society as well as individuals, envisioning a community of citizens bound to one another in "brotherly love":

> If we are to live together in mutual amity and justice, if we are to be dignified without being proud or overbearing, we must be givers rather than receivers; we must be quick to discharge our duties and modest about our rights. For the

---

[3] Robert Menzies, "The Nature of Democracy", *Forgotten People*, p 172.

harmony and brotherly love of a family is not maintained on the basis of claims. In the wise language of the Bible, the family are "in honour of preferring one another".[4]

This was essentially the conception of democracy that informed the philosophy of the Liberal Party. The party platform he co-drafted in 1954 affirmed that "rights connote duties", warning that "sectional and selfish policies are destructive of good citizenship".

Menzies' understanding of the critical relationship between freedom, virtue and faith accorded with what the Anglo-American public intellectual, Os Guinness, termed the "Golden Triangle of Freedom".[5] According to this paradigm, the flourishing of freedom is reliant upon virtue, which in turn requires faith, which again requires freedom, and so the triangular cycle continues *ad infinitum*. In the spirit of the American founders, Edmund Burke and Alexis de Tocqueville, Menzies held that freedom and democracy did not rest on the preservation of the Constitution or on laws alone, but on the virtue and character of the nation's citizens. In his own words, "the love of freedom" would not be found in "Acts of Parliament or blue books or dusty records, but in the hearts of the people themselves.[6] For democracy to succeed moreover, it demanded all the skill and unselfishness of its citizens.[7] For Menzies, the apex of personal moral character was "selflessness", and this, in turn, had an essential foundation in faith. Menzies once remarked that "religion gives to people a sensitive understanding of their obligations".[8] For religion to thrive, it, in turn, required the "freedom to worship, to think, to speak and to choose".[9] All this was never to imply that for Australia to be free, it needed to be made officially Christian. Rather, it was based on the understanding, shared by both the American

---

[4] Ibid.

[5] Os Guinness, *A Free People's Suicide: Sustainable Freedom and the American Future*, Downers Grove [Ill]: IVP Books, pp 93-121.

[6] Robert Menzies, Constitutional Guarantees, 27 November 1942.

[7] Robert Menzies, "Democracy and Sir Alan Newton", 4 September 1949.

[8] Robert Menzies, Motion on Education, *CPD*, House of Representatives, 26 July 1945, Robert Menzies Papers, NLA, MS 4936, Box 253, Folder 15.

[9] Menzies, "Election Speech", 10 November 1949.

and Australian constitutional framers, that voluntary faith, made manifest in the moral character of the people, provided the optimal foundation for freedom to thrive. In the historical context of Menzies' Australia, such faith was typically either of a Protestant, Catholic, Eastern Orthodox or Jewish kind.

The essential interconnectedness between faith, character and freedom helps to explain the supreme importance Menzies accorded to religious freedom and this is ever applicable to the present day. The freedom of religion in teaching, practice, worship and observance remains highly prized in contemporary Australia which is home to a multiplicity of Christian traditions and religious faiths, that, for the most part, amicably coexist. With the sectarian rancour and discrimination of earlier generations banished to the past, religious freedom is in some respects less inhibited now than in Menzies' time. On the other hand, the advance of secularism has brought new challenges to the free exercise of religious beliefs and practices that had hitherto gone largely unchallenged. This has been particularly pronounced in the realm of sexual ethics where traditional attitudes to marriage, typically informed by religious sensibilities, have been on a collision course with the modern, mostly secular outlook affirming of same-sex marriage. With the right for such attitudes to be expressed in the public square becoming increasingly contested, questions of religious freedom have been brought into sharper focus.

This became evident when the Australian parliament legalised same-sex marriage in December 2017 after a protracted public debate and postal plebiscite.[10] Responding to some concerns of the public that the passage of the *Marriage Amendment (Definition and Religious Freedoms) Act* 2017 (Cth) could abridge the freedom of religious bodies committed to the traditional, heterosexual conception of marriage, the then Prime Minister, Malcolm Turnbull, announced appointment of an Expert Panel. Chaired by the former Attorney-General, Philip

---

[10] The postal plebiscite referred to the Australian Marriage Law Postal Survey that asked each respondent the question: "Should the law be changed to allow same-sex couples to marry?" The Australia-wide, non-compulsory survey returned a "Yes" vote of 61.6 percent and a "No" vote of 38.4 percent.

Ruddock, and a team of legal experts, the Panel would examine and report on whether Australian law adequately protects the human right to freedom of religion.[11] Under the Terms of Reference, the scope of the Panel's review was to "consider the intersections between the enjoyment of the freedom of religion and other human rights". The obvious challenge for the Panel was to navigate the tension between respecting the new rights for individuals afforded by the *Marriage Amendment Act* and to uphold the freedom for religious bodies to freely express and practice their beliefs.

With the tension between religious freedom and non-discrimination on sexuality grounds surfacing only relatively recently, this was not a predicament Menzies faced in his own time. The religious freedom principles he enunciated, however, suggest that he would most likely have lent firm support to legislative measures to protect religious freedom from undue impingement by competing rights to non-discrimination. His ardent support for church schools to practice their faith and his express resolve to protect the rights of citizens to think, worship, pray and assemble according to their own conscience stand decidedly at odds with modern threats to some of these liberties. These include instances of employees being fired for religious beliefs or calls to strip religious schools of their rights to engage staff in accordance with their faith and values. Accordingly, he would endorse many of the proposals of the Religious Freedom Review to accord religious liberty greater protection.[12] As he said in his broadcast on Constitutional Guarantees, he would be "among the first to act promptly to destroy the threat" to religious freedom

---

[11]   Religious Freedom Review: Report of the Expert Panel, Canberra, 18 May 2018. Accessed from https://www.ag.gov.au/sites/default/files/2020-03/religious-freedom-review-expert-panel-report-2018.pdf

[12]   The Panel of the Review proposed a number of recommendations to strengthen religious freedom. Amongst other proposals, these included changes to Australian charity law to ensure that faith-based charities did not face disqualification for advocating a traditional view of marriage (4); ensuring that religious schools could discriminate on the basis of sexual orientation, relationship status or gender identity, providing this accorded with the religious precepts of the institution (5); and making it unlawful to discriminate on the basis of a person's religious/non-religious belief or activity, but with appropriate exemptions for religious bodies (15).

in Australia. Thus, for all the radical changes in the religious beliefs and moral mores of society since the 1960s, the guiding principles of Menzies maintain a timeless quality and urgency.

The importance Menzies attached to the cultivation of moral character also give his thoughts on education a contemporary resonance, carrying multiple lessons. The first is that universities must recover their original purpose. Instead of being mere commercial enterprises fixated on churning out the greatest number of graduates, they need to return to their founding purpose as being cultivators of character and culture. Critical to this, is the importance of investing in liberal arts faculties that offer studies in disciplines such as history, philosophy, literature, languages and theology. Menzies understood such disciplines as critical to fostering human understanding and nurturing civilisation. In this vein, the establishment of the Ramsay Centre for Western Civilisation in 2017 was a welcome development. By offering to contribute greater resources to the arts faculties of selected public universities, it will seek to draw more students to the riches of Western civilisation bequeathed from the Jewish, Classical and Christian traditions. The trenchant opposition to the Ramsay Centre from some quarters, however, underscores the extent of the task required for public universities to recover their original mission to be both "homes of pure culture and learning" and "trainers of character".[13] The second lesson is that independent schools must continue to be supported, not so much as status symbols or bastions of exclusive privilege, but as training grounds for building faith and personal character. Finally, the state must afford such schools the greatest possible freedom to instruct pupils in the precepts of their founding faith.

To understand the spiritual inspiration that Menzies brought to his conception of Liberal democracy, articulation of Liberal Party principles, dedication to religious freedom and philosophy of

---

[13] Menzies, "Place of a University", 1939.

education, this study has sought to explore how Menzies absorbed his broad form of Presbyterian Christianity and the essential tenets of faith that he held to. With Menzies subscribing to a sincere yet uncomplicated and practical Christianity, it has analysed how he applied his faith to the political philosophy and major themes of his time. The religious outlook of Menzies was such that, through a combination of broad sympathies and political mastery, he was able to identify with Protestants in their love of the Bible, with Catholics in their dedication to their schools, with Jews in their links to Israel, with all freedom-loving people in their renunciation of communism, and with all liberally-minded citizens in their affirmation of religious freedom. In an age where the great pillars of faith have been weathered by secularism and where religious liberty is increasingly contested, Menzies' own sturdy belief and broad embrace of Australia's faith communities provides a way forward for a flourishing society nourished by things beyond the material.

In a Western world preoccupied with materialistic imperatives such as economic growth, prosperity and productivity, the high premium Menzies afforded to faith, moral character, freedom, civilisation, community and personal relationships remain eminently instructive for today. As Menzies led Australia through the post-war period, he presided over a country becoming more prosperous with increased home ownership, car ownership and acquisition of consumer goods such as refrigerators and appliances. Whilst he welcomed this rising standard of living as a positive sign of national progress, he also reminded his fellow citizens that:

> We could easily become man for man, woman for woman, the richest country in the Southern Hemisphere, but it won't matter very much unless we can say that we are the most civilised country in the Southern Hemisphere. Civilised because we understand the unselfish duties of citizenship; civilised because we have come to understand the importance of the human being, the dignity of the human

being, the dignity of labour, the responsibility of riches. These are the tests of civilisation, and our great task is to produce a civilised nation.[14]

True to form, Menzies appealed to ideals anchored in Judeo-Christian notions of humanity and society, yet capable of resonating with citizens of all faiths or none. Even in our society which is that much more culturally diverse and religiously plural than in 1962, his faith-inspired call to seek the common good is a timeless message, appealing as it does to universal human values.

---

[14] Robert Menzies, WA Convention of the Liberal Party, South Perth Civic Centre, 30 July 1962, Robert Menzies Papers, NLA, MS 4936, Box 274, Folder 167.

AFTERWORD

The Hon John Anderson AO

I t is one thing to be Australia's longest-serving Prime Minister, but it is quite another to be arguably Australia's most important and 'nation-shaping' Prime Minister. In truth it is hard to deny either, and so the interest in his life and career needs no justification.

Menzies' life has now been exhaustively documented in several biographies, as has his political career and lasting legacy in Australian history. Happily, earlier caricatures of Menzies as merely a seller of pig iron to Japan, mere Cold War warrior, or a backwards-looking Anglophile are now superseded by more subtle and even-handed analyses of his mind and legacy. Long may this much-needed exercise in historical recovery continue.

In this respect, David Furse-Roberts' *God & Menzies* is a welcome addition to the growing interest in the founder of the Liberal Party. Furse-Roberts shows at the very least that, even if Menzies was no Christian enthusiast in the evangelical mould, his world-view and vision for Australia's future cannot be adequately explained without uncovering his deeply held conviction that Christianity is absolutely essential for democracy and a healthy civilisation. Even if Menzies, like many of his generation, was shy about speaking at length about what his Christian beliefs meant to him personally, he was not shy in discussing their importance to a democratic, free, and peaceful Australia.

If Menzies had never mentioned the role of Christian belief in the image of God in all people, as a foundation for democratic equality, or ornamented his speeches throughout his career with Bible verses and allusions, or repeatedly stressed that a full education ideally includes religious instruction, he would not have been very different from other prime ministers. In other words, Australians would not have judged him harshly for it. He spoke of these things because he believed in them.

To understand any Australian prime minister's effect on the country, indeed, any great historical figure, it is necessary to get inside the mind to find the principles animating the policies. Perhaps the most significant aspect of Menzies' religiosity was his aversion to sectarianism – unusual during a period in Australia's history in which Catholic-Protestant rivalries still raged. Certainly the extension of Commonwealth funding to denominational schools, starting incipiently in the 1950s and becoming robust from 1964 onwards, was one of the greatest contributions Menzies made to Australian society. But importantly for Furse-Roberts' study, resuming funding for Catholic schools after two generations of its absence was a startling demonstration of Menzies' Christian ecumenical spirit.

Furse-Roberts has written the most detailed account to date of Menzies' religiosity, his relationship to communities of faith, and the way his religious convictions informed his activities as a legislator. Certainly this book will never be surpassed for its detail and scope.

Menzies famously remarked, "Human nature is at its greatest when it combines dependence upon God with independence of man." Likewise, analyses of Menzies are at their best when they acknowledge, not only the intellectual and strategic brilliance of the man, but also his sense that everything hinges, in the end, on a nation's response to the God whose existence is presupposed, even demanded, by the principles of freedom, equality, and democracy, principles which characterised the very civilisation he spent his life trying to serve and defend.

REFERENCES

Archival sources

Irving Benson Papers, 1939-1970, National Library of Australia, MS 7695 (two boxes)

Robert Menzies Papers, 1905-1978, National Library of Australia, MS 4936 (multiple boxes)

Government documents

Australian Bureau of Statistics (ABS), Chapter 12, Culture and Recreation, Religious Affiliation, 1301.0, Year Book of Australia, 2006. Accessed from https://www.abs.gov.au/ausstats/abs@.nsf/bb8db737e2af84b8ca2571780015701e/bfdda1ca506d6cfaca2570de0014496e!OpenDocument#

Religious Freedom Review: Report of the Expert Panel, Canberra, 18 May 2018. Accessed from https://www.ag.gov.au/sites/default/files/2020-03/religious-freedom-review-expert-panel-report-2018.pdf

General sources

Ahdar, Rex and Leigh, Ian, *Religious Freedom in the Liberal State*, New York, Oxford University Press, 2005

Apple, Raymond, *The Jewish Way: Jews and Judaism in Australia*, Sydney: The Great Synagogue, 2002

Bebbington, David, *Evangelicalism in Modern Britain: A History from the 1730s to the 1980s*, London: Unwin Hyman, 1989

_____, "Drummond, Henry (1851-1897)", *Oxford Dictionary of National Biography*, Oxford University Press, 2004

Bessant, Bob, "Robert Gordon Menzies and Education in Australia", *Melbourne Studies in Education*, 2006, 47: 1-2, pp 163-187

Boland, T P, "Duhig, Sir James (1871-1965)", *Australian Dictionary of Biography*, Volume 8, Melbourne University Press, 1981

Bramston, Robert Menzies: *The Art of Politics*, Melbourne: Scribe, 2019

Brett, Judith, *The Australian Liberals and the Moral Middle Class: From Alfred Deakin to John Howard*, New York: Cambridge University Press, 2003

____, *Robert Menzies' Forgotten People*, Melbourne: Melbourne University Press, 2007

____, *The Enigmatic Mr Deakin*, Melbourne: The Text Publishing Company, 2017

Bukharin N. and Preobrazhensky, E., *The ABC of Communism: A Popular Explanation of the Program of the Communist Party of Russia*, with a preface and an introduction by Sidney Heitman, Ann Arbor, Mich: University of Michigan Press, c1988

Burla, Shahar and Lawrence, Dashiel, *Australia & Israel: a diasporic, cultural and political relationship*, Chicago: Sussex Academic Press, 2015

Chavura, Stephen, "The Christian Social Thought of Sir Robert Gordon Menzies", *Lucas: An Evangelical History Review*, 2.12 (December 2018), pp 19-46

Chavura, Stephen, Gascoigne, John and Tregenza, Ian, *Reason, Religion, and the Australian Polity: A Secular State?*, New York: Routledge, 2019

Chavura, Stephen and Melleuish, Gregory, "Utilitarianism contra Sectarianism: The Official and the Unauthorised Civic Religion of Australia", William Coleman (ed.), *Only in Australia: The History, Politics and Economics of Australian Exceptionalism*, Oxford: Oxford University Press, 2019, pp 62-80

_____, "The Forgotten Menzies: Cultural Puritanism and Australian Social Thought", *Journal of Religious History*, 44(3), 2020, pp 356-379

_____, *The Forgotten Menzies: The World Picture of Australia's Longest Serving Prime Minister*, Melbourne: Melbourne University Press, 2021

Chilton, Hugh, *Evangelicals and the End of Christian Australia: Nation and Religion in the Public Square, 1959-1979*, PhD Thesis, University of Sydney, 2014

Clark, Tim, Belsham, Bruce and Goward, Pru, *The Liberals: Fifty Years of the Federal Party* [videorecording], ABC Video Enterprises, 1994

Clements, M A, "Adamson, Lawrence Arthur (1860-1932)", *Australian Dictionary of Biography*, Volume 7, Melbourne University Press, 1979

Connors, Jane, "The 1954 Royal Tour of Australia," *Australian Historical Studies*, vol. 25, no. 100 (April 1993), 371-382

Cowan, Zelman, "Ashkanasy, Maurice (1901-1971)", *Australian Dictionary of Biography*, Volume 13, Melbourne University Press, 1993

Cramer, John, *Pioneers, Politics and People*, Sydney: Allen & Unwin, 1989

D'Arcy, Martin C., *Communism and Christianity* (Mitcham: Penguin Books, 1956)

Deery, Phillip, War on Peace: Menzies, the Cold War and the 1953 Convention on Peace and War', *Australian Historical Studies*, vol. 34, no. 122, (October 2003), 248-269

Duncan, Bruce F., *Crusade or Conspiracy: Catholics and the Anti-Communist Struggle in Australia*, Sydney: UNSW, 2001

Duncan, Graham A., "John Knox and Education", *Theological Studies*, 73(3), 2017, pp 1-9

Eggleston, Frederic W., *Search for a Social Philosophy*, Melbourne: Melbourne University Press, 1941

Einfeld, Billie, "Australia", *The Australian Jewish Yearbook*, Volume 58, 1957, pp 369-373

Frydenberg, Josh and Kemp, David, "Menzies: An Enemy of Tyranny and Friend of Freedom", *The Australian Jewish News*, 24 January 2013

Furse-Roberts, David, *Menzies: The Forgotten Speeches*, Brisbane: Connor Court, 2017

Guinness, Os, *A Free People's Suicide: Sustainable Freedom and the American Future*, Downers Grove [Ill]: IVP Books, 2012

Gunson, Neil, "Murdoch, Patrick John (1850-1940)", *Australian Dictionary of Biography*, Volume 10, Melbourne University Press, 1986

Hazlehurst, Cameron, *Menzies Observed*, Sydney: George Allen & Unwin, 1979

Hempenstall, Peter, *The Meddlesome Priest: A Life of Ernest Burgmann*, St. Leonards [NSW]: Allen & Unwin, 1993

_____, "Burgmann, Ernest Henry (1885-1967)" *Australian Dictionary of Biography*, Volume 13, Melbourne University Press, 1993

Henderson, Gerard, *Menzies Child: The Liberal Party of Australia, 1944-1994*, St Leonards [NSW]: Allen & Unwin, 1994

_____, Gerard, *Santamaria: A Most Unusual Man*, Carlton [Vic]: The Miegunyah Press, 2015

Henderson, Anne, "Robert Menzies (1894-1978)", Geoff Lindsay and Wayne Hudson (eds), *Australian Jurists and Christianity*, Sydney: Federation Press, 2021, pp 156-166

Henderson, Heather, *Letters to My Daughter*, Millers Point [NSW]: Murdoch Books, 2012

_____, *A Smile for My Parents*, Sydney: Allen & Unwin, 2013

Hilliard, David, "God in the Suburbs: The Religious Culture of Australian Cities in the 1950s", *Australian Historical Studies*, 24:97, 1991, pp 399-419

Hilliard, David, "Church, Family and Sexuality in Australia in the 1950s", *Australian Historical Studies*, 27:109, 1997, pp 133-146

Hilliard, David, "The Religious Crisis of the 1960s: The Experience of the Australian Churches", *Journal of Religious History*, Vol 21, No 2, June 1997, pp 209-227

Himmelfarb, Gertrude, *The Roads to Modernity: The British, French and American Enlightenment*, New York: Vintage Books, 2005

Hocking, Jenny, "Robert Menzies' 'Fundamental Authoritarianism': The 1951 Referendum", Love, Peter and Strangio, Paul (eds), *Arguing the Cold War*, Carlton North, Red Rag Publications, 2001

Hogan, Michael, *The Catholic Campaign for State Aid: A Study of a Pressure Group Campaign in New South Wales and the Australian Capital Territory, 1950-1972*, Sydney: Catholic Theological Faculty, 1978

_____, *The Sectarian Strand*, Ringwood: Penguin Books, 1987

_____, *Justice Now! Social Justice Statements of the Australian Catholic Bishops. First Series: 1940-1966*, Sydney: Department of Government and Public Administration, University of Sydney, 1990

_____, *Australian Catholics: The Social Justice Tradition*, Melbourne: Collins Dove, 1993

Howard, John, *The Menzies Era: The Years that Shaped Modern Australia*, Sydney: HarperCollins, 2014

Howe, Renate and Swain, Shurlee, *The challenge of the city: the centenary history of Wesley Central Mission 1893-1993*, South Melbourne: Hyland House, 1993

Howe, Renate, "Benson, Sir Clarence Irving (1897-1980)", *Australian Dictionary of Biography*, Volume 13, Melbourne University Press, 1993

_____, Renate *A Century of Influence: The Australian Student Christian Movement*, Sydney: UNSW Publishing, 2009

Howe, Renate and Howe, Brian, "E. H. Sugden and civic liberalism in Melbourne". In Howe, Renate (ed.), *The master: the life and work of Edward H. Sugden*, Uniting Academic Press, Parkville, Vic., 2009, pp.85-96.

Hudson, Wayne, *Australian Religious Thought*, Melbourne: Monash University Press, 2016

Hutchinson, Mark, *Iron in our Blood: A History of the Presbyterian Church in NSW, 1788-2001*, Sydney: Ferguson Publications and the Centre for the Study of Australian Christianity, 2001

Johnston, Elizabeth, "O'Brien, Eris Michael (1895-1974)" *Australian Dictionary of Biography*, Volume 15, Melbourne University Press, 2000

Kemp, David., *Society and Electoral Behaviour in Australia: A Study of Three Decades*, St Lucia, QLD, University of Queensland Press, 1978

_____, *The Land of Dreams: How Australians Won their Freedom 1788-1860*, Melbourne: The Miegunyah Press, 2018

_____, *A Free Country: Australia's Search for Utopia 1861-1901*, Melbourne: The Miegunyah Press, 2019

_____, *A Democratic Nation: Identity, Freedom and Equality in Australia 1901-1925*, Melbourne: The Miegunyah Press, 2019

_____, *A Liberal State: How Australians chose Liberalism over Socialism 1926-1966*, Melbourne: The Miegunyah Press, 2021

Lake, Meredith, *The Bible in Australia: A Cultural History*, Sydney: NewSouth Publishing, 2018

LeRoy, Doris, *Anglicanism, Anti-communism and Cold War Australia*, PhD Thesis, Victoria University, 2010

Levi, J. S., "Sanger, Herman Max (1909-1980)", *Australian Dictionary of Biography*, Volume 16, Melbourne University Press, 2002

Lewis, Donald M., *The Origins of Christian Zionism: Lord Shaftesbury and Evangelical Support for a Jewish Homeland*, Cambridge: Cambridge University Press, 2014

Livingstone, Richard, *On Education: The Future in Education and Education for a World Adrift*, Cambridge: Cambridge University Press, 1954

_____, *The Rainbow Bridge and other Essays on Education*, London, Pall Mall, 1959

Locke, John, "A Letter Concerning Toleration" (1685) in David George Mullan (ed), *Religious Pluralism in the West: An Anthology*, Oxford: Blackwell, 1998

Lowe, David, *Menzies and the 'Great World Struggle'*, Sydney: University of New South Wales Press, 1999

Lyons, David, "Defence, the Family and the Battler: The Democratic Labor Party and its Legacy", *Australian Journal of Political Science*, Vol 43, No 3, September 2008, pp 425-442

Macintyre, Stuart, "Rentoul, John Laurence (1846-1926)", *Australian Dictionary of Biography*, Volume 11, Melbourne University Press, 1988

Mallon, Ryan, "A Church for Scotland? The Free Church and Scottish Nationalism after the Disruption", *Scottish Church History*, 49(1), 2020, pp 1-24

Mansfield, Joan, "Flockhart, David John (1889-1964)", *Australian Dictionary of Biography*, Volume 14, Melbourne University Press, 1996

Martin, A. W., *Robert Menzies: A Life: Volume 1 1894-1943*, Carlton [Vic]: Melbourne University Press, 1993

Martin, A. W., *Robert Menzies: A Life: Volume 2 1944-1978*, Carlton [Vic]: Melbourne University Press, 1999

Martin, A. W., "Sir Robert Gordon Menzies", Grattan, Michelle (ed.), *Australian Prime Ministers*, Sydney: New Holland Publishers, 2000, pp 174-205

McKenzie, Maisie, *Outback Achiever: Fred McKay Successor to Flynn of the Inland*, Brisbane: Boolarong Press, 1997

Melleuish, Gregory, *Cultural Liberalism in Australia: A Study in Intellectual and Cultural History*, Melbourne: Cambridge University Press, 1995

Menzies, Robert Gordon, *The Forgotten People and Other Studies in Democracy*, Sydney: Angus & Robertson, 1943

_____, *Speech is of Time: Selected Speeches and Writings by Robert Gordon Menzies*, London: Cassell, 1958

_____, *Afternoon Light: Some Memories of Men and Events*, Melbourne: Cassell Australia, 1967

_____, *The Measure of the Years*, Melbourne: Cassell Australia, 1970

Mill, John Stuart, *On Liberty*, Second Edition, Boston: Ticknor and Fields, 1863 (originally 1859)

Mullins, Patrick, *Tiberius with a Telephone: The Life and Stories of William McMahon*, Melbourne: Scribe, 2018

Murphy, John, *Imagining the Fifties: Private Sentiment and Political Culture in Menzies' Australia*, Sydney: Pluto Press, 2000

Nethercote, J. R. (ed.), *Menzies: The Shaping of Modern Australia*, Brisbane: Connor Court, 2016

O'Brien, Glen, *Methodism in Australia: A History* (edited with Hilary Carey), Farnham, Surrey and Burlington, VA: Ashgate, 2015

O'Brien, Glen, "Irving Benson: Preacher, Writer, Mission Superintendent (1897-1980)," in *Out of the Ordinary: Twelve Australian Methodist Biographies*, (ed.), William Emilsen and Patricia Curthoys, Adelaide: Mediacom, 2015, 217-38

O'Brien, "Christian Perfection in Australian Methodism," in Sean Winter, ed. *Immense, Unfathomed, Unconfined: Essays on the Grace of God in Honour of Norman Young*, Melbourne: Mosaic Press, 2013

O'Farrell, Patrick, *The Catholic Church and Community: An Australian History*, Sydney: UNSW Press, 1992

Ormonde, Paul, "The Movement – Politics by Remote Control," in Ormonde, Paul, (ed.), *Santamaria: The Politics of Fear: Critical Reflections*, Richmond: Spectrum Publications, 2000

Osmond, Warren G., *Frederic Eggleston: An Intellectual in Australian Politics*, George Allen & Unwin, Sydney, 1985

Pabst, Adrian, *Story of our Country: Labor's Vision for Australia*, Redland [Qld], Kapunda Press, 2019

Palmer, H M. "Livingstone, Sir Richard Winn (1880-1960)", *Oxford Dictionary of National Biography*, Oxford University Press, 2004

Paproth, Darrell N, *Failure is Not Final: A Life of C. H. Nash*, Sydney: Centre for the Study of Australian Christianity, 1997

Piggin, Stuart, *Spirit of a Nation: The Story of Australia's Christian Heritage*, Sydney: Strand Publishing, 2004

_____, "'The Bible says and so say all of us: Decades of Equipoise or Entropy? Evangelical Currents in Australia, 1946-65", *Lucas: An Evangelical History Review* 2.6, December 2013, pp 17-38

Piggin, Stuart and Linder, Robert D., *The Fountain of Public Prosperity: Evangelical Christians in Australian History 1740-1914*, Clayton [Vic]: Monash University Publishing, 2019

_____ *Attending to the National Soul: Evangelical Christians in Australian History 1914-2014*, Clayton [Vic]: Monash University Publishing, 2020

Rack, Henry D., "A Man of Reason and Religion? John Wesley and the Enlightenment", *Wesley and Methodist Studies*, 2009, Vol 1, pp 2-17

Rowse, Tim, *Australian Liberalism and National Character*, Melbourne: Kibble Books, 1978

Rubinstein, Hilary L., *The Jews in Victoria 1835-1985*, Boston: Allen & Unwin, 1986

Rubinstein, Hilary L, "Brodie, Sir Israel (1895-1979)", *Australian Dictionary of Biography*, Volume 13, Melbourne University Press, 1993

Rubinstein, W. D. (ed.), *Jews in the Sixth Continent*, Sydney: Allen & Unwin, 1987

Rutland, Suzanne D., *The Jews in Australia*, Melbourne: Cambridge University Press, 2005

_____ "Australia and the Struggle for Soviet Jewry: 1961-1972", *Australian Journal of Politics and History*, Vol 60, No 2, 2014, pp 194-213

Sandys, Jonathan & Henley, Wallace, *God & Churchill: How the Great Leader's Sense of Divine Destiny Changed His Troubled World and Offers Hope for Ours*, London: SPCK Publishing, 2016

Santamaria, B. A., *Against the Tide*, Melbourne: Oxford University Press, 1981

Sawer, Marian, *The Ethical State? Social Liberalism in Australia*, Melbourne: Melbourne University Press, 2003

Semmel, Bernard, *The Methodist Revolution*, New York: Basic Books Inc, 1973

Siedentop, Larry, *Inventing the Individual: The Origins of Western Liberalism*, Milton Keynes, Penguin Books, 2014

Smart, Judith, "The Evangelist as Star: The Billy Graham Crusade in Australia, 1959", *Journal of Popular Culture,* vol. 33, no. 1, (Summer 1999), 165-76

Stanton, Timothy, "Locke and the Politics and Theology of Toleration", *Political Studies*, Vol 54, 2006, pp 84-102

Starr, Graeme, *The Liberal Party of Australia: A Documentary History*, Redmond [Vic]: Drummond/Heinemann, 1980

____, Graeme, *Carrick: Principles, Politics and Policy*, Ballan [Vic]: Connor Court Publishing, 2012

Steinback, John, "Sectarianism's Last Stand? Mannix, Menzies and the 1954 Duntroon Colours Controversy", *Australian Defence Forces Journal*, no. 146, January February (2001). 19-26. http://www.adfjournal.adc.edu.au/UserFiles/issues/146%202001%20Jan_Feb.pdf

Stonebraker, Johnathan and Irving, Sarah, "Natural Law and Protestantism: A Historical Reassessment and its Contemporary Significance", *Oxford Journal of Law and Religion*, 2015, 4, pp 421-441

Stoneman, David, "Richard Bourke: For the Honour of God and the Good of Man", *Journal of Religious History*, Vol 38, No 3, September 2014, pp 341-355

Terracini, Paul, "Moyes, Menzies, and the Vietnam War: New Insights into the Public Correspondence Between the Prime Minister and the Bishops", *Journal of Religious History*, Vol 36, No 1, March 2012, pp 70-88

Thompson, Yvonne, Brandis, George and Harley, Tom (eds), *Australian Liberalism: The Continuing Vision*, Melbourne: Liberal Forum, 1986

Thompson, Roger C., *Religion in Australia: A History*: Walker, David (ed.), Australian Retrospectives, Melbourne: Oxford University Press, 1994

Tiver, Peter, *The Liberal Party: Principles and Performance*, Milton [Qld]: Jacaranda Press, 1978

Treloar, Geoffrey R, *The Disruption of Evangelicalism: The Age of Torrey, Mott, McPherson and Hammond*, London: Inter-varsity Press, 2016

Warhurst, John, "Catholics, Communism and the Australian Party System: A Study of the Menzies Years:, *Politics*, 14:2, November 1979, pp 222-242

Wilken, Robert Louis, *Liberty in the Things of God: The Christian Origins of Religious Freedom*, New Haven: Yale University Press, 2019

Williams, Roy, *In God they Trust? The Religious Beliefs of Australia's Prime Ministers, 1901-2013*, Sydney: Bible Society, 2013

_____, *Post God Nation: How Religion Fell off the Radar in Australia and what Might be Done to get it Back on*, Sydney: HarperCollins Publishers, 2015

Acknowledgements

I wish to acknowledge the following people for their invaluable assistance in the composition of this book, *God & Menzies*.

First, I wish to recognise the Executive Director of the Menzies Research Centre (MRC), Nick Cater, for inspiring me to embark on the timely project of researching and writing about the faith that shaped Australia's longest serving Prime Minister. This publication will enable readers to appreciate the important, yet often underestimated, spiritual values that guided Sir Robert Menzies. Nick's encouragement throughout this project has been invaluable and much appreciated.

I would like to thank my colleagues at the MRC, Tim James, Susan Nguyen and James Mathias, for their encouragement, support, guidance and abiding interest in this publication.

I especially appreciate the generous support of those who have made this project possible including   Nick Moll, A. Anthony McLellan and Senator Eric Abetz.

I am very grateful to the Prime Minister, the Hon Scott Morrison, and the former Deputy Prime Minister, the Hon John Anderson AO, for their respective Foreword and Afterword. Written by two national leaders of faith, with an acute appreciation of the spiritual values that informed Menzies, these provide a fitting adornment to the volume.

With the editing of the publication, I am especially indebted to the assistance of Professor J. R. Nethercote, Dr Stephen Chavura, Dr Geoff Treloar and Rev Peter Kurti. Their wealth of scholarship, editorial experience and meticulous eye-for-detail have indelibly enhanced the quality of this publication.

In bringing this volume to print, I am grateful to Dr Anthony Cappello, Michael Gilchrist and the team at Connor Court for overseeing the process of publication with their professionalism and precision. Gratitude also to Vanessa Schimizzi of Branded Graphics for her creativity with the cover design.

I conclude by offering my profound appreciation to my family, friends, church and fellowship communities who have supported me through this endeavour with their love, good humour, interest and encouragement.

David Furse-Roberts
Sydney, June 2021

INDEX

www.ingramcontent.com/pod-product-compliance
Lightning Source LLC
Chambersburg PA
CBHW060837100426
42814CB00016B/406/J